Looking for Jesus

Looking for Jesus
Virginia Stem Owens

Westminster John Knox Press
Louisville, Kentucky

Book design by Sharon Adams
Cover design by PAZ Design Group
Cover art: Yellow Crucifixion, *Marc Chagall,*
Collections Mnam/Cci-Centre Georges Pompidou,Photo Philippe Migeat

First edition
Published by Westminster John Knox Press
Louisville, Kentucky

Published in association with the literary agency of Alive Communications, Inc.,
1465 Kelly Johnson Blvd., Suite 320, Colorado Springs, Colorado 80920

This book is printed on acid-free paper that meets
the American National Standards Institute Z39.48 standard. ∞

PRINTED IN THE UNITED STATES OF AMERICA
99 00 01 02 03 04 05 06 07 — 10 9 8 7 6 5 4 3 2

Library of Congress Cataloging-in-Publication Data

Owens Virginia Stem.
   Looking for Jesus / Virginia S. Owens. — 1st ed.
      p.   cm.
   Includes bibliographical references and indexes.
   ISBN 0–664–25819–0
   1. Jesus Christ—Biography—Meditations.   2. Bible. N.T.
Gospels—Meditations.   I. Title
BT306.4.O94   1999
232.9′01—dc21
   [B]   98–39671

Contents

Introduction: Looking for Jesus
Where I Started

I didn't go looking for Jesus till I was in my thirties. Only gradually had I become aware he was even missing. When I was a child, he had lived in our house, easily accessible, if invisible. I could talk to him, picture him standing at the foot of the bed in his white nightgown, listening as I asked him to keep my soul safe. This was in contrast to his Father, who was so infinitely expandable that, like air, he was everywhere at once, and also like air, impossible to picture.

I was taught early to look to Jesus not only for protection but for guidance. Any morally ambiguous situation could be resolved by simply asking myself, What would Jesus do? The answer was, inevitably, whatever was hardest. Gradually, however, between junior high and college, I stopped asking that question, sometimes because I was no longer sure of the answer, sometimes because I was.

In the '60s, when I left home, I figured I was leaving Jesus behind. I didn't see him fitting into the kind of adventures I intended to have. Imagine my surprise when I found his face on posters tacked on college dorm walls with Che Guevara's name stenciled across his chest. Students with biblical hair and Jesus sandals wandered the campus, espousing peace and love. I went to antiwar rallies, where the old question "What would Jesus do?" lurked behind the rhetoric about burning children with napalm. I decided maybe I'd been lucky to make his acquaintance at such a young age. When the Revolution came, he'd be right there with me on the barricades.

Instead, the war ended. I felt relieved, but not jubilant. The clear moral divisions between good and bad guys had disappeared too. By the time Nixon's helicopter lifted off from the White House lawn for the last time in 1974, most Americans simply wanted to know what would work now, what was best for the country. Our boat had been rocked quite enough for a while. Practically the only ones still asking what Jesus would do were diehard Jesus freaks and people whose bumper stickers proclaimed they'd found "it"— and they didn't necessarily agree on the answer.

Like a number of people, I had been reading Thomas Merton's *Seven Storey Mountain.* This autobiographical account of how he came to be a Trappist monk sounded more adventurous than packing up the leftovers from the Revolution. So I went to seminary, where I expected to immerse myself in the works of great mystics like St. John of the Cross, Jan van Ruysbroeck, Julian of Norwich, Dorothy Day. Instead, we studied Freud and Alfred North Whitehead. The only mystics offered were Zen. Jesus, it seemed, had dissolved into an underground lake of nonsectarian spirituality, indistinguishable from Lao-tzu or Baba Ram Dass.

As the '70s gave way to the '80s, I found myself with three degrees, two children, and a house in the suburbs. I could see that even Hare Krishnas and Moonies were on their way out. The pop mysticism of Shirley MacLaine became slightly embarrassing. Even old hippie poet Allen Ginsberg wore ties and formed a tax-exempt nonprofit institute. Instead of mystics, I read information theory. Returning to teaching, I found the curricula now stressed process over product. Jesus, meanwhile, had been reduced to a stylized metal fish you attached to the rear of your car in place of the manufacturer's logo. Though modeled after the secret sign by which Christians recognized one another during times of Roman persecution, ironically, the little metal fish now targeted the driver not as a subversive but as a potential member of the Christian Coalition.

Then in the '90s, that abandoned underground lake of spirituality began to heat up, oozing like magma through deep fissures of cultural and personal dissatisfaction. As it surfaced, it hardened into various consumer products—movies about UFOs, books about angels, witch paraphernalia, crystals for health and channeling. Even politicians began to talk about spiritual hunger. And, lo and behold, who shows up again but Jesus. Museum portraits of him appear on the covers of national newsmagazines. The gospels, indeed the entire Bible, are translated and paraphrased in myriad idioms. This century began with Albert Schweitzer's *The Quest of the Historical Jesus;* as it draws to a close, the Jesus Seminar is still trying to ferret out his identity.

Why this persistent and insatiable hunt for Jesus by scholars and archaeologists, even novelists and filmmakers? Humanity's two-thousand-year obsession with this figure is hard to ignore. He has outlived even those cultures that made him into their mascot. Considering that we live in the most secular age in the history of the world, one would think interest in this itinerant rabbi from Galilee would have petered out after the triumph of the scientific method. Just the opposite is true. He has had more books written about him than anyone else in history—and most of them in the latter half of this century. Far from washing our hands of him, we cannot seem to be done with him.

What do we want from this figure, obscured by two thousand years of accumulated history and cultural debris? Why is Jesus' identity still an issue? Why am I still intrigued enough by Jesus to go looking for him again?

I confess I was enamored of the crisis-Jesus, the one who asked the hard questions and propelled people into staking their lives on a moral wager. But historical forces beyond my control had marginalized and co-opted this Jesus of the barricades. I liked the mystical Jesus too, the one who operated like quarks on some ahistorical quantum level, probably because a quarklike Jesus promised a connection to an as-yet-untapped spiritual force. But I ultimately found such an insubstantial figure too thin and vaporous, mixing like mist with Emerson's Over-Soul. Subatomic particles, after all, are interesting only in theory. Being indistinguishable from one another, they have no history, one could almost say—as some physicists do—no reality.

Jesus may submit to being marginalized, but not to being

generalized. With other great religious leaders, we are satisfied
once we have extracted the essence of their teachings from their
sacred texts. Stories about Buddha, for instance, are didactic rather
than dramatic; the narrative arc of his life is relatively unimportant
to his message. The Tao-te Ching yields useful instructions for ordering one's perceptions of life. No one worries about discovering
the "real" Lao-tzu behind the words. But with Jesus, the story is
important, and we want it to be about a real person. Where did he
come from? What did he do? Who were his friends and enemies?
Why did he die? What happened next?

Reflected Reality

The search is not easy—not because the clues are scarce, but because they are so many and varied. Everyone, it seems, has a description of him. Museums display his portraits. The problem is
that none of them are alike. After Constantine declared his empire
safe for Christianity, Byzantine icons depicted Jesus as an exalted,
if weary, world ruler. The Middle Ages, a period of plague and political disintegration, produced meditations on the crucifixion emphasizing his patient and obedient endurance. In the eighteenth
century, Rousseau depicted Jesus as a rebel born too soon for the
French Revolution. The Victorians turned Jesus into a gentleman
more at home in a drawing room than in fishing boats and on dusty
roads. In our own sexually fixated century, Nikos Kazantzakis
gave us Jesus fueled by testosterone.

Using Jesus as a mirror for cultural or personal ideals seems a
tendency we can't escape. What I learned about him in Sunday
school has, I can see, been colored by my teachers' agenda. Wanting us to be good, cheerful children, they gave us a kindly Jesus,
sitting on a flower-studded hillside, handing out box lunches and
comforting aphorisms. He was supposed to be our friend and example. The songs we sang told us he walks and talks with us, keeps
us singing, and doesn't care what color we are.

As an adult, though, I have come to distrust those early simple
images. I know that flower-studded hillsides get turned into slag
heaps. That there aren't enough lunches to go around. That my

singing may only be whistling in the dark. At times, a fear has crept over me that Jesus may be no more than a psychological crutch, wish-fulfillment, the result of self-hypnosis. Has the Jesus I am looking for been no more than a grown-up version of the lonely child's imaginary playmate? I don't want to configure a Jesus to fit my private fantasies. How can I, a woman at the end of the twentieth century, avoid making Jesus into a replica of the qualities I value most?

Should I merely trust professional biblical scholars who approach these stories like detectives looking for clues to a crime? Modeling their research on what they believe to be scientific methods, they begin with an absolute skepticism about the text, assuming that only such an uncontaminated approach will yield reliable facts. Let me say that there is a certain intellectual nobility in such an attempt, based on a commendable hunger for certainty.

But this very fear of the text is itself, I soon realized, a part of our cultural baggage. This Hamlet-like paralysis when faced with questions of meaning is the plague of the postmodern world. Literary critics have learned from contemporary physics that the old scientific ideal is a myth, that it is impossible to stand outside an experiment, no matter how much you want to avoid influencing the outcome. The researcher always remains a component in the experiment.

Physicists measuring light waves, for example, cannot simultaneously track individual photons. Deciding to measure light as waves automatically precludes finding photons. Or inserting a thermometer into a solution inevitably changes the temperature of the original sample. This principle operates in other fields as well. When people are polled for their opinions, for instance, those opinions are often altered in the process. In other words, the very act of gathering data inevitably tampers with the evidence.

You will notice, however, that this state of affairs has brought neither physics nor sociology to a standstill. Wall Street does not shut down simply because multiple meanings can be assigned to tensions between China and Taiwan. The world has always operated with ambiguity and muddle. What we have discovered—or perhaps have simply been reminded of—is that investigators, whether in laboratories or armchairs, are well advised to examine their agendas and methods and to take them into account in their search.

Searching for Clues

Only four references to Jesus occur in first-century documents outside the New Testament: two in the Jewish historian Josephus, one from the Roman historian Tacitus, and one oblique allusion in a letter from Pliny the Younger to the Emperor Trajan, recommending the persecution of the Christian sect. Just enough to confirm that such a person as Jesus actually existed, but little more. This makes it even more fortunate that the gospels give us four separate accounts of Jesus' short life. Since they are all told from different perspectives by people of diverse background and temperament, they provide points from which we can sight our target. We can compare details, weigh evidence, fill in information lacking in one report with that supplied by another.

In addition to these four accounts, there are also apocryphal gospels which the early church councils decided were not sufficiently authentic to sanction as official scripture. Some of these are obvious fabrications in the manner of fairy tales: they have the boy Jesus turning clay birds into living ones or zapping insolent playmates with invisible power-rays. A Greek manuscript of the *Gospel of Thomas,* unearthed in Egypt in 1945, is as ancient as any of the canonical gospel manuscripts. Instead of stories, however, this manuscript contains only pithy sayings and parables attributed to Jesus, some of which parallel passages in Luke and Matthew. These few artifacts, then, are all anyone, including expert biblical scholars, has to work with.

The four canonical gospels do not, of course, agree in every particular. If they did, I believe that in itself would make me suspect collusion. Testimony from witnesses to accidents or crimes rarely agrees either; we expect discrepancies among individual perceptions of an event. Yet despite the variations in witnesses' testimonies, courts routinely manage to reach verdicts.

Besides, I am not really interested in discovering if Jesus fed five thousand people with five loaves or four thousand people with seven loaves. I don't care that Luke provides one genealogy for Jesus while Matthew gives us a different list of his forebears. If Jesus went to Jerusalem three times in John's gospel and only once in the other three accounts, that doesn't bother me. I expect these four writers to have made choices about how to tell their story based on their particular concerns. This is how all kinds of writing—from newspaper articles to corporate reports—get done. Yet I rely on both those sources to give me information I can evaluate and use profitably. And what I want from the stories of Matthew, Mark, Luke, and John is a picture of Jesus.

Negative Space

To a modern audience, their expectations trained by novels and movies, the storytelling techniques of both the Hebrew and the Greek scriptures are exceedingly aggravating. We are accustomed to the careful descriptions, precise time indicators, and nuanced vocabularies supplied by contemporary writers. The gospels provide none of those frills. In fact, they contain scarcely any adverbs or adjectives. All the contextual marrow that once filled its narrative structure has long since dried up and disappeared along with the original authors and audience. The details of setting, motivation, tone of voice are lost to us now. All that's left are the bare bones of act and speech.

But that negative space, it turns out, is the genius of the gospels. Narrative, it seems, like nature, abhors a void. Leave an open space in a story, and the perceiving consciousness rushes to fill it. Listen to even the sparest narrative, and soon you'll find yourself constructing sets and designing costumes to fill your own interior stage. So powerful is the pull of the story that, before we know it, we are sucked into those empty spaces.

Anyone with a red-letter edition of the New Testament can tell that the teachings of Jesus are remarkably abundant compared to the amount of space devoted to describing him. To get a picture of what he was like requires more than evaluating his teaching. To assemble such a profile, we turn to the narratives, which are as rich in range of characters as they are poor in description. From Jesus' encounters with other people, we see his own character take shape. A border begins to emerge around this figure. How he acts, especially in relation to other people, reveals as much about him as his teachings. Indeed, his actions are a way of testing his teaching against his life.

A good deal of implicit information can be garnered from the gospel scenarios of encounters with Jesus. They show us the kinds of people he met and under what conditions, what these people wanted from him, whether they got what they asked for, and even sometimes if it did them any good. Unfortunately, in sermons and devotional writings these encounters have often been reduced to a one-size-fits-all model. The pattern goes something like this: people approach Jesus as suppliants, usually falling on their knees at his feet. He compliments them on their faith, heals either them or their relatives, then tells them to follow him. The point is that we should emulate this pattern.

But when I read scenes where Jesus has face-to-face meetings with people, I find that not everyone swoons in ecstasy at the sight of this man. Not everyone is immediately convinced of his powers nor even aware of who he is. Not everyone comes begging for healing. Sometimes people approach Jesus warily. Or even belligerently. Sometimes he actually makes the first move or asks a favor of a stranger. And when people do make a request, it's not always for healing. Sometimes they simply want information or his opinion. His responses vary as well. At least once he tries to shake someone off, to turn down the request. At other times his petitioners get more than they bargained for. And he doesn't always tell the people he meets to follow him. Most often he moves on and leaves them standing there in their own lives.

A Note on Method

Trying to standardize these encounters minimizes their truth. In this book, I have tried to recount twenty-three of these stories in a way that does justice to their variations, rather than forcing them into a single mold. First-century Palestine was more, after all, than a factory for manufacturing Christians. People neither came to nor left Jesus like products on an assembly line. In fact, just the opposite. These accounts show that people came to Jesus from every level of society, in differing situations, with specific concerns and attitudes. Since they were a varied lot, they did not all receive the same treatment. Nor did they all leave equally satisfied. In order to emphasize what is unique in each of these stories I have told them from the point of view of the people meeting Jesus, to reconstruct as nearly as I can the angle of vision from which they might have seen him.

I have not arranged these stories in chronological order, but instead have grouped them according to the seeker's purpose in looking for Jesus. This plan allows me to compare the results of their searches more easily. Be aware, therefore, that each category contains episodes from different stages of Jesus' public life. While this chronological hopscotching may be somewhat confusing, I have tried to indicate at the beginning of each story where it fits into his brief career.

Supplying a context for these encounters has meant gathering relevant information about the setting—the social and political conditions, the geography and history of the region—and inserting information we require for understanding. The research literature on these four novella-length accounts literally fills libraries. Yet I have wanted to keep the stories as free of scholarly apparatus as they were for their original audience. Therefore, I have avoided footnotes and other intrusions into the text. Instead, I have provided a short list of books that were useful to me in my own search, and which supply a large part of the historical and sociological information with which I stuff the descriptive gaps in the gospels. Most direct quotations from the Bible are taken from the Authorized or King James Version. A few are from the Revised Standard Version. The frequent paraphrases are my own.

Keeping the Story Straight

Our surest and most spontaneous way of testing any story's truth is to measure it against our own lives. The implicit question we put to any movie or novel or even a family tale is always "What does this have to do with me? How does it match my own experience?" The gospels are no different. We must recognize the full human spectrum of the encounters presented in these stories. If we try to force them to conform to a single, inadequate mold formed by our own agendas, the mold will eventually crack under the pressure, contorting our own experience and falsifying the stories.

Interestingly, however, the gospels have a way of resisting our pushing and pulling to make them fit our molds. Whether one is ideologically committed to the inerrancy of scripture or takes a more cautious view of its accuracy, these stories after two millennia still act as touchstones for testing our own perceptions of reality. Is sacrifice actually the way to fulfillment? Do you really lose your life by trying to hoard it? This is why it is so important to keep the story straight, to see its central character clearly, to forgo inventing a Jesus who never existed. A fantasy-Jesus has neither enough substance nor sufficient strength to shatter our illusions about ourselves or the world we live in.

These sketches of meetings with Jesus are meant to illuminate and clarify the gospel narratives, while also making them permeable enough for entry. For only by entering his story can we hope to meet Jesus.

PART I

LOOKING FOR EXCITEMENT

Jesus became a celebrity when he was roughly thirty years old. Until then he had merely been the eldest son of a working-class family living in an otherwise insignificant village in the backwater province of Galilee. According to Matthew, the household was headed by Joseph, a carpenter, and Mark tells us that Jesus followed that trade himself until he left home. This didn't mean he built houses, however. Most Palestinian buildings were made of stone or adobe bricks. He probably made a living constructing and repairing common tools like plows, sledges, yokes, and household furniture. Except for Luke's account of the family's trip to Jerusalem for the Passover when Jesus was twelve years old, we know nothing of these early years and thus assume Jesus led an altogether quiet and unremarkable life in Nazareth, a stranger to fame.

Nevertheless, the city of Sepphoris, Galilee's capital, was only four miles north of Nazareth. During Jesus' lifetime the Romans rebuilt the city to house its provincial government. Included in the capital's renovation were public baths, a forum, a gymnasium, and a four-thousand-seat theater, evidence that the Empire relied on public entertainment—"bread and circuses"—to keep its provinces pacified. Joseph and Jesus may actually have worked as subcontractors on some of these projects. At the very least, trips to Sepphoris would have given the small-town boy his first taste of city life—and the capricious psychology of crowds drawn to public amusements. Familiarity with the theater also supplied him with a name for pretentious phonies: hypocrites, he called them, the Greek word for actors.

So how did a handyman from Nazareth get to be famous up and down the Palestinian provinces from Syria to the Negev? Certainly no one from his home village would have voted him their "young man most likely to succeed." After his first excursion into the larger world as an itinerant rabbi, Nazareth gave him a distinctly chilly homecoming. He certainly didn't fit their picture of a national hero. Even John the Baptist, who had been drawing huge crowds himself down in Judea, didn't recognize Jesus—his cousin, according to Luke's gospel—when he first appeared on the banks of the Jordan.

Despite this inauspicious beginning, Jesus doesn't seem to have worked on a marketing strategy to improve his public name recognition. In fact, just the opposite. In contrast to modern evangelists, he repeatedly cautioned his small band of followers, as well as the strangers he healed, *not* to broadcast either his deeds or his identity. Why? Not because he was shy, certainly. The most obvious answer is simply crowd control. Several times the gospels comment on how the crowds made even getting a meal difficult. Yet how can Jesus repeatedly insist on anonymity while performing feats that commonly draw crowds?

Not that Jesus was the only show in town. Palestine was known for its itinerant religious teachers—rabbis who traveled from town to town (much as conference speakers do today) expounding their particular take on the Torah. These roving rabbis found eager listeners as obsessed with Jewish scriptures as modern audiences are with spiritual self-help programs. Inevitably, such teachers were claimed by various political and theological factions among the Jews—Pharisees, Sadducees, Essenes, Zealots—and the conflict their open-air talk shows generated drew large crowds. Still, John the Baptist may well have been a more electrifying preacher than Jesus, since, according to Mark, it was only after the enormously popular John had been arrested that Jesus began speaking publicly.

Words alone, however, would not have been sufficient to draw the thousands Jesus was soon attracting. Not until news spread of his miraculous healings did his audiences begin to grow. Jesus' teaching may have been interesting, even provocative, but it was his miraculous cures that drew the crowds. After that, Mark tells us, though he tried to travel incognito, he was immediately recognized wherever he went. People "ran about the whole neighborhood and began to bring sick people on their pallets to any place where they heard he was. And wherever he came, in villages, cities or country, they laid the sick in the marketplaces, and besought him that they might touch even the fringe of his garment."

Yet even as a miracle worker, Jesus was not without precedent in Palestine. An order of Galilean rabbis called the Hasids, or Devout Ones, were believed to effect miracles through their powerful prayers. The region also produced at least two other miracle-working rabbis: Honi the Circle Drawer, who reportedly could produce rain in response to prayer, and Hanina Ben Dosa, who the Mishnah claims could heal people from a distance. Also, in the Acts of the Apostles we meet Simon the Sorcerer, who drew great crowds in Samaria with his magic show and tried to buy the secret of their healing power from the apostles. Miraculous cures were obviously the biggest draw for any itinerant wonder-worker, including Jesus.

While the percentage of intellectuals and scholars interested in theological debate would have been small among the crowds who came to see Jesus, not everyone was carrying sick kin on stretchers to be healed either. Most were simply thrill seekers, the first-century equivalent of groupies and autograph hounds, hoping to get a glimpse of the latest celebrity stirring things up in the provinces. This was Jesus' own unflattering assessment of his audience in Matthew. Speaking to the crowds he inherited from John the Baptist, Jesus accuses them of flocking to the prophet expecting a freak show—"a reed shaken by the wind"—a wild man whose antics would entertain them. He compares the crowd to children calling irritably to playmates who refused to play their game:

> "We piped to you, and you did not dance;
> we wailed, and you did not mourn."

After deserting John, they were now mobbing Jesus, hoping to gratify their childish craving for excitement and diversion.

Nevertheless, Jesus ends this tirade against the crowd's superficial expectations by praying for them. He thanks God for revealing himself, paradoxically, to these "babes," peevish and impulsive though they be, instead of to the "wise and prudent," those sensible, stable folk who always show up for work instead of taking the day off to chase celebrities.

Chapter 1

Bread and Circuses:

Feeding Thousands

A cast of thousands"—that's how Hollywood used to advertise its biblical epics like *The Ten Commandments* and *Ben Hur*. When the gospels claim these same numbers for the multitudes that flocked to see Jesus, scholars have sometimes called them inflated. On the other hand, no one denies that even larger numbers of people followed Gandhi as he trekked around India, and any reasonably successful rock star today easily draws triple the biblical figures.

However, I probably wouldn't have been among the throngs who spilled like lemmings from the Palestinian villages to see this miracle worker. I don't like crowds myself. I'm a stay-at-home, pay-per-view person who'd rather spend the price of a concert ticket on the album. Nor do I enjoy mass sporting events. Why endure inclement weather and parking hassles when you can watch a game on TV? So it's hard to imagine myself among the mass of shoving, shouting humanity surrounding the rabbi from Nazareth.

I'm also a wary person. Like most skeptics, I consider myself less gullible than the average person who browses the magazine rack at the checkout counter or watches *Unsolved Mysteries* on television. However, had I lived in the first century and heard about Jesus and his extraordinary healings, I wouldn't have had the luxury of waiting for *60 Minutes* to investigate Jesus or of catching even the edited coverage of his exploits on the nightly news. At that point in history, you either had to be there in person or settle for picking up rumors at the village well. And Jesus, at least for a couple of years, was the best, if not the only, show in town.

Whether or not you had any sick relatives to bring along, just the prospect of seeing a miraculous healing would have been enough to make most people swarm out into the countryside. Add the possibility of the proverbially elusive free lunch, and the crowds were bound to materialize.

Not that Jesus planned it that way. In fact, he probably thought he had settled the issue of whether to bait his message with bread at the outset of his preaching career. After his baptism by John at the Jordan River he had gone on several weeks' retreat in the wilderness to meditate on the task that lay before him. As frequently happens during extended periods of solitude, his worst nightmare showed up, turning his meditation into a kind of spiritual war game. Satan, the same spirit who had tried to wear Job down, presented him with the temptations. The first—and a powerful one, considering that Jesus had been fasting—was an invitation to turn stones into bread. On that occasion, Jesus had refused to appease his own hunger by disrupting the natural order. But how would he respond when it came to feeding others?

He got the chance to find out after several months—and in a setting curiously similar to the location of his original temptation.

Jesus' followers, having just returned from their own trial run of preaching, exorcism, and healing, find themselves besieged by demanding crowds. So great is the crush of curiosity seekers, in fact, that they have "no leisure so much as to eat." Thus, Jesus decides to take them off to "a desert place," hoping there they can rest and reflect on their recent experience without the distraction of the "many . . . coming and going."

Jesus has already procured a boat to take them across to the eastern shore of Lake Galilee. Since his fame has not yet spread to that region, he hopes to find the necessary solitude there for his pupils. The crowds catch on to this scheme to elude them, however, and set out for the far shore on foot. As they go, they spread the word in the towns ringing the lake, and their numbers swell even more. Thus, when Jesus steps out of the boat, a crowd is already there waiting for him. His plan has misfired. And this horde is hungry for a show.

The gospels, never long on overt interpretation of a scene, give us a rare glimpse of Jesus' emotional response to the situation: "he had compassion on them, because they were like sheep without a shepherd." He sympathizes with these people, far from their homes and neighbors in a district dominated by pagans. Who knows how the local authorities may feel about this sudden influx of strangers? How will they react to this aimlessly milling crowd?

And what is the crowd feeling? Tired and hungry. They've missed a day's wages. It's going to take something pretty spectacular to make the ten-mile hike worth it. The situation could easily turn nasty. It's a real challenge in crowd control.

Jesus neither denounces them as mere thrill seekers nor caves in to their expectations by dazzling them with magic. Instead, Mark reports that he began to "teach them many things." Luke adds that he "spoke to them of the kingdom of God, and healed them that had need of healing." Usually, teaching has been reserved for Jesus' inner circle of twelve or for his debates with Torah scholars who come to him with technical questions. And whether they are too tired to protest or genuinely interested in what he has to say, the crowd settles down to listen. In fact, they are still there when the sun begins to set.

At that point, though, despite Jesus' words of wisdom, their stomachs remember that it's been hours since they've eaten. What had begun as a lark—unplanned, impulsive—has left them cut off from all their ordinary resources. There are no friendly homes, no shops, no street vendors nearby.

Of course, they could just turn around and go home. But no one's looking forward to another ten-mile hike, especially on an empty stomach. Besides, it will be dark before they reach home again. And as for those who brought their sick relatives and friends all this way, there's no question of making it back tonight.

Still, there's no indication in any of the four gospels (and this is the single miracle story that all four record) that anyone in the crowd demands that Jesus feed them. While the crowd may have earlier acted "like sheep without a shepherd," they do not respond now the way one might expect of a hungry mob.

Jesus, no doubt, appreciates the irony of the situation; he's brought his disciples on this retreat so they could eat in peace, only to end up with thousands of hungry people on his hands, uninvited and unprovisioned.

In Mark's account, the disciples, growing uneasy with the hungry mob, point out to Jesus what a deserted place they're in and how late it's grown. They urge him to send the crowd away so they can buy supper in the surrounding villages. In John's gospel, Jesus turns to Philip, a native of the nearby town of Bethsaida, and asks if they can buy food there for the crowd. Philip immediately points out that it would take six months' wages just to give everyone a snack.

Both the question and the response indicate that Jesus' band of followers had a common treasury, funds we learn elsewhere were administered by Judas. Their assets could not, however, have been very large, certainly not enough to feed five thousand people. And blowing their resources on food for the crowd is obviously not Philip's idea of responsible money management.

Nevertheless, much to the consternation of his disciples, Jesus refuses to send the people away, "lest they faint in the way." In every story in which the multitudes are fed (six in all), this same interchange occurs. First, the disciples want to get rid of the crowd, but Jesus forestalls their dismissal, instructing the disciples to feed the people themselves. Then the disciples protest their lack of financial resources, at which point Jesus, bypassing any cash reserves, calls for an inventory of available food.

The crowd, meanwhile, are ignorant of these negotiations. Their appetite for words and deeds has been satisfied; now they're hungry for a real meal deal. They realize they're a long way from home, yet they don't wander off and scatter. They wait.

After all, that's what they've learned from Jesus' teaching that day about the Kingdom. They're like seed, he's told them. Like the birds of the air, flowers of the field. So they're not worrying about where their next meal's coming from. They're just waiting for it to be served.

The inventory of the crowd's resources, meanwhile, yields only five loaves and two fish. Mark and John agree that it is an unnamed boy who supplies the loaves (no more than buns really) and salted sardine-size fish, probably one of those children we're told to emulate if we hope to enter the kingdom of heaven. Nevertheless, if I had been in the crowd that day and watched this transaction, my question would have been the same as Andrew's: "But what are they among so many?" The crowd, now orderly and obedient, sits down on the grass in rows as they've been instructed; their faith is at least temporarily superior to the disciples'.

In fact, the crowd's behavior is the most astonishing, yet the most overlooked, aspect of this story. When Jesus first stepped out of the boat, they were no more than a mob—sheep without a shepherd. Yet in the course of the next few hours they have become something different. Their chaos gets ordered into a congregation, a flock that recognizes its shepherd. They neither demand bread, like an unruly rabble, nor doubt that it will be provided when promised. The member who has resources offers them up for the good of all, the rest divide themselves into groups and sit as they've been instructed. They watch as Jesus offers the traditional thanks for the bread, hands it off to his helpers, along with the fish, and then wait patiently while it's distributed.

In none of the gospel accounts does Jesus pull food out of a hat like a magician. He always begins with actual, material bread and fish that someone in the crowd has handed over. What happened next? How were the loaves and fishes "multiplied"? Did the cells of the barley meal and fish flesh replicate themselves, blooming into bountiful basketfuls?

Some interpreters of this story claim that, under the influence of the boy's example, other people in the crowd sheepishly take out provisions they've been holding back and share them with their neighbors. All the gospels say is that there was enough. More than enough actually. Twelve baskets—not wastebaskets, but containers travelers used to pack provisions for a journey—were afterward filled with the leftovers. So not only was the crowd fed, but the doubting disciples, in the end, become the beneficiaries of this mysterious largesse.

Neither the magical nor the moral explanation for the feast entirely satisfies me. The first implies that supernatural cell reproduction is a greater wonder than changed hearts. But the second explanation posits a multitude who came prepared to camp out, a condition the story itself does not support. Certainly Jesus thinks they have no food or he wouldn't have been concerned about their hunger. He knows these people acted on impulse when they set out to follow him to this lonely place. No one took time to go home and pack a picnic lunch.

Still other theologians have made much of these stories as symbolic representations of the Eucharist, artfully inserted into the text by the gospel editors to provide literary foreshadowing of the church's later ritual. More likely, it happened the other way around. The story is the real thing, the way faith works on those rare occasions we can pump ourselves up for it. The story chronicles an actual instance when, at least once in this world's history, people took Jesus at his word. They didn't panic. They waited. In consequence, they were bound together into a common body. To my mind, the rituals are the shadowy recollection of that fact.

We often choose our interpretation, I believe, because we are like the disciples rather than the crowd. Some of us, worried about how we're ever going to meet the needs of the hungry and diseased masses of the world, miss what Jesus says about the flowers of the field and the birds of the air. The crowd, however, undistracted by feelings of obligation, hears those words and takes them to heart. Thus, when they're asked for their resources, they hand them over, confident that they will meet the present need, not troubled about the mechanics of the process.

Sure, they're a gullible lot. Any would-be messiah can—and frequently does—deceive such crowds. "People will believe anything," skeptics like myself often say in disgust. And it's true. But believing anything, in the hope of hitting on the real McCoy once in a while, may be superior to never believing, never being duped, and thus missing your one chance at a miraculous meal.

Despite myself, I find I like this crowd. They, after all, are the true heroes of the story. Compared to them, the disciples come off as tightfisted misers. I would have been glad to join this multitude hiking around the lake, if only, for once, I could feel a part of something larger than myself—that I had entered into a partnership with providence, had received its profuse bounty.

Superstar Status:

Entering Jerusalem

*T*he shouting masses who welcomed Jesus to Jerusalem at the end of his career were a different kettle of fish from the rural Galileans he had fed in the wilderness earlier. This was a big-city crowd, mostly from Jerusalem and its outlying suburbs, though augmented by Jews from all over the known world who had come to the holy city to celebrate Passover, the event that had first marked them as distinct and given them their identity as Jews. Passover was the time of year when people would be feeling most passionate about that identity. Many among the crowd had, at great expense and trouble, traveled back to their spiritual capital just to eat the Passover seder there. Even today, wherever Jews gather to celebrate this meal, they end the evening with the cry, "Next year in Jerusalem!"

We would call their passion nationalism today, though that wouldn't have been quite accurate in Jesus' time. For one thing, Israel had ceased to be a nation, in a political sense, hundreds of years earlier, when the country was conquered by a series of foreign powers and large segments of its inhabitants deported, often to other continents. By the first century A.D. between seven and eight million Diaspora Jews lived scattered across the far reaches of the Roman Empire. But they considered themselves no less Jews for all that. And for good reason. Though repeated attempts to throw off foreign domination and reclaim control of their country had all failed disastrously, Jews still managed to maintain their religion intact.

Syrian kings had first tried to force Greek culture, including polytheism, on the region. When the Jews resisted, thousands had been slaughtered for their obstinate orthodoxy. Then, the Maccabee rebels still lived in the popular imagination as heroes and martyrs of this quasi nation two centuries after they had reclaimed the Temple from the Greek god Zeus. In recent years, however, a more pragmatic Jewish religious establishment had worked out a deal with Rome whereby the Empire granted them immunity from the prescribed emperor worship in deference to their monotheistic religious sensibilities. In exchange, the chief priests at the Temple promised to maintain peace and suppress any disruptive elements among their people.

And they had their hands full doing it. Certain factions among the Jews still clung tenaciously to the notion of themselves as a people apart, whose link to the land of Palestine, given by divine decree, endured over time and despite political exigencies. A Galilean named Judas, along with a revolutionary Pharisee named Zadok, had founded the Zealot party, which urged all Jews not to pay taxes to Rome and, in general, not to acknowledge their foreign masters. Twice already they had incited their compatriots to riot in Jerusalem.

This mixture of political xenophobia and religious idealism both amazed and irritated the rest of the civilized world. Sure, everyone feels a certain nostalgia for his place of origin—the hometown, the region, even a country—so long as it continues to exist. But in the eyes of the Empire the Jews had turned an attachment into a obsession. Pride in our own regional roots pales in comparison to that of the first-century Jews. The lingering devotion of certain Southerners to Dixie, a country that abides only in the imagination, comes closest, perhaps.

At any rate, when you picture the people who lined the road into the city of Jerusalem that day, don't think of the sedate processions many churches stage on Palm Sunday, the congregation timidly shaking thin palmetto stalks ordered from a Florida florist. Think instead of the ecstatic faces of French soccer fans whose team unexpectedly won the World Cup in 1998. Or a bunch of rednecks and fraternity boys waving the doomed Stars and Bars at the approach of a reincarnated Robert E. Lee.

Jesus, the latest man of the people (there had been others before him and others would follow), embodied the Jews' dream of independence from Roman rule and the triumph of traditional values over a perverted secular culture. The crowd saw him as their champion who would redress inequity, reclaiming their rightful heritage. In contemporary terms, someone who, depending on your preferred agenda, could (a) restore family values in America, (b) put an end to discrimination against gays and lesbians, (c) halt illegal immigration, (d) give women and minorities their fair share of the work and wages. A figure on whom you could pin your highest hopes.

Jesus begins his final journey to Jerusalem knowing he will be perceived this way. He is returning there against the advice of his disciples, who remind him that, on his last visit to Jerusalem, he was almost stoned for certain incendiary remarks that had been interpreted as blasphemy. He starts out from Bethany, a village about two miles northeast of the city where, in a public display of his supernatural powers, he had resurrected a friend from the tomb in which he had been interred for three days.

News of this spectacular event, along with Jesus' reputation as a healer and teacher who dares to challenge the Temple hierarchy, has inflamed the popular imagination. People are talking in terms of a messiah, a hero, a deliverer, alongside whom other rabbis and the priests look weak and ineffective. The chief priests know this man is a threat to their own power, which depends on their ability to keep the crowds under control. No doubt at least some members of the hierarchy are genuinely concerned for the security of the common people, who will suffer if the Passover crowds get out of hand. So great is their combined fear and concern that they make common cause with the Pharisees, not ordinarily their allies. Worried "the whole world has gone after him," they conspire to put a price on this would-be messiah's head.

Jesus understands that, mob psychology being what it is, he will not be able to enter the city without drawing a crowd. Unlike the multitude in Galilee who were content to sit down in orderly groups and listen to him teach, this horde is not interested in a sermon. Thus he chooses a visual image, a type of performance art, if you will, to emphasize his peaceful intent. In an attempt to undercut the crowd's perception of him as a military figure challenging imperial authority, Jesus sends his disciples ahead to procure a young donkey for him to ride. Those Jews well versed in scripture would remember that at least one of the prophets had pictured the redeemer of Israel appearing in such a guise. And any Middle Eastern audience would recognize the donkey as the sign of a king coming in peace, not as a conquering hero.

And when the crowd sees the man on the donkey, the people go wild. They rampage through the neighborhood, just as the religious leaders predicted they would—ripping off tree branches to wave like flags, even stripping off their clothes to carpet the road where it descends from the Mount of Olives to the eastern gate of the city. As the man on the donkey rides by, they shout "Hosanna," an Aramaic term which most English Bibles translate as "Peace."

But other, less peaceful, acclamations ring out as well. "Son of David," "he that cometh in the name of the Lord," even "king," and—most inflammatory of all—"the King of Israel." These titles would have done little to reassure either the establishment Jews or the Roman authorities. And, in fact, it will be "King of the Jews" that appears on the notice nailed atop Jesus' cross only days later.

The Pharisees, mingling with the throng, not as supporters but as potential witnesses against him, push through the shouting masses to appeal to Jesus. "Rabbi," they plead, realizing the danger these politically charged slogans put them all in, "for heaven's sake, tell them to shut up!"

But for once Jesus appears powerless to bend the will of the crowd. "If I told them to be quiet," he replies, "the stones themselves would immediately cry out."

His old adversaries the Pharisees no doubt hear his response as a boast; rather, it signals his resignation. Jesus pauses before the final descent to the city, looking at the shining Temple below, recently restored to its former splendor as a goodwill gesture by the pagan Herod. He is not pausing to bask in his popularity with the masses nor to gloat over his discomfited enemies. Instead he is crying.

We only see Jesus in tears one other place in the gospels, at the tomb of his friend Lazarus. But he is weeping now for another death—and not his own. He is mourning for the capital whose name means City of Peace, and for the crowds who have been crying "Peace," but who want something else. He foretells in graphic terms the death of that city, the tragedy that will come from its embrace of war rather than peace. In roughly forty more years, his vision will become a reality when the Roman armies level the city. No stone will be left standing. The Temple of which the Jews are so proud will be torn down. The very earth will be sown with salt so that nothing grows. "Jerusalem, Jerusalem," he cries, "if you had only known the things that make for peace! But you just can't see it, can you?"

The crowd, meanwhile, pays no attention to the tears of its hero. They have turned the figure of sorrow into a symbol of defiance and rebellion. A figurehead for their fantasies of vindication.

Of course, they had no access that day to the dramatic irony with which we read this story today. We know what they cannot—that their hero will die shamefully, like all the other messiahs who arose to threaten the Roman Empire, and that they will play a part in that death. In a few more days, these archpatriots will be shouting, "We have no king but Caesar."

Chapter 3

Excitement:
Reconsidering Crowds

I have already said that I don't like crowds. I think my aversion started in high school when we were regularly herded into the gym for assemblies. There we sat on concrete bleachers while the principal made speeches on topics like good citizenship or how smoking could lead to drug addiction. The worst assemblies, however, were the ones called on the eve of major football games. First the cheerleaders in their letter sweaters and short, pleated skirts breathlessly told us how the guys on the team really needed the support of the student body to beat the crap out of the team of another school, across town. Our part was to supply "school spirit."

Having an incurably literal mind, I would sit, while everyone around me went wild, pondering that term "student body." Did all the students in the gym make up some kind of conglomerate organism? Did we meld into a clumsy, lumbering mound of studenthood? What *was* a student body? And even more puzzling, what was "school spirit"? All my prior reference points for the word "spirit" were religious. As in Holy Spirit, or unclean spirits—the kind Jesus cast out of people. I felt some faint, intuitive understanding of those terms. But surely we weren't being asked to invest a football game with religious significance, were we?

That was precisely the case, of course, though I'm certain both the principal and the cheerleaders would have denied any such implication. Yet I have since figured out that school spirit—like party pride or patriotism or even clan loyalty—is nothing more than that fierce sense of cohesion which enters large groups of people simultaneously. Sometimes it persists over fairly long stretches of time—during war, for instance. Sometimes it lasts only for the length of a football game.

Despite the darker side of crowd psychology, there's nevertheless something to be said for throwing caution to the winds, for getting caught up in shared emotion, especially joy. I got the same psychic charge from choral singing in high school that others did from football games. Therefore, I like to think that, given their circumstances, I might have joined either the crowd on the lakeshore or the one welcoming Jesus to Jerusalem. I hope I'm not so wary of crowds that I wouldn't have dropped what I was doing that morning if a friend stopped by, breathless, to tell me Jesus was in the neighborhood and I'd better get a move on if I wanted to see this miracle man. I don't like to see myself, prudent like the Pharisees, trying to shush the crowd shouting their hosannas.

Wanting excitement, wanting to see miracles and marvels, hoping that this time it really *is* the Messiah—those are not evil desires or dreams. And while Jesus did his best to escape celebrity hounds, he never rebukes either the Galileans' curiosity nor the Passover rabble's enthusiasm.

At the same time, however, he knows that crowds can get out of control. In the first instance, he divided the mass of people into smaller segments, defusing some of their energy, which might have become destructive. He made them sit down to keep them from milling around, stirring up dust and trouble. Then he gave them what they only dimly perceived they wanted. Along with healing the diseased, he also spoke to their hearts and minds, and in such a way that, tired and hungry though they were, they trusted him for their daily bread. This crowd, then, like the prodigal son, got more than they asked for.

The Jerusalem crowd, however, had perhaps too definite an idea of what they wanted from the man they went out to welcome to the city. Along with their hope of a messiah, they brought their job description for him. They imposed on the man riding the donkey their own vision of a messiah as defiant rebel. Many of them, caught up in the spirit of revolt, might have willingly died with him.

But their vision quickly faded. This so-called messiah issued no call to arms, submitted meekly when he was arrested, offered no further challenge to either ecclesiastical or political authority. Fame is fragile, hinging on an implicit transaction between celebrities and their fans. If the celebrity doesn't live up to the crowd's expectations, its mood can quickly turn ugly. No one buys a ticket to see Madonna in a shirtwaist singing hymns.

Unlike the Galileans on the hillside, this Passover crowd, who knew only too well what they wanted from Jesus, were not open to receiving what he had to give. As individuals, they might have heard him out, listened to his pitch for the true kingdom, but as a crowd their corporate vision, centuries in the making, was too fixed, too obdurate to allow for alteration. It was impossible to hear his voice above the shouting.

PART II

LOOKING FOR RELIEF

The ancient world had no hospitals. Nor any medical insurance or disability pay. Sick people were either cared for at home or, lacking family support, ended up on the streets. You couldn't go to a shop or the synagogue without stumbling over some paraplegic beggar. Disease, deformity, and death were highly visible, a common sight in everyday life of first-century Palestine. Even lepers, required by law to live outside the city limits, were not shut away; as soon as travelers ventured outside their village, they were often set upon by lepers announcing their presence with bells and begging bowls.

Nowadays, we isolate the ill—in hospitals, nursing homes, rehabilitation centers, schools for the blind and deaf. Sometimes this is for good reason, to avoid the spread of infection or for efficiency's sake. But we mainly keep sick folk out of sight to spare ourselves—the healthy ones—the sights, sounds, and smells of disease. I certainly don't want to romanticize the way the sick were treated in the ancient world, nor would I want to do without the modern benefits of antibiotics and sterile operating instruments. But, if nothing else, the first century at least allowed the sufferers a certain visible reality whereas we store them someplace away from view. Surely people then feared physical calamity as much as we do now, but their constant exposure to the ill and infirm kept them acquainted with the frailty of their own flesh.

Yet despite all our precautions, disease—or rather, its denial—has become our national obsession. We spend more on medical research and treatment, insurance, health clubs, running shoes, diet plans, and exercise videos than on the basics of food and shelter. Yet the very sight of the sick or elderly fills us with dread. I know a number of people too squeamish to visit friends in the hospital. We maintain the childish belief that what we don't see doesn't exist.

New vocabularies are invented to disguise disease, words that gloss over uncomfortable realities. Doctors, for instance, prefer to say "carcinoma" rather than "cancer." And instead of using the blunt biblical terms "blind," "deaf," "crippled," we now say "visually challenged," "hearing impaired," "handicapped." Supporters of these circumlocutions justify them as less destructive to the sufferer's self-esteem, and perhaps they're right. Surely no one wants to be defined by a disease. But do they want the reality of their condition denied?

Jesus would have seen plenty of sick people as he walked through the streets of Galilean towns and along the highways to Jericho and Jerusalem. They were everywhere—in the markets, beside the doorway of every public building, in the homes where he was invited. You didn't have to visit the sick; you had to step over them. Especially those whose disabilities made them dependent on begging for a living—the blind, the lame, and lepers.

And once Jesus began healing the diseased and deformed, he was soon surrounded by them. He became a one-man walking emergency room. If you want to know what the crowds that followed Jesus looked like, try visiting the trauma unit at a county hospital. No matter how often he implored the person healed to keep quiet about it, the word always got out. Soon a veritable tide of diseased and crippled folk packed the courtyards of the homes where he stayed and the streets of the towns he visited. An epidemiologist's nightmare. It wasn't long before the crowds became so great that he could deal with them only out in the open countryside.

Now for the big question: so how did he do it?

That's really what we want to know. As creatures of the technological age, we want to understand the mechanics of healing, whether medical or miraculous. If we're skeptics, we want to know how Jesus created the illusion of health. If we're believers, we still want to pin down the necessary ingredients, develop a reliable do-it-yourself guide.

The usual technique for analyzing any problem is to break it down into component parts in the hope of seeing how they all fit together, the same way curious children dismantle household machinery or medical students learn anatomy. And there are, in fact, a number of ways to classify the cases Jesus took on. We could, for instance, divide them into types of diseases—blindness, leprosy, paralysis, and the like. Or by gender or age. Or sort those who asked to be cured from those whose healing was solicited by friends or relatives, or from others who were restored without anyone requesting it. A roughly equal number, we find, fall into each of those last three categories. There are examples, in fact, to illustrate all the classifications I've mentioned. The stories represent diverse diseases and conditions, different ages, sexes, and stations, as well as various methods of connecting with the healer.

So what does this analysis tell us about the mechanics of healing? Is there a right time and place? Is there a system to it? Can it be codified? Is faith necessary or not? If so, what kind? Is there a protocol? a rubric? a magic word?

Such questions, one way or another, underlie all the commentaries and scholarship—including the debunking sort—written about these stories. I confess these same questions drive my own inquiry. Not because I have any personal aspiration to be a healer myself but because, like all those sick and broken people in the gospels, I too fear pain and depletion.

Almost every day now I hear about some friend or relative being tested or diagnosed for their death sentence. As I write this, my aunt is dying in North Carolina. She will not live to see these pages in print. Last night I heard that a friend, only two years older than I, is undergoing tests for throat cancer which may well have already spread to her lymph glands. My father has just added a fifth heart medication to his daily pharmacological regimen. Tomorrow I go for my annual mammogram. Last week the doctor sent the bad news from my husband's cholesterol test. All of us know that, despite what we like to call "modern medicine," we are fighting a war of attrition against disease and death. We all eventually fail our diagnostic tests.

When I reach that point, I know I'm going to be looking for relief. And I want to know what I can expect Jesus to do about it.

Chapter 4

A Bloody Shame:
The Woman with the Issue of Blood

A section of the law code contained in Leviticus, the third book of the Bible, covers "uncleanness," a technical term designating, in this case, a discharge of bodily fluids. This section, which includes proscriptions and precautions against contamination, sounds like a contemporary manual for safeguarding against AIDS. Since the germ theory of disease hadn't been invented yet, all discharges from the body—semen, pus, mucus, and blood—were treated similarly—including menstrual blood. Every article of clothing or bedding touched by anyone secreting these fluids had to be washed and the person quarantined.

A subsection in Leviticus deals specifically with a gynecological condition, probably that known to us as endometriosis: "When a woman has a discharge of blood for many days at a time other than her monthly period or has a discharge that continues beyond her period, she will be unclean as long as she has the discharge, just as in the days of her period. Any bed she lies on while her discharge continues will be unclean, as is her bed during her monthly period, and anything she sits on will be unclean, as during her period. Whoever touches them will be unclean; he must wash his clothes and bathe with water, and he will be unclean until evening."

Such restrictions would obviously put a crimp in one's social life. If the woman were single, it would mean the end of her marriage prospects until the condition cleared up. If she were married, her husband could not sleep with her. If it went on for an extended period, he could divorce her. She would radically complicate the lives of anyone with whom she lived, family or not.

The woman in this story has not stopped bleeding for twelve long years. The physical weakness resulting from such anemia would be bad enough, but the social consequences would be, if anything, worse. She would have been isolated, shamed, fearful of appearing in public. Because Mark's gospel tells us that the woman "had suffered much under many physicians, and had spent all that she had," we may assume she began her ordeal as a woman of some means, though she may be down to her last dollar by the time she goes looking for Jesus.

The story is set in Galilee, probably in the town of Capernaum. Jesus, by now famous for his teaching and healing, has just returned from yet another unsuccessful attempt to elude the crowds by crossing the region's large inland lake. He has no sooner stepped out of the boat than a man called Jairus approaches him. Because Jairus is a well-known and important figure in the town, in fact a member of the board of directors for the local synagogue, the crowd would have parted, opened a space for him to speak to the rabbi. The crowd would have been aware of his extreme need also. The man's daughter, only twelve years old, is sick and at the point of death. Jairus begs Jesus to come home with him and heal his little girl before it's too late. Jesus immediately starts out with the man to his house, the crowd pushing and shoving around them, eager to be on hand to see this next miraculous cure.

Now is the worst possible moment for this woman with the secret uncleanness to stop Jesus and make her own petition. He is, after all, dealing with a life-and-death situation. Her own condition is not quite so desperate. She's waited twelve years already; surely she can wait for a more convenient time. What are a few hours, even an extra day, when a child's life is at stake?

Consider too that the woman is extremely reticent. Socially ostracized for twelve years, she probably shrinks from speaking to anyone publicly. Though her ailment is not obvious, like blindness or a crippled limb or leprosy, by now the whole town must know her situation. She would find it hard to work up the nerve to speak to Jesus even if he had not just received another and more pressing appeal.

Yet even shy people can be desperate. And quick-witted. Finding herself near the miracle worker and knowing she may never get this close to him again, she reaches out and touches the tasseled fringe on his outer cloak, the sign of a devout Jew. Just this physical contact with his clothing will be enough to cure her, she feels.

To our modern noses, this gesture smells of superstition. We like our healing accomplished by antibiotics or hormone therapy, not amulets or fetishes. Even the orthodox believer may feel a little uneasy with the woman's belief in Jesus' magic tassel.

But it works. I like the drama of the King James Version's description here: "And straightway the fountain of her blood was dried up; and she felt in her body that she was healed of that plague." The text emphasizes the physicality of her cure. Instead of a vague spiritual sense of assurance, the woman feels the blood flow stop; she feels the healing *in her body*.

Her relief is short-lived, however. Jesus immediately stops and whirls about. "Who did that?" he demands. "Who touched my clothes?" For he too has felt a reciprocal flow of energy draining from his body.

The disciples, acting as their rabbi's bodyguards to clear his path through the crowd, are exasperated by the question. "All these people pushing and shoving, and you want to know *who* touched you?"

But Jesus is already peering into the faces nearest him. His eyes fall on the woman.

Realizing she's been found out, she's now afraid. Her fleeting boldness deserts her. She knows she has breached the law even by being there, that all the people who have jostled against her in the crowd are now technically unclean as well, that even by touching the rabbi's robe, she has defiled this important figure on his way to save a child's life. She falls at the rabbi's feet, spilling out her story as quickly as she can, waiting for the blow of his denunciation to fall.

But even as she confesses, she is no doubt hugging the knowledge of her body's renewed health, aware that, if she had it to do over again, she would change nothing.

Miraculously, however—the second miracle in as many minutes—the rabbi neither scolds nor exposes her. In fact, the very name he calls her acts as a balm to her wounded spirit: "Daughter," he says, and with that one intimate word rakes her back inside the circle of Abraham's family, "your faith has made you whole." He discounts his own part in the miracle, as if he has only been a conduit through which the healing power flowed into her. He had been focused on Jairus's child, not her. He therefore attributes the woman's healing to her own belief in his efficacy.

To be "made whole" indicates more than to be healed. It carries the larger meaning of "made blessed," a more comprehensive state than simple restoration of proper bodily functioning. The words encompass the cloud that has isolated her from other people for twelve disastrous years. "Go in peace," the rabbi adds, "and be healed of your disease."

Chapter 5

Let Down by Friends:
Paralyzed on a Pallet

*V*acation Bible school was one of the few places where I was able to shine as a child. Never good at sports—not even jacks—I could nevertheless beat out the other six-year-olds in games requiring quick recall of Bible stories. Why my church fostered competition using material manifestly meant to discourage rather than promote pride, I don't know, but all the teacher had to say was "a certain man," and my little hand would shoot up, waggling my eagerness to identify the parable of the Good Samaritan.

Another thing I liked about vacation Bible school was the models we got to build. Tiny biblical villages with snippets of hedge for trees and a round mirror for the Lake of Galilee. We patted clay into square Palestinian houses and folded strips of heavy construction paper accordionwise for the steps running up the outer wall to the flat roof. There, we were told, the family spent their evening hours to escape the heat and darkness indoors. We all wanted to live in houses where you could go up on the rooftops. We used twigs to simulate the roof beams on our models, stuffed the spaces between them with pine needles, and plastered them over with clay to fill in the chinks. Whatever damage vacation Bible school did to my spiritual development, at least it taught me the logistics involved in the story of the paralyzed man let down through a rooftop on a stretcher by his friends.

Mark's version mentions Capernaum, Peter's village, as the site of this story. Jesus has just returned from a successful tour of regional synagogues and is trying to get some rest, possibly in the same house where he had previously healed Peter's mother-in-law.

His popularity in the town is at its height, however, and the house is soon mobbed, its common room filled to capacity. Even the courtyard outside the single doorway would be packed.

Inside the house with Jesus, the most important people—scribes and representatives of the Pharisee party—are listening to what the young rabbi has to say about Torah. Scribes got their name from their occupation of copying the Torah, a task that made them more familiar with finer points of the Law than the ordinary people. Scribes moved in the same intellectual circles as the ascetic Pharisees, laymen who lived by a higher standard of conduct than the average Jew. Some of these may have also been Hasids, a charismatic offshoot of the Pharisees. Several Hasids were also known as healers, and, in fact, Luke's account remarks that on this particular occasion, the healing power of the Lord was present. Nevertheless, the true passion of Jewish scholars and religious enthusiasts of every stripe was *talk*. They minutely dissected and debated the finer points of Torah interpretation with as much fervor as men rehash football games today.

Meanwhile, the people crammed into the courtyard outside have the common expectations of crowds. They want to see a little action, maybe even have their diseases treated. They're already growing restless when four men arrive, each carrying the corner of a sleeping mat on which a fifth man, a paraplegic, lies. At first they try to push through the crowd to the doorway. They're not particularly interested in the theological debates going on inside, but they figure if they can deposit their friend at the rabbi's feet, he can make their friend walk again. Simple as that. No lessons necessary, no debate required. Unfortunately, however, access is.

My vacation Bible school teacher liked to dwell on the devotion of the man's friends, whom she portrayed as selfless Red Cross workers. In that peculiar tone of urgency with which she always signaled the point of a story, she told us we should be like the man's friends—helpful, resourceful, determined. Then nothing would discourage us from bringing our friends to meet Jesus in Sunday school.

Reading the story now, though, I wonder what these fellows

were really like. Judging from the crowd's unwillingness to clear a path for them, they can't have been very important people in Capernaum. Even the man on the stretcher didn't seem to arouse much pity in the hearts of the villagers.

With the Bible being distressingly skimpy on description, we can only speculate from the few, spare details the story includes. For one thing, the paraplegic has to rely on his buddies, rather than family members, to haul him to the house in Capernaum. This makes me question my vacation Bible school teacher's sentimental portrayal of them. They may just as easily have been a bunch of rowdies, the rough-and-ready sort who do their male bonding in bars and never spend a day in vacation Bible school. Maybe they'd been drinking already. In fact, this seems a distinct possibility, given how they deal with their access problem.

Barred from the house by the crush of unsympathetic people, they make for the outside stairs. After hauling the stretcher up the steps, they don't even hesitate but, like some first-century motorcycle gang, start ripping up the roof. Which wouldn't have been particularly difficult. They would only have to break up the clay coating, dig out the brushwood and thin branches beneath, and, through the three-foot aperture between the beams, stuff their paraplegic friend, pallet and all. Probably the four friends attached rope to the corners of the mat (though we used twine in vacation Bible school)—Capernaum was a fishing village where rope was ready to hand—and let their surprise package down, hand over hand, into the midst of the astounded intellectuals below. They probably even laugh when the dislodged clods of dirt rain down on the upturned faces of the stunned scholars.

Jesus looks up at the hole in the roof, rimmed by the grinning faces of the men. They must feel pretty pleased with themselves at that moment. They've managed to outsmart the unsympathetic crowd blocking the door of the house, and they've certainly surprised the big shots inside. For them, it would have been like those satisfying moments described in the Psalms, when the proud get their comeuppance. I picture gratification on those faces peering down through the hole in the roof, maybe even vindication.

Yet the gospels call what Jesus sees faith. He studies the inert body they have deposited at his feet and addresses their friend. "Son," he says, "your sins are forgiven."

To this day, we're still wondering just what he meant by that. It sounds like a tremendous non sequitur to the modern ear. Lacking is the hearty "How are you doing today?" with which doctors greet patients now, or even a tender word of commiseration with the man's condition. In fact, the rabbi appears to ignore the man's paralysis entirely and to focus instead on his spiritual health.

Some scholarly interpreters point to the close connection in all ancient religions between illness and infraction of some divine code. Others think Jesus was just using the situation to set up the Torah experts, baiting them by making a declaration only God has the authority to pronounce. I have even wondered if Jesus, glancing up at the roof just torn apart on the paraplegic's behalf, didn't remark, half jokingly, "Look at the mess your friends have made — and all for you! Well, okay, I forgive you."

Or did it go deeper than that? Was there, in fact, some connection between the friends' faith and the man's sins? All three of the synoptic gospels emphasize this link, as if this were an essential point. The man hasn't asked for forgiveness, though it's possible his paralysis is so extensive he can't speak. No one, not even Jesus, delineates just what the man's sins might be. Was there some difficulty between the five of them that needed straightening out? The gospels preserve this privacy with a cloak as impenetrable as a confessional. But supposedly Jesus knows forgiveness is necessary before the paralysis can vanish.

The scholars, meanwhile, stroke their beards and frown. They obviously do not question the man's need for forgiveness. But how dare this young rabbi presume to grant him amnesty? To joke about such matters is sacrilege. To utter words that can be spoken only by God himself — it's unthinkable. In fact, unforgivable. But Mark reports they are silent, hesitant to confront the rabbi with their objection. Unlike the men who have torn up the roof, the scholars lack the courage of their convictions.

Biblical commentators, especially those who take the scriptures seriously, often delight in beating up on Pharisees and scribes every chance they get, casting them as defensive, turf-protecting pedants. Jesus, however, has little difficulty figuring out why they're offended. He knows as well as they do that forgiving sins is God's prerogative and can hardly expect them to feel other than outraged at his presumption. Was he necessarily upset by their response? Again, we have no description of his tone when he speaks to their silent grievance—whether angrily or with wry humor. As it is, we have only the words themselves.

"Okay," he says, "so what do you think? Is it harder to say 'Your sins are forgiven' or to say 'pick up your pallet and walk'?"

The question, whatever his tone, is a teaser. *Is it harder to say . . . ?* The question doesn't strike me as rhetorical. In fact, I'm still not sure of the answer. It makes us wonder about the link between disease and what we prefer to call destructive behavior, rather than sin. But changing such behavior sometimes seems harder than healing disease. I expect we will discover a cure for cancer before we stop polluting the planet or addicting ourselves to drugs. Can your neighbor's diabetes be controlled with medication? Yes. Can she and her husband learn to stop fighting? Don't count on it.

The scholars sitting around the young rabbi fear that his words may be just cheap talk. Is the question he throws at them mere braggadocio? The man is gambling a lot by offering to validate his authority with miracle. Which position is worse, he's asking: to risk charges of blasphemy or to risk humiliating failure? He'll reveal himself to be either a blasphemer or a huckster. Or something too enormous to think about.

"Fine," he concludes, when they maintain their silence. "Just so you know I do indeed have authorization to perform the invisible act of forgiving his sins, I'm going to also perform the visible act of healing this man's paralysis." Here he turns to the man lying immobile at his feet. "You," he says, and the words in Greek sound brusque, "get up. Pick up your pallet and go on home."

The man rises up, probably first testing his weight on his elbows, then rolling onto his knees and bundling the mat like a sleeping bag. Finally, he scrambles to his feet, stuffs his bedding under his arm, and heads for the door. He wastes no time arguing. He couldn't care less what the theological debate is about—he's out of there.

Inside the house the scholars listen to the man's yelps of joy as he hurries away home. And though many well-meaning commentators seize this opportunity to gloat over the reaction of the Pharisees and scribes, we should give those Torah experts credit for once. According to Mark, they are not only properly astonished at the miraculous healing, but praise God for it—another indication that this particular assortment may have contained Hasids. They openly admit they've never seen anything like it before. Luke leaves them ruminating, "We have seen strange things today."

But what did the paraplegic, once he calmed down, think about this strange twist in his fate? We never know. Throughout this story, he is little more than a pawn, a passive spectator to his own healing. We don't know if he shared his friends' confidence that this rabbi would heal him or if they took him to Peter's house under protest. Other than his shouts of joy, he never speaks a single word during the entire encounter.

And those men still up on the roof, did they stare at one another with their mouths open when they saw their friend get to his feet? Did they slap their palms together in an ancient version of a high-five? In my imagination, they descend the construction-paper stairway no more soberly than they went up. Like their friend who's already hightailing it for home, they do a good bit of whooping and hollering themselves.

As the scene fades and the figures recede into the distance, we have to accept that we don't know the rest of their story. The former paraplegic goes home to his family, but did he join those buddies the next day in the field or the fishing boat, happy to finally be earning his living? Did he acknowledge his debt to their faith? Was the psychological adjustment difficult? None of these questions is answered. Jesus himself does not inquire further about the man's circumstances, nor does the gospel say he paid a follow-up visit. He had his own friends to worry about, after all.

Chapter 6

Breaking the Silence:
The Deaf and Dumb Man

Geography is important in Mark's version of this story. It begins with Jesus and his band of followers on the Mediterranean coast of Phoenicia, one of the three gentile regions surrounding predominantly Jewish Galilee. The gospels usually refer to Phoenicia as "Tyre and Sidon" after its two principal cities. Jesus' motives for leaving his home turf of Galilee are not explicitly stated, but since Galilee's ruler, Herod Antipas, has recently executed John the Baptist, prudence may have prompted Jesus to make himself scarce for a while, especially since John's old crowds are now mobbing him.

But now Jesus is leaving the Phoenician coast and heading inland to the Decapolis, another gentile region at the north end of the Sea of Galilee. Some scholars have wondered about the route Jesus takes when he leaves Tyre. He travels north first, skirting the coast to Sidon; then he dips south again to the Decapolis. That's a bit like going from Los Angeles to Denver by way of Seattle. This circuitous route makes more sense if, as some scholars estimate, Jesus and his band spent as long as eight months making the journey to give the political climate back in Galilee time to cool down.

At any rate, he has just reached the Decapolis, this gentile region bordering Herod's territory, when a man who can neither hear nor speak is brought to him for healing by a group identified only as "they."

The English teacher in me always wants to mark such frustratingly indefinite pronouns, which constantly crop up in the gospels. Who are "they"? Not the disciples, strangers in the region themselves. Is it the man's friends, like the paraplegic's buddies, who bring him to Jesus? Family members? Or is the poor man simply being used as bait by a crowd that wants to see this Jewish magician do some trick?

Like the paraplegic, the man plays a passive role in his own drama. Because he is deaf, he can understand little of what's going on. He's probably used to people pushing and tugging him in one direction or another for reasons he cannot easily comprehend. Sometimes people try to pantomime their intentions for him, other times they just haul him around by his sleeve or push him out of the way. He's no doubt been the butt of jeers and practical jokes brought on by the unearthly, gargling noises sometimes made by those profoundly deaf since birth. (Tyndale's translation describes him as "stambed in his speech.") Since he survives by reading people and situations from strictly visual clues, he may have identified Jesus as an observant Jew from his clothes.

Still, when they shove him in front of this stranger, the man very likely has no idea what's going on. In his silent world, there is only the swirling confusion of the crowd. He's not even aware that his advocates, whoever they might be, are asking Jesus to lay hands on him to heal him. The paraplegic in a previous story was at least aware of what was happening to him. The deaf man, however, doesn't have a clue. Nevertheless, he can tell that the stranger exerts power enough to magnetize the crowd. And he knows all eyes are on him. But in response the deaf man can only grin in that apprehensive, ingratiating way the powerless rely on to protect themselves.

Whatever he's expecting next—another practical joke, the strange Jew's scorn, public humiliation—what happened is likely a surprise. First, the stranger takes him by the arm and leads him away from the crowd. (In the next healing Mark recounts, Jesus does the same thing—leads a blind man all the way out of town in order to restore his sight.) But why would this foreigner, the center of the crowd's attention, single him out? And where is he taking him, and for what purpose?

Once they are away from the commotion, the stranger turns and they study each other. The deaf man warily appraises this unpredictable Jew. What next? he wonders. Then he sees the stranger reaching out his hand, feels him insert his fingers into his ears. He flinches, perhaps even backs away a step. The stranger's touch, so peculiarly intimate, is either violation or love. Which is it? What's going on here?

But the man holds still, and, after a moment the fingers are withdrawn from his ears. The deaf man is just releasing his suppressed breath in relief when the stranger does an even more outlandish thing: he lifts his hands to his mouth and spits on them. Then, grasping the deaf man's dropped jaw with one hand, he sticks the saliva-moistened fingers of the other hand into the man's open mouth, laying them along the slack tongue.

Remember that, at this point, the man still can hear nothing. He can only watch the stranger performing this curious act. His jaw still in the stranger's grip, he sees the Jew turn his eyes skyward where even pagans know lies the region of ultimate appeal. He watches the stranger's face contort and feels the vibrations of his groan, a sound, if he could only hear it, as inarticulate as his own slurred wailing but with all the passion of the cosmos yearning for its perfection.

At last, the stranger, having delved into these private orifices of mouth and ears, opens his eyes and drops his gaze to the man's face. The man watches the stranger's lips move—and, for the first time, hears a sound he recognizes as speech.

"*Ephphatha*," the Jew says, the muffled fricatives of the Aramaic nuzzling the whorls of the man's ears. "Open up!"

Immediately the glass wall of silence between the man and the world shatters. As if a window has suddenly been thrown open, letting in that multiplicity of subtle noises which forms the aural background of life, he can hear.

Next, his own lips move in imitation of the stranger's: he speaks. And plainly. His tongue performs cleanly all those minute adjustments it ordinarily takes the muscles months to learn, as if, along with opening the neural pathways to his brain, kinetic memory has also been implanted.

Such swift and thorough change would be staggering to the

psyche. The man, mute for perhaps all his life, would, ironically, be struck dumb by such a miracle. What do you say when the limits that have always defined you are suddenly dissolved?

I think he must have kept to nouns for a good while—*grass,* he probably whispered, then *rock, sky, tree.* And the greatest gift of all—his own name, the syllables that held his whole silent history.

Nevertheless, we the readers never learn the man's name. Whatever words he spoke are lost to us in the clamor of the mob. His place in the story is appropriated once more by the conglomerate "they," whom Jesus orders to keep this miracle under their collective hat. But the rabbi who can command creation, cannot, it seems, control the crowd's will: "The more he charged them, so much the more a great deal they published it," Mark tells us.

The crowd operates much like a Greek chorus in this drama. In the Genesis account of creation, at the end of every day's production the antiphon rings out: "And God saw that it was good." In Mark, the crowd echoes: "He hath done all things well." They supply a voice for the silent stones, the bedrock of creation, which Jesus says elsewhere would cry out were they to keep quiet.

Meanwhile, the man, who never asked to be healed, who did not even realize what was happening to him at the time, moves off into the great silence of history to which even the articulate are relegated. We don't know what happens to him now that he can hear and speak, if he is able to lead a normal life, whether he is afterward kindly and sympathetic toward others who suffer similar handicaps.

I imagine he stayed clear of crowds for a while, though. For someone still learning language—in fact, discovering sounds of all kinds—the confusion of voices would be overwhelming. I think he went and sat on the shore of the great inland lake of Galilee, listening to the waves lap against the sand and rocks for a long time. Maybe he, more than most, could still hear what Paul described as the groaning of creation, the wordless world's deep agony, waiting, as he had, for rescue from futility.

And when he heard, some months or years later, about the death of this strange Jew who had given him this great gift of hearing and speech, what words did he find to console himself then?

Chapter 7

Sick unto Death:
The Official's Son

*T*he man who goes looking for Jesus in this story literally stands out from the crowd. In fact, the crowd, always pushing and shoving to get closer to the miracle worker, would have parted like the Red Sea when he appeared on the scene. Unlike the woman who touched Jesus' cloak or the paraplegic barred from the house in Capernaum, this man is an important personage. John's gospel calls him a *basilikos,* which translates literally as "king's man." The King James translators took this to mean "nobleman," though the term probably meant an administrator for the king, in this case Herod, the tetrarch of Galilee. It's possible that this *basilikos* is Chuza, Herod's steward. Luke identifies one of the women who followed Jesus as "Joanna, the wife of Chuza, the manager of Herod's household." Whoever the man was, his entire family would have been profoundly affected by what happens in this story.

A similar account appears in Matthew and Luke, both of whom may have adapted theirs from John's. Both of them identify the man as a centurion, however, an officer in the Roman army. In either case, the man is most likely a gentile, though sympathetic to Jewish culture. Thanks to the deportation of Jews by a series of Palestine's invaders, most of the lands ringing the Mediterranean and even regions farther east had been exposed to Jewish monotheism. And a significant number of gentiles had found the notion of one universal deity preferable to their own indigenous panoply of gods. They also appreciated how the Torah strengthened the social fabric by its emphasis on morality and communal responsibility. Josephus, the Jewish historian who also served as a Roman general, claimed that gentiles "showed a keen desire to adopt our religious observances; and there is not one city, Greek or barbarian, not a single nation, to which our custom of abstaining from work on the seventh day has not spread."

Some gentiles, in fact, converted to Judaism, submitting to circumcision and becoming, in effect, naturalized Jews. Many more were satisfied simply to belong to a category called "God-fearers," uncircumcised yet devout supporters of Jewish law and custom, who attended local synagogues where they were permitted limited participation in worship.

This *basilikos* who comes to Jesus not only wields significant secular authority in Galilee but probably understands and reveres Jewish observances. When his son falls ill, he turns for help to the charismatic young rabbi operating in his district. Galilee indeed produced more than its share of such holy men, whose unconventional manners made them favorites in the province, though Jerusalem frowned on their practices.

The young rabbi has, in fact, just returned to Galilee from Jerusalem, where, word has it, he caused a quite stir in the Temple. These rumors don't concern the official, however. For one thing, Galileans who cause trouble in Jerusalem are often heroes at home. For another, the official's boss, Herod Antipas, is no particular friend of Pilate, who represents Rome in Jerusalem. Besides, politics are not uppermost in this man's mind right now. His son is suffering from a severe illness; his life hangs by a thread.

Leaving the child in Capernaum, fearful he will never see him alive again, the official hurries to the village of Cana, twenty miles to the west. The rabbi, he's heard, has already performed one miracle there, turning water into wine at a wedding feast.

We know little else about the setting for this encounter, except, as we learn later, it's early afternoon. Was Jesus still staying at the home where the now-famous wedding feast took place? Did the official just knock on the door and inquire if Jesus was in? Or did he come upon the rabbi in the street, ringed by a host of other suppliants? The man's non-Jewish status makes that option the more probable. Even if he is a God-fearer, ethnic and social differences still separate him, a gentile representative of a foreign power, from the Jewish miracle worker. And the desperate father would not want to challenge those differences of class and heritage at this critical moment.

Wherever the meeting takes place, other people may well be present. Very little in the ancient world happened in private. Unlike modern consultations with a doctor or minister, this encounter probably has an audience.

The official asks the rabbi to come to Capernaum and save his son's life.

"Unless you people see miraculous signs and wonders, you won't believe," Jesus replies.

What? the official must wonder. Did I miss something here? Is this rebuke meant for me and my pagan ancestry? Or is the rabbi speaking to the people crowded around us?

The official may be uncertain, but he's also persistent. This is no time for discussions about multiculturalism. He doesn't argue or attempt to defend himself. He simply repeats his original request, emphasizing the urgency of his son's condition. "Sir," he says, "come down before my son dies."

The rabbi replies, almost offhandedly. "Go on now. Your boy's all right."

And—this is the most astonishing part—the man believes him. He turns around and starts back to Capernaum immediately.

It makes a certain kind of sense, I suppose. He's already opened himself up to ridicule by a crowd to whom he represents gentile oppression. If he, a man of high rank, has been willing to grovel publicly before a Jewish rabbi, then he'd better believe the risk has been worth the humiliation. He's put his pride on the table already; it hardly makes sense to back out now.

Still, emotional situations rarely call forth rational responses. And Jesus' words, a rather preemptory command in the Greek, aren't aimed to show cultural sensitivity or even sympathy.

But the official doesn't care about sympathy at this point. He prefers results. Has this rabbi really cured his child? He hurries back up the road to Capernaum. Another twenty miles, remember.

It would have been almost morning before he makes it. The first thing he sees is his servants, running down the road to meet him, eager to tell him that the boy is alive and well.

When, he asks them, when did his son begin to mend?

Yesterday, they say. Right after noon. About one o'clock, in fact.

And the man, exhausted from his journey to Cana and back, would, I imagine, drop into the nearest seat and begin to laugh. I knew it, he keeps telling the servants, I just knew it.

When he has seen his son again, washed up, and had something to eat, he tells the others in the household what happened, about his encounter with the young rabbi in Cana. How he had at first been dismissed as just another superstitious pagan, how he had struggled to make clear the hopelessness of the case. He mimics the abrupt command and equally blunt promise of the rabbi. They are all as amazed as he is. No one dares mention coincidence. How could they, with the living, breathing boy before them? Command and obedience; promise and trust. The combination worked. Who will argue with that?

The following is a similar story that appears in the Talmud, about another rabbi, a contemporary of Jesus, Hanina ben Dosa, who healed a person from a distance.

It happened that when Rabban Gamaliel's son fell ill, he sent two of his pupils to Hanina ben Dosa that he might pray for him. When he saw them, he went to the upper room and prayed. When he came down, he said to them, "Go, for the fever has left him." They said to him, "Are you a prophet?" He said to them, "I am no prophet, neither am I a prophet's son, but this is how I am blessed: if my prayer is fluent in my mouth, I know that the sick man is favored; if not, I know that the disease is fatal." They sat down and noted the hour and wrote it down. When they came to Rabban Gamaliel, he said to them, "By heaven! You have neither detracted from it, nor added to it, but this is how it happened. It was at that hour that the fever left him and he asked us for water to drink."

The similarities between the two stories are striking. In both cases, the healing occurs without the healer touching the sick person or even being in his presence. Also, in each instance, the time of the healer's pronouncement coincides with the actual healing.

But the differences are also instructive. In the Talmudic story, it is a rabbi's son, not the child of a foreign official, who is healed. Also, Hanina ben Dosa relies on the feel of the prayer's fluency to know whether it has been efficacious. Jesus does not pray for healing, but pronounces it. And while Hanina ben Dosa obviously has faith that the healing has occurred, in John's gospel it is the official who supplies the faith. Later, upon hearing the whole story, the official's entire household believes as well. The Talmud story actually bears more resemblance to accounts of healing by prophets, particularly Elijah, than it does to the healing by Jesus.

We find differences between this account of the official's son and other gospel stories of healing as well. For one thing, Jesus never sees this boy he heals from a distance of twenty miles. He does not follow the father home as he sometimes does when he heals a member of a Jewish family. The father's faith is the only link between Jesus and the boy.

Another element missing from this story is any display of emotion on Jesus' part. He calls the woman with the hemorrhage "Daughter," and tells her to go in peace, commending her for her faith. Likewise, he groans in pity for the deaf man's condition. There are no groans, no terms of endearment, no tender words recorded in this story of Herod's official.

But wouldn't emotion be suspect here? Jesus has not, after all, seen the sick child. When I hear reports of war casualties on the radio or hear about a tragic illness befalling a relative stranger, it's not exactly pity that I feel but something more like mild affront, aggravation that the world should contain such incongruity, such inequity. Jesus' emotion, or lack of it, seems properly placed throughout the gospels. Whereas dramatic reproductions of the gospels often portray him with a face constantly contorted by compassion, the truth is that, like all of us, he is able to *feel* only when he knows the person or has the suffering visibly present to him. To manufacture emotion, or even the semblance of it, was not his way. If he truly operated within the same human limits we do, he could have felt little, except in a generic way, for the official's sick child. Sympathy for unseen strangers can be only vague at best; instead, it is reason that recoils from a child's death.

For the official's son to die would be an offense against the natural order, and Jesus appears to assess objectively the father's faith by the man's willingness to risk his position. As any good doctor would, Jesus heals in this story because it is the right thing to do and because he has the power to do it. And for the father, as well as the boy, this cognitive response proved just as beneficial as an emotional reaction.

Chapter 8

Been Down So Long:
At *the Bethzatha Pool*

*T*he encounter with Jesus described in the fifth chapter of John's gospel supplies an uncommon number of details about the setting. It occurs on a second trip to Jerusalem, where John, unlike the other gospels, brings Jesus on three different occasions. The Temple, the most important building in the city, is situated on a high hill. To the west is a commercial mall, or agora, which, in addition to other wares, sells sheep for sacrifice in the Temple. Nearby, just north of the Temple, is a pool called Bethzatha surrounded by five colonnaded porticoes.

The earliest manuscripts of this gospel do not contain the short section, now assumed to be a later insertion in the text, which explains a popular legend about the Bethzatha pool. At certain times the water in the large rock basin bubbled up, possibly from an underground spring. Local lore had it that the water's disturbance was caused by an angel "troubling" the water, imparting to it power to heal disease. This supernatural effect lasted only fleetingly, however. The first person into the water after its disturbance apparently soaked up all the angelic energy, leaving none for anyone else.

The porticoes surrounding the pool had turned into something like a perpetual waiting room at a doctor's office. A variety of sufferers with every affliction from blindness to birth defects waited day after day for their turn at the healing waters. But there were no scheduled appointments. Treatment was on a first come, first served basis. John's gospel describes one man waiting there as having "an infirmity," which could mean anything from paralysis to Parkinson's disease. At any rate, he has been in this crippled condition for thirty-eight years and has yet to beat out the competition for a cure.

One might think the man would have given up by now. After so long, it's hard to know whether habit or hope still brings him there. But then what are his options, given his condition? Drowsing in the shade of the portico has become a way of life. He probably knows the other old-timers, is familiar with their ailments, their histories. At least it gives him someplace to go every day. The pool and its clientele provide a certain structure to his days.

He appears to be a man singularly alone in life. No family member stays with him, waiting to hoist him into the pool. Unlike the Capernaum paraplegic, he has no buddies eager to lend their aid either. Perhaps he's been crippled since childhood, cut off from the ordinary means by which one acquires friends—work, marriage, worship. Or maybe he's turned into an ungrateful curmudgeon over the years, whose crankiness drives away people's sympathy or help.

I think I have a pretty good idea of what this man's life looked like. Last summer I sat in the modern "portico" of a major medical center, waiting day after day while my mother underwent a long string of tests and examinations. Newcomers there for their initial diagnoses often looked concerned or even fearful as they waited for their tests and then for the results. The old-timers, however, the ones with chronic conditions, had lost their worried look. It had been replaced by an expression of resignation or simply boredom. Tests and treatment had become a way of life.

After a few weeks of my mother's routine, I understood how this transformation happened. Once you've read all the magazines and pamphlets in the rack, learned the hospital maze necessary to negotiate the tests, and memorized the cafeteria menu, there's not a lot to do. Very few people brought a book or handwork to ease the time. Instead, we all sank into a state of suspended animation, the sick and well alike. We merely waited.

We understood what was happening in the tests inflicted on us or our loved ones about as much as the people in the Bethzatha porticoes understood what stirred the water in the pool. My mother was "shot" with invisible rays in all manner of postures, was shunted prone through large white tubes, had her blood sucked up into glass and metal tubes, which then disappeared to undergo mysterious processing in some invisible lab. The foul, chalky brews she was ordered to drink might just as well have been magic potions, for all we knew. A magical element inevitably creeps into any culture's healing arts, even when practiced in modern skyscrapers.

Likewise, all religions, even the most austere and ethically based, eventually get translated on a popular level into a kind of primitive or folk magic. First-century Judaism, unlike its more fluid and emotive pagan rival religions, was based on Torah and the Mishnah, a codification of rules governing behavior and meant to benefit the entire community. Because of this legal framework and foundation, Jewish piety was based on erudition, not superstition. Men *studied* Torah, in order to learn what God required. Unlike the gods of the Greeks and Romans, the Jew's deity was impervious to bribes or cajoling. The panoply of pagan gods were whimsical and unpredictable; with Yahweh you knew exactly what he expected. In fact, you could look it up. Judaism was, then, by far the least superstitious of all first-century religions.

Nevertheless, when people are sick, they feel powerless, the pawns of inscrutable fate. Almost inevitably they fall back on some kind of magical thinking. The people waiting beside the Bethzatha pool represent that intractable human propensity. The people in the medical center felt just as impotent. Neither group had the vaguest notion how either the water or the tests would heal them. They simply trusted some mysterious process.

Some of my companions in the waiting rooms had passed even that point. Some had already lost limbs or organs. Some were too weak to make the effort to dress properly anymore and showed up in pajamas and robes. Their treatment was obviously losing ground to the disease. But still they came, day after day, doggedly. For them, a ritual begun in hope had ended as mere routine. They showed up at the reception desk, gave their patient number, received an assignment slip, got on the elevator, and ascended to another level, where they surrendered the slip to a receptionist. Then they waited some more. Why not? Was sitting at home any better? They were going through the motions of hope long after they'd lost the reality.

This is the state of our man in the portico. After thirty-eight years, he is defined by his illness. Where, literally, would he be without it?

It's a slow day in the shade of the colonnades—the Sabbath, actually—when an unfamiliar figure shows up. Seemingly healthy himself, the newcomer doesn't appear to be attached to any of the pool's regulars. The old-timer notices the stranger looking at him. After a moment, the newcomer approaches and hunkers down beside him.

The new man is younger, and, judging by his accent, not from Jerusalem. Nevertheless, the *tsitsit,* or fringes on the corners of his cloak, mark him as a pious Jew. The stranger doesn't waste any time with small talk. "You want to get well?" he asks abruptly.

Does he want to get well? The old-timer almost chokes at the question. It is so blunt, so ridiculous—almost an affront. *What do you think? You suppose I enjoy lying here day after day with all the rest of these losers? You think I like living this way? You think I chose this life?* All this the man might have protested. But the question, unanswered, lodges somewhere inside his brain and sticks like a burr.

The man turns toward the stranger, frowning, weighing the possibilities. This inquiring outlander, he figures, must be ignorant of the pool's history. And of his. But maybe he can get something out of the bumpkin, perhaps appeal to his sympathy. So the crippled man begins his tale: how he's been coming there every day for more years than the young visitor has been alive, how he has no one to help him—that's why he's still in this condition. You know what people are. The others push and shove to get ahead of him. And with no family, forsaken by friends, well . . . He peers up pitifully, already extending his hand toward the stranger.

But the newcomer is getting to his feet again, obviously not as easy a touch as the man had hoped.

"Get up," the stranger says brusquely.

The man squints up at him. What?

"Come on. You heard me. Get up."

And for some reason, perhaps just to demonstrate the absurdity of the command, the man pushes his palms against the pavement and struggles to lift his weight—only to discover that it's not as much of a struggle as he anticipated. In fact . . .

The stranger locks him in a resolute gaze. The man feels strength rise through all his limbs, a sensation he'd almost forgotten. He wavers to his feet.

"Now then," the stranger continues, pointing to the man's mat, "roll that up too and take it along with you."

Shaken, giddy, the man obeys. He rolls up the mat, sticks it under his arm, and hurries off, still with no idea who the stranger is and not waiting to find out.

This man has not, strictly speaking, gone looking for Jesus at all. Nor does he appear to have much interest or curiosity about him afterward. If he did, it is soon squelched by what happens next. He is scurrying away from Bethzatha, bedroll under his arm, when he is stopped by the unofficial Sabbath police, pious Jews who immediately take offense at his carrying the mat. "You can't do that," they protest. "Carrying your bed on the Sabbath is work. You're breaking the law!"

The fourth commandment expressly forbade work on the seventh day of the week. But work—what's work? The commandment didn't spell that out. In order to clarify that omission, as well as a thousand finer points of the original Ten Commandments, centuries of legal precedents had gradually accreted, first in an oral, then in a written collection of rules called the Mishnah. It contained thirty-nine categories of activity considered off-limits on the Sabbath, most of which concern obvious restrictions on agricultural labor and hunting. But domestic chores are covered in almost excruciating detail. No one, for instance, was to tie or untie a knot, sew or rip out two stitches, write or erase two letters, or put out a fire on the Sabbath. The last item on the list—"taking out aught from one domain to another"—is the particular offense the Sabbath police accuse our man of committing.

He reacts to the charge defensively. "Hey, it's not my fault," he protests. "This stranger told me to go home and take my bed with me."

"What are you talking about? Who told you to do this?" they demand.

"I don't know. Just some guy. From out of town, I think." He looks around, scanning the crowd that has begun to gather. "I don't see him now."

Then, perhaps out of genuine gratitude for his good fortune, perhaps to pacify his pious accusers, he sets off for the Temple, probably to offer the required thanksgiving sacrifice for his healing. At any rate, he is in the Temple when, for a second time, the mysterious stranger seeks him out.

If the stranger was curt before, he is positively stern now. "You'd better watch out," he warns the man. "You've been given back your health and strength. Don't waste it. Get yourself a real life now. If you go back to your old ways, you'll be worse off than ever."

An alcoholic being released from a detox center is always told that his future health and happiness depend entirely on the choices he makes from now on. And this is what our man hears now. He has spent the last thirty-eight years as a passive sufferer in the grip of a malady he can no longer count on to provide him with either an excuse or an identity. His body is strong now, but he will need an equally strong spirit to invent a new life for himself.

These are not words anyone is particularly eager to hear. Almost everyone in those waiting rooms at the medical center was sent home with a new diet, a new exercise plan, a new therapy— some regimen that aimed at changing their lives for the better. The sad truth is that a certain percentage of patients there found it easier to sit passively waiting, mere bystanders to their own treatment, than to take the actions necessary to maintain health. They preferred a situation where their responsibility was minimal. Medication was a ritual they could handle. But change? Constructing a new mode of living?

Jesus is telling the man that a one-shot cure won't last forever.

His future health depends on his own choices. But his injunction is met with the same reaction physician's orders, particularly those which require us to change, often do.

The man is affronted. Making certain of the stranger's identity this time, he hurries off—on those newly restored legs—to turn his healer in to the Sabbath police.

What might some of the old-timers at the medical center have done if this same stranger had taken the chair next to them in the waiting room and asked them, "Do you want to get well?" How many, like the man at the pool, would have avoided answering? And what if, even so, he had miraculously made the person's body sound again? Suppose the fellow wheezing with emphysema had felt his lungs fully inflate for the first time in decades? Would the smoker have given up cigarettes forever, once he could breathe again? Maybe. Maybe not. We can't predict individual reactions, only statistical averages.

This story of the man at the Bethzatha pool remains one of the strangest healing stories in the gospels. The man, as we've noted, did not go looking for Jesus. The cure was totally unprovoked and gratuitous. Unlike the Capernaum paraplegic, he did not lope off shouting with joy. He was willing enough to accept his new strength, but felt no personal connection to his healer. "I didn't ask to be healed," he might have protested. When, almost immediately, his new health gets him in hot water, he seems eager to shift the blame to his benefactor. And when cautioned about necessary changes in his life, he is offended and, ironically, in his first display of initiative, seeks out Jesus' critics to turn him in. Obviously, the health restored to his body has not caught up with his spirit.

Chapter 9

Relief:
A Second Glance

*S*o what do we post-Enlightenment types find in these stories that we can squirrel away for the inevitable rainy day when a cloud appears on the X-ray or an embolism explodes in the brain? What can you expect when you go looking for Jesus then? Should we throw away our crutches, cancel our health insurance, empty the medicine cabinet in the expectation that all we have to do is ask and Jesus will make us well?

Before we claim to have found in Jesus the ultimate miracle drug, we need to assess what we've seen in these stories of healings. Though the crowds, especially in Galilee, came to think of him as some kind of healing machine, we should remember that Jesus did not make every sick person in ancient Palestine well. He left untouched and uncured any number of blind, deaf, leprous, and paraplegic sufferers. Nor did he heal people en masse, but singly. His healing power, apparently, was a one-on-one affair. This method necessarily limited the number of cures.

Another point. Everyone he cured eventually died. There are no survivors of the first century still around today. Even Lazarus, snatched back once from death, finally died again. Being healed by Jesus did not guarantee perpetual health or immortality.

On the up side, however, there's no mistaking his dedication to healing. Jesus wanted people well. He restored the health of as many human creatures as he could get his hands on during those short years of his residency on earth. Sometimes people who didn't even ask for it got healed anyway. Besides the man at the Bethzatha pool, at least five other people in the gospels fit this category of unsolicited healing: a woman bent double for eighteen years, a man with a withered hand, a man blind from birth, a man with dropsy, and the servant whose ear Peter cut off during a scuffle over Jesus' arrest. Jesus either comes into all these lives unannounced, or they are brought to his attention by seeming chance. Once confronted with illness, he always takes the opportunity to correct these flaws in nature. As the Creator's envoy, he feels obliged to clear up, as it were, any glitches in creation he comes across. As he tells the pious Jews who take him to task for healing the man at the pool, "My Father is still working and I am working too."

Those sick or maimed people Jesus stumbles across in the course of his perambulations were fortunate; they got the overflow of his healing potency. His creating energy immediately fills the vacuum of disease or waste with health. He doesn't stop to question afflicted persons about their former life or even consider whether they *deserve* to have their bodies restored. The body in itself seems worth putting right. And in this, I think, he resembles physicians in general who, without inquiring too closely into the character of sick people, always approach broken or malfunctioning bodies with the intent of making them work right, do what they were meant to do. Better a bad man in a sound body than the same man in a broken one.

When John the Baptist, languishing in Herod's prison, begins to wonder about his career choices, he sends two messengers to ask Jesus if he really is the Messiah. Jesus tells them to report to John what they have seen: "The blind receive their sight, and the lame walk, the lepers are cleansed, and the deaf hear, the dead are raised up, and the poor have the gospel preached to them." Notice that preaching comes last on the list, preceded by restoring a list of bodily imperfections. Restoring bodies to proper functioning—renewing creation—is apparently a messianic duty.

Today, however, despite two centuries of sentimentalizing (and capitalizing) Nature, we bracket ourselves off from it, think it occurs only outdoors. Healing, we think, is something different from, say, reforestation or reclaiming strip-mined land. But our bodies are as much a part of creation as mountains and trees. Our own

groans contribute to the general chorus of frustrated creation, waiting, as St. Paul told the Romans, to be "set free from its bondage
to decay." Maybe this failure to see ourselves as part of creation
results in our belief that health is wasted on bad people. It may be
difficult for some of us to countenance, but Jesus never balked at
restoring health to any body, whatever a person's spiritual state.

Why, then, did he tell the man healed at Bethzatha to "sin no
more"? Or announce to the paraplegic that his sins were forgiven?
What's the connection between sin and sickness?

In another story, in John's gospel, Jesus makes clear that a man
he has healed of congenital blindness was not being punished for
his sin, nor even for the sins of his parents. He was no more responsible for his lack of sight than diseased elm trees are to blame
for Dutch elm disease. Nonetheless, once given his sight, the man
must value it enough to safeguard the gift. Jesus never required a
background check before he agreed to heal anyone. But once the
body got fixed, he didn't want it abused. It's always *after* healing
that he warns against sin. We should desire the goodness of creation ardently enough to tend that portion assigned to us—our own
bodies. Sustaining health, once it has been restored, requires the
will to cooperate with the body.

Then there's the question of mechanics. We're as interested in
how Jesus healed people as why. On a couple of occasions Jesus
simply sent home people who had come to intercede for a friend
or relative, saying the deed they sought was as good as done. Usually, the intercessor's exceptional degree of faith appeared to play
a part in these healings. But more often, Jesus actually handled the
sick person. What part did touch play, for instance, in the deaf and
dumb man's healing? Why that probing of orifices, sticking fingers
in ears and mouth?

One obvious answer is that Jesus communicates with the man
the only way he can, by visual and tactile methods. Here and here,
he says, is what needs fixing. But why didn't Jesus simply point,
maybe to his own ears and mouth? Why this physical intrusion,
that application of saliva?

Healing, miraculous or not, seems to benefit from touch. "Open," the doctor orders, "say 'ah'," and sticks a wooden paddle on our tongue. We lie stripped before strangers, waiting to receive the benefit of their diagnosis. Though we've invented all manner of medical apparatus to interpose between the physician and the patient, from stethoscopes to CT scanners, machinery cannot communicate the intention, the desire to heal. Only the human hand palpating the human body can do that.

These are the only curative devices the stories show us: touch and faith. And faith appears to be the more complex. If Jesus always healed upon request and often even without it, what relation does faith have to healing? The woman who reached out surreptitiously to touch Jesus' robe in the crowd is told her faith made the difference. In the case of the Capernaum paraplegic, his friends had faith on his behalf. Also, the story claims the official "believed the word that Jesus had spoken unto him" on behalf of his son. So important was faith, in fact, that the gospels of both Mark and Matthew recount how Jesus' miraculous powers were thwarted in his hometown because his neighbors refused to believe in them. "He could there do no mighty work," Mark says, "*save that he laid his hands upon a few sick folk and healed them.*" The exception is noteworthy, I think, showing that his touch could convey his desire to heal.

So these questions remain: Why did faith seem necessary in some cases while in others it was superfluous? How can we know if we're producing faith in sufficient quantities to work? How much is enough? And how does one produce it? We come at faith with questions of mechanics, but I'm not sure those are the right questions. We might, in fact, get farther asking why we frame our questions this way.

Growing up in a culture with little taste for risk, we like to hedge our bets as much as possible. Instead of waiting for the divine eye to fall on us and notice our condition, we naturally want to do as much as possible to ensure that we'll get relief when we need it. That's the way the game of life is played now, at least in what we call the developed nations of the world. We've learned to rely on safety nets and insurance policies, diversified mutual funds and

managed health care. Once in a while, some of us get the itch to
feel the thrill of living close to the edge, but we do it by hang-
gliding or stock-car racing, something that makes us look bold and
adventurous, not ridiculous. We want risk to be something we
choose, not something—like faith—we're forced to rely on out of
desperation.

Faith probably came a lot easier to people who'd never experi-
enced the benefits of antibiotics or known they were covered by disability insurance. But desperation is the true country of faith, the
place where all the props have been knocked out from under us.
And though we train ourselves to think it's a land we'll never visit,
any day now we might find ourselves wandering where nothing
looks like the scenario we expected or planned for. Any number of
circumstances can catapult us into that dark region—divorce, bank-
ruptcy, betrayal. But the most common one is illness.

Then we may go looking for Jesus, reaching out to feel him, as
fearful as the woman in the crowd. Or someone may do it for us.
On the other hand, we may simply find ourselves pondering the
same question put to the man by the Bethzatha pool. *Do you want
to get well?* Our answer may depend on both our desire and our
desperation.

PART III

LOOKING FOR A WAY OUT

In the latter half of our century, in our effort to outdo Marx, his secular rival as savior of the poor, we have often portrayed Jesus as the champion of the downtrodden and oppressed. In the '60s, posters featured Jesus in the guise of Che Guevara, the Cuban freedom fighter. Scholars mined the scriptures for proof that Jesus was actually a rebel leader of a Palestinian peasants' revolt. Theologies were systematically constructed from Jesus' words and acts to show that his primary goal was liberating the masses from political and economic oppression.

How accurate is this picture? We know Jesus wasn't rich—he died homeless, his clothes his only possessions. But was he also a revolutionary, challenging the ruling powers on behalf of the powerless? Is there any evidence to support a rebel Jesus?

This section contains stories from the gospels showing Jesus responding to people who seek him out because they feel powerless and want him to do something about it. But, fortunately, archaeological and historical evidence is also available that can supplement the sparse sociological and political information of the gospels.

What made the Jews in Jesus' day feel powerless? Consider first the economic and political situation of the region of Palestine. At the time Jesus was born, Rome controlled the entire Western world. Herod the Great ruled the region from Syria down to the Negev desert as a puppet king. Though not a Jew himself, he tried to placate his Jewish subjects by reconstructing their dilapidated

Temple in Jerusalem, employing a thousand of their priests to oversee the job and ten thousand workers to carry out their instructions. The Jews nevertheless considered Herod little more than a bloodthirsty savage, a pagan given to murdering his own children and ignorant of God's ways. Levying the heavy taxes necessary to pay for his many extravagant building projects—the Temple was only one of them—didn't improve his standing with the people, especially since he confiscated land from those who didn't pay up. At his death, he had thus acquired from half to two thirds of the region as his personal property.

When Herod the Great died not long after Jesus' birth, the Emperor Augustus divided his kingdom between his surviving sons. One inherited the southern section, called Judea, which included the city of Jerusalem. Unfortunately, he used his first few months in office to execute three thousand of his Jewish subjects. Augustus, rather than see the region depopulated by such a madman, declared Judea a province of Rome and appointed his own deputy, whose duties were primarily collecting taxes and keeping the peace. Galilee, the northern section of the old Herod's kingdom, went to another son, Herod Antipas, whose immorality became a national scandal. Herod Antipas finally beheaded the popular prophet John the Baptist for publicly criticizing his marriage to his sister-in-law. Consequently, the Jews had little respect for either the Roman deputy in Judea or Herod Antipas in Galilee, and resented them both as pagan interlopers whose extravagance the people paid for with oppressive taxes.

Given that the Jews had already been living as conquered people under foreign rulers for at least four centuries, it is amazing that they still retained their national identity intact in the first century. Almost two hundred years before Jesus was born, a Syrian overlord had desecrated the Jerusalem Temple and begun a series of pogroms against the Jews. The Maccabees, a clan of Jewish patriots, had led a successful guerrilla war against this persecution and taken back their land—at least until Rome later conquered it for the Empire.

Rome's rule proved to be comparatively tolerant, particularly toward the Jews. Because imperial policy indulged the provinces in their local customs, the Jews were exempted from emperor worship. Memories of the Maccabean revolt, however, still inspired periodic uprisings in Palestine, most of them led by rebels from Galilee, giving that region a reputation as a hotbed of revolution.

The irritation of living under foreign domination and the burden of heavy taxes were only half the problem, though. Another kind of oppression came from the Jerusalem priesthood. The chief priests at the Temple there, acting as intermediaries between the people and the Roman government, wielded considerable political power. On the one hand, the imperial henchmen needed the priests' backing in order to control their Jewish subjects. On the other hand, the people counted on the priests to safeguard those nonnegotiable religious privileges on which their Jewish identity hinged.

The priesthood, in fact, constituted a second layer of government. And it imposed its own kind of taxes on the people. Many of the prescribed religious obligations caused considerable economic hardship on the working class. For example, in addition to the religious tax or tithe (10 percent) all Jews were expected to pay, they also had to buy specially approved animals for the required sacrifices from a Temple concession, pay fees for regular cleansing ceremonies, and contribute to the operating expenses of the Jerusalem Temple. Scholars have estimated that the common man had to spend up to half his annual income to pay for these various religious obligations. Also, certain occupations, such as herding goats, were declared off-limits to observant Jews, restricting their ways of making a living.

Another problem came from the hereditary nature of the priestly class, which made it vulnerable to the abuses of nepotism. A rabbi's lament, written during the period when Herod was building the new Temple, included this complaint: "Woe is me . . . for they are high priests and their sons are treasurers and their sons-in-law are trustees and their servants beat the people with staves." Thus, the people felt oppressed by the very religious establishment meant to protect them from their foreign overlords.

In addition to these tensions, demographic shifts in the Middle East from a land-based to an urban-based economy put even more pressure on the people. The Hebrew and the early Greek ideal citizen had been the independent farmer producing crops, providing for his clan, and coming to the defense of his country in time of need. Rome, however, had replaced that agrarian model with urban centers of power and commerce to which agricultural lands were only satellites supplying the more centralized population's needs. Yet Jewish Palestine remained stubbornly rural. Jerusalem was the only true city in the region, though Sepphoris and Tiberias in Galilee qualified as large towns. The coastal cities—Caesarea, Ashkelon, Gaza, and Joppa—though important ports, were, except for Joppa, essentially gentile.

For farmers, dependent on uncertain variables like the weather, fluctuating prices, and interest rates, the only constant was taxes. Though the Maccabean revolt had redistributed property and returned farmland to the peasant class, by the first century those land reforms had been undone, and small farmers were in constant danger of being forced off their property. This peasant class, some of them dispossessed, made up the majority of those multitudes who heard Jesus teach in agricultural metaphors, peopling his parables with characters they could identify with—farmers uncertain about crops, day laborers waiting to be hired for work in the fields, rebellious farm workers rising up against absentee landlords.

Conditions such as these account for the frequent appearance of bandits in Jesus' stories as well. The historian Josephus notes that robbers were a particular aggravation to travel in Palestine. Like their ancestor David, who centuries earlier had gathered an army from the dispossessed and disaffected, some of these bandits were also political activists. Josephus tells of such Robin Hoods breaking into the public archives and burning "the contracts belonging to their creditors" in order to "gain the multitude of those who had been debtors, and that they might persuade the poorer sort to join in their insurrection with safety against the wealthy." During another uprising, Galilean soldiers mutinied against their Herodian officers and drowned them.

But a power even more fearsome than imperious political rulers or a despotic priesthood waited to oppress people in that age—an invisible hostile force that threatened to swallow up a person's mind and spirit. We feel a lot more comfortable analyzing demographic shifts and tracking political power bases than considering such bizarre phenomena. What the first century called demon possession we prefer to attribute either to physical ailments such as epilepsy or to psychological aberrations like schizophrenia. The difference in language alone shows the dissimilarities between the two ages' understandings of this dark world. In Jesus' day people attributed wild behavior to uncontrollable and malevolent spiritual forces. We devise more detached, less personified terms for such afflictions in order to give ourselves a sense of control over them. I suspect, though, that our modern sense of control is largely a linguistic chimera. Call it what we may, the human personality today is still subject to grotesque deformities and at times complete disintegration. About someone suffering such affliction we may well say, "She's just not herself anymore," indicating that a more powerful but unnamed force has obliterated the person we knew. Whether the cause is biochemical or evil spirits, we sense that the true personality is trapped, caged someplace inaccessible to us.

Demon possession in the first century may strike us as bizarre or simply an ancient version of alien abduction stories. (Such stories do not occur in the Old Testament.) But if you doubt the reality of the kind of madness that drives people to inflict harm on themselves in the same way the gospels describe the phenomenon, just visit any mental hospital. People still live trapped inside themselves, powerless to break through the invisible walls of their private hell. And whether we call that prison addiction or Alzheimer's, one factor hasn't changed: they all long for release.

Chapter 10

Death and Taxes:

Herod and Caesar

*I*n the year A.D. 6, having banished Herod the Great's son Archelaus, who had proved such a disaster as Judea's ruler, the Emperor Augustus sent a Roman senator named Cyrenius with specific instructions to straighten out that province's finances and make an assessment of its wealth and possible benefit to the Empire. To this end, Cyrenius ordered a census and a poll tax, levied on every male from fourteen to sixty-five and every female from twelve to sixty-five. Thus we have the famous passage from Luke, read as a prelude to countless Christmas pageants, describing the "decree from Caesar Augustus, that all the world should be taxed."

Not everyone, however, proved as compliant with this decree as Joseph who had returned to his hometown of Bethlehem with the pregnant Mary. In fact, this poll tax, amounting to a denarius, roughly a day's wages for a laborer, sparked the beginning of an underground insurrection by a guerrilla group popularly known as the Zealots. The historian Josephus calls the movement the Fourth Philosophy to distinguish it from the other main Jewish sects of Pharisees, Sadducees, and Essenes. A Galilean named Judas, either a hothead or a patriot, depending on your political persuasion, was the original fomenter of the tax rebellion, which would, in the next generation, explode into open warfare. He exhorted the people to resist, claiming that taxation was only the first step on the slippery slope to slavery. Josephus, who had capitulated to the Romans during the war, described the Zealots' intransigent nationalism as "an infection" which appealed particularly to "the younger sort."

Theologically, Zealots were most closely aligned with the Pharisees, a popular faction intent on right living. But their political pacifism irked the Zealots whose own peculiar take on how to be holy meant acknowledging only God as their ruler, not some heathen in Rome. Their objection to paying the imperial poll tax was not economic but theological. Our coins today say "In God We Trust," but at the time that Jesus was teaching in Palestine, the coins used to pay the tax were stamped with these words: "Tiberius Caesar, son of the divine Augustus, the high priest." The person spending a dime today or a denarius then probably pays little attention to either motto; however, in the Zealots' eyes, paying the poll tax was tantamount to conceding divinity to the Roman emperor.

Knowing where to draw the political and theological line was more difficult for first-century Jews than we in the twentieth century can easily understand. After their kingdom had been conquered four hundred years before Jesus, many of them had been deported to the outer reaches of the civilized world. Ever since then, the Jews had struggled to maintain their cultural and religious identity. From Rome to the Black Sea and beyond, communities of exiled Jews still gathered for prayers, the reading of the Torah, the celebration of Passover and other holy days. At the same time, however, they had to put down roots as citizens in whatever country they found themselves. This often meant adapting their customs and practices to survive in alien soil. In the Egyptian city of Alexandria, for example, the Jewish philosopher Philo was working on allegorical interpretation of the Torah so that Jewish law could merge with Greek wisdom. Between the two extremes of fundamentalists like Judas, the Galilean insurrectionist, and the watered-down liberalism of Philo, the exiled intellectual, the majority of Palestinian Jews had to find their narrow way.

Still, neither they nor anyone else in the ancient world would have dreamed of separating church and state in the manner we do today. One thing both Romans and Jews agreed on: the state depended for its validation on whatever gods it honored. God, goodness, and power were a triumvirate, and if these were separated, society and possibly the cosmos itself would certainly dissolve.

But what if you lived under the domination of a nation whose gods were an abomination to you, among people who worshiped a mere mortal as divine? How was it possible to maintain your own spiritual balance under such conditions? The Jews in Palestine had suffered enough from foreign invaders already. While everyone revered the Maccabean heroes of the past, most people also wanted to live in peace, without the threat of wholesale slaughter from nervous officials. Thus, sacrifices were offered every day at the Temple in Jerusalem for the emperor—a part of the accommodation policy that the Jews had worked out with Rome during the previous two decades.

But the Zealots wanted no part of accommodation. In fact, they put out contracts on the priests who offered those prayers for the emperor. The rebels exhorted the people to believe that God would intervene on their behalf, if only enough Jews were willing to put their lives on the line. Even Josephus reveals a grudging admiration for the Zealots; he describes them as "indifferent to dying any kind of death, nor indeed do they heed the deaths of their relations and friends, nor can any such fear make them call any man Lord."

This, then, is the volatile political climate when Jesus rides into Jerusalem on a donkey, greeted by a throng of enthusiastic supporters expecting him both to relieve them of the Roman occupation of the holy city and to challenge the current bureaucracy running the Temple. And so far he appears to be living up to the crowd's expectations. After his hero's welcome, he visited the Temple, where he behaved much like a Zealot revolutionary himself, driving out the merchants who sell doves to the poorest Jews for their sacrifices and overturning the tables of the tellers who exchange for special Temple currency the Roman coins with their blasphemous Roman imprint. "This is supposed to be a place of prayer," he'd shouted at them, "not a hideout for bandits."

Naturally, this had not gone down well with the priests who ran the Temple. The president of the priesthood was already well aware that the Pharisees, always sticklers for the rules, questioned his authority to hold that office. According to the Torah, the priesthood was to be kept within the clan of the Levites. But Herod the Great and the Roman deputies who followed him, realizing how strategic this office was to controlling the Jews, wanted their own handpicked man to fill that key position.

But how to get the Pharisees and their many supporters to recognize their choice? A compromise had finally been worked out whereby the Pharisee party would agree to tolerate the chief priest and his administration if they could set the Temple's calendar and control the liturgy. Still, the Pharisees and their followers considered the current chief priest and his administration as a poor substitute for the real thing. And the Zealots looked on them as outright impostors.

The Temple administration, nervous about any challenge to its shaky authority, can only react defensively to any disturbance of the sort Jesus has caused. In their eyes, he is quite obviously a Zealot—especially since he comes from Galilee. The riot in the Temple has been no mere symbolic act, like pro-lifers picketing abortion clinics or environmentalists chaining themselves to trees. They know about the death threats against some of their priests. If they let things get out of hand, the Romans will dump them. At the same time, they can't afford to offend the huge following Jesus has built up. If things go on like this, their credibility with the Roman deputy will be ruined. Yet if they bar this popular young rabbi from the Temple or put him in jail, his supporters might well stage an uprising.

The strategy the Temple administrators devise to meet this challenge shows a good deal of political savvy. Knowing they have no influence with the masses in town for the Passover, they solidify their shaky power base by enlisting the aid of the Pharisees—ordinarily their enemies rather than their allies. After all, the Pharisees have some stake also in seeing that the schedule at the Temple is not disrupted. The Pharisees agree to go along with the chief priests' strategy: by drawing him into a debate over the hated poll tax they will cause Jesus either to lose face with the people or to incriminate himself with some incendiary statement than can get him arrested.

In order to implement this plan the Pharisees must also bring along members of a faction called the Herodians, Jews who, for one reason or another, find it in their interest to publicly endorse Rome's puppet governor of Galilee, Herod Antipas. Their pro-Roman position should act like a red flag in the face of a Galilean rebel. Together they will pose a question to Jesus in such a way that whatever answer he gives will be the wrong one. Either Jesus will say something to disenchant his followers or his reply will provoke the Romans into arresting him for sedition.

Their interview with Jesus probably takes place in the outer courts of the Temple, where representatives of various religious factions have already engaged him in debate. This unlikely coalition of Pharisees and Herodians begin by attempting to disarm their victim's suspicions and ingratiate themselves with his followers. "We realize that you are only concerned with the truth," they commence. "You tell it like it is, no matter who's listening. You're no bootlicker—you don't care what people think."

The record shows no reaction from Jesus to this bit of flattery. He merely waits for them to continue.

Now comes the question they've so carefully devised: "Is it right to pay taxes to the emperor or not? That's what we want to know."

They do not, observe, ask about the Temple tax or the tithe or any of the tariffs levied on them by the religious establishment. Their question concerns only the tax that has been such a bone of contention in Palestine, the one paid to the emperor. They sit back to wait for the clever young rabbi's reply.

Jesus, of course, sees through both the flattery and the question itself. "Hypocrites," he calls them in Matthew's account, letting them know he hasn't been fooled by their charade, "why are you trying to trick me?" But despite their intentions, he doesn't dodge the question. He realizes this tax problem has been plaguing the Jews for decades now, and despite the hidden agenda of his questioners, he sees an opportunity to address a thorny issue that concerns all the people listening to him.

But first he requires a prop. "Anybody have a denarius?" he asks, and someone drops the coin into his hand. "Okay, look," he says, holding it up for everyone to see. "Whose picture do you see stamped on it?"

"The emperor's," someone answers.

"Right. Now, what does the inscription say around the edges here?" He points to the familiar Latin characters, known even to the illiterate.

They repeat the words to him, the Herodians speaking up firmly, the others only muttering the hated title: "Tiberius Caesar, son of the divine Augustus, the high priest."

"Right again. So the answer's simple really. The emperor's picture is on the coin, along with his name. It must belong to him. So give it back."

The Herodians begin to smile and look around smugly at their Pharisees. See there? the look says. You fanatics are just making a big deal out of nothing. You have to go along to get along. Nothing wrong with that.

But Jesus isn't through yet. "On the other hand," he continues, "whatever has God's image stamped on it is his by rights. Give God what belongs to him as surely as you give the emperor his due."

Any Jew, of course, would catch the allusion. Right at the start of the Torah, when God makes the first human beings, he stamps them with his own image. Like the coins of God's realm, he owns them all. Their very existence is a debt owed to him.

The Pharisees begin to stroke their beards and the Herodians to frown. So what's the answer here, they're all wondering. On the one hand, Jesus has just condoned the controversial poll tax, but on the other hand, he's said all things human belong to God. Does that mean the emperor too?

The Herodians are satisfied to let the matter drop, having had their own position exonerated—at least they think that's what happened. And the Pharisees leave to go off and explore the point among themselves.

And here we are, two thousand years later, still pondering questions about taxes and the authority of the state. As I write this, a contingent of modern-day Zealots in Montana calling themselves Freemen are on trial for, among other things, tax evasion. A few years ago a confrontation with a more overtly religious group calling themselves the Branch Davidians ended in a fiery disaster. Underground cadre dissidents who consider themselves true patriots are on trial in Denver for bombing a federal office building in Oklahoma City. Despite our freedom from foreign despots and our democratic form of government, the same issues that triggered violence in ancient Palestine still set us off today.

And just as with the Palestinian Jews, those issues are not merely economic. Like Judas the Galilean rebel, we see taxation as a symbol of power and control. We question how much government, even one elected by a majority of the citizenry, should or can control our lives. We fear handing over too much control to the impersonal power of the state, instinctively feeling that, even with the best safeguards, that power cannot be completely trusted.

Does Jesus' aphoristic answer still have any relevance? Can a reply meant for a conquered people living under foreign occupation have any relevance for us? If he were asked the same question today, wouldn't Jesus have to include something about electing responsible candidates, staying informed on the issues, working for tax reform?

Not exactly. His attitude toward Caesar—and whatever form of government we live under, I think we all regard it as "Caesar"— appears strangely indifferent. Neither belligerent nor obsequious, urging neither insurgence nor collaboration, Jesus accepts Caesar as a fact of life—we might even say a necessary evil, though he never directly labels government either necessary or evil. On the one hand, he condones paying the tax and obeying the law. If you are going to use the things of Caesar to make a life for yourself here on earth—and that includes using his highways, attending his schools, depending on his army to protect you—then you have to be prepared to live by Caesar's rules.

On the other hand, Jesus has to borrow a coin just to illustrate his point; he himself owned nothing that belonged to Caesar. His band of followers did, of course, carry money, which was held by the treasurer, a man named Judas. We know too that money figures largely in the stories that Jesus used as teaching devices, the parables of the lost coin, the talents, and the workers in the vineyard being only a few examples. His attitude toward money itself in these parables is never supercilious. The woman is elated when she finds her lost coin, the man who multiplies his investment is praised, and the owner of the vineyard pays the same wages to the latecomers as to the early risers. But while Jesus does not disparage using money, he does treat it with almost childlike nonchalance. Sometimes a small coin such as the housewife's is a big deal and at other times large sums are spent whimsically.

What he does not treat lightly are matters of life and death. Especially where life comes from, what its source is, who can give it and take it away. Beside these questions, taxes look like a trifling affair.

Chapter 11

Climbing in the Kingdom:
The Mother of Zebedee's Sons

Jesus has left Galilee on his final trip to Jerusalem, accompanied by an indeterminate number of followers, some of whom are dispossessed peasants, unemployed laborers, disaffected patriots, all with no particular place to go and nothing better to do. For the most part, they are poor. Nevertheless, they are shocked when Jesus tells them that wealthy people have a hard time making it into heaven's kingdom. "A camel can get through a needle's eye easier than a rich man can come before God."

How could that be? they wondered. It's poor people who have a hard time affording even pigeons to sacrifice at the Temple. Rich people don't have to worry about keeping the rules—buying from the right butcher, keeping a kosher kitchen. If the rich couldn't get it right, who could?

"If it was just up to them, they couldn't," Jesus said. "But God can do anything, don't forget."

Peter, one of his right-hand men, wanted to push the point though. "Well, look at me," he said. "I might not have been rich, but I had a good fishing business going, owned my own boat. And I did just what you said. I gave it all up to follow you here. So what am I going to get for it?"

Everyone was glad he asked the question. It had been on everybody's mind—whether they were really going to be better off once this Poor People's March reached Jerusalem.

"Don't worry," Jesus told Peter. "Once things have been set straight, and the right man is on the throne again, you twelve will have your own thrones and judge your fellow Jews." Then he had turned to the rest of them and added, "This goes for all of you. Anybody who's left a home and family behind, or given up his land or livelihood to follow me, he'll get it back a hundred times over, along with the life beyond death."

Now that's the kind of speech they'd been waiting to hear! It would be like the legendary jubilee years of their ancestors, when all the debts were supposed to be written off and everyone got his fair share of land. Let the Gang of Twelve have their judge's benches, so long as the people got their farms back.

"Many of the first will be last, and the last will be first," the rabbi added.

Right on! they all muttered. Let those fat cats find out what it's like on the bottom, and give working people a chance at the trough for a change.

Then the rabbi told one of his stories to calm them all down again. Something about a rich landowner hiring workers for his vineyard. He goes down to the marketplace and signs up one batch, then about noon decides he needs some more help. He goes back a third time in the middle of the afternoon. Finally, he goes back once more, right before quitting time, and hires a fourth bunch. But when the workers come to get their wages at the end of the day, he pays them all the same. Of course, the ones who got hired first complain about the last ones getting as much as they did. Tough luck for them! The owner doesn't back down. He tells the early birds he can be generous if he wants to.

A generous landowner? Now that's a stretch for the imagination. Still, it was a good story, and Jesus finishes it off with that battle cry again: "The last shall be first, and the first last!" They figure the rabbi means they're the workers who got hired last—the ones who didn't get a chance to earn a full day's wages. But Jesus is going to take care of that now. Once he gets to Jerusalem, he's going to see that they get what's coming to them.

The rabbi, however, seems troubled, as if he's afraid they haven't yet gotten the message. So, as they begin the final leg of the journey, he calls aside the twelve men he's picked as his apprentices. "Look," he tells them; "it's not going to be like you think when we get to Jerusalem. The people who run things there aren't going to welcome me with open arms. In fact, they're going to do everything they can to get me arrested and executed by the Romans. It won't be a pretty sight."

On the sidelines, the mother of two men in this inner circle grows impatient. Her name is Salome, and her boys, James and John, have been with Jesus from the very beginning. Fishermen like their father Zebedee, they've been hard workers—not like some of these down-and-out deadbeats following Jesus now. Zebedee expected the boys to take over the business he's worked hard to build. He owned his own fleet of fishing boats, even hired extra hands. A good thing too. He'd need them now with the boys gone.

The boys had been out with their father one day, mending the fishing nets, when Jesus had come strolling along the shore. "Come on and go with us," he'd said, gesturing to Simon and his brother Andrew, two other fishermen the boys teamed up with sometimes. Then the rabbi made some joke about fishing for men instead of mullet. Maybe that's what had tipped the scales. The promise of something bigger and better. It was almost like a dare. And her boys weren't ones to hang back or let others outdo them.

Still, their father would never forgive them for leaving him in the lurch like that, all to follow some fool who was likely to get them killed. Don't rock the boat—that was Zebedee's motto.

It hadn't taken Salome long to make up her mind to join them too. She didn't want to stay behind with old Thunderbolt, whose temper, always unpredictable, hadn't improved after the boys left. So when she heard how this little handful of fishermen had swelled to hundreds, sometimes thousands, and that her boys were now leaders in this small army, Salome had slipped away and followed them.

Not that it hadn't taken guts to leave everything behind. Respectable women don't abandon their home and husband to go traipsing off across the countryside, chasing after some idealistic guru. Sometimes she still asked herself what she, the wife of a prosperous fisherman, was doing here—if, in fact, she was still Zebedee's wife. For all she knew, he may have drawn up divorce papers as soon as he heard where she'd gone. Well, let him. Jesus had already made it clear that he was against men discarding their wives the way they might throw away an old pair of sandals. When the rabbi set up his new kingdom, wives would have a few safeguards. They wouldn't have to settle for being a whipping post for bad-tempered husbands anymore.

All the same, she was grateful not to be the only woman in the company. And not all of the women were poor, homeless creatures like that Mary from Magdala, either. Why, even Joanna, married to Herod's own bookkeeper, had joined them. It wasn't an easy life. They never knew where their next meal was coming from. And despite the rabbi's fine words about living like flowers and birds, these men couldn't get along without women to make sure there was something to eat and a place to stay every night.

Thank heaven, they wouldn't be living like vagabonds forever. Hadn't Jesus just promised everyone who left home to follow him a hundredfold compensation for what they'd left? She just hoped that didn't mean a hundred Zebedees.

Even better had been Jesus' promise to his handpicked lieutenants. They were going to have positions of real power in the new government. Judges, princes. Generals, maybe. Just like the Maccabees. And her sons were right up there with the best of them. The only problem was Peter. He was always trying to take over, setting himself up as Jesus' second in command, pushing in ahead of her boys. Maybe, she reflected as she trudged along the road, it was time to take a hand in this business herself.

At their next stop she hunts up James and John and, taking them each by the hand, leads them to where Jesus is resting. She kneels down, to let him know she has an important favor to ask.

"What is it you want?" he asks her.

"Sir," she says, "when you set up this new kingdom of yours, I hope you won't forget these two sons of mine. Put them on either side of your throne, right next to you."

Did James and John know what their mother was going to ask on their behalf? Maybe. Maybe not. But now that she's asked, they certainly don't mind hearing what Jesus has to say.

The rabbi looks up at the trio standing before him. "You don't know what you're asking for," he tells them. "Can you drink of my cup? Can you let yourselves be overwhelmed by what's going to overcome me?"

Salome's boys aren't bashful. "You bet," they say. "We can do it."

Jesus shakes his head. "Well, it doesn't make any difference. That's what's going to happen to you anyway. But as for making promises, handing out rewards—I can't do that. It's not up to me, but to my Father."

Were the boys disappointed? Was Salome angry? Embarrassed? We don't know. The story doesn't say.

What we do know is that the other ten members of that inner circle are decidedly put out by such a display of naked ambition. Just where do those two get off, they mutter, asking for favors like that? And hiding behind their mother's skirts as well. Didn't they all hope to get a piece of the action? What made James and John think they were so special?

Jesus is quick to squelch this dissension. "Okay, hold it," he says. "Everybody over here." When they're all huddled around him, he begins: "You all know what the Roman rulers are like. And the Syrians. And the Egyptians. It's always the same, never any different. The people with the power push the little guys around. Whatever they say goes. But I don't intend for you to act like that. Now, I know all of you want to be the big cheese. But this is what I want: for the strong to take care of the weak; for the bosses to be the kitchen help—the ones who wait tables, serve the food."

And here he might well have caught Salome's eye, as if directing his next comment especially to her. "The people who make sure we all get something to eat—they're the ones who really do the world some good. In fact, they're doing just what I am—serving. Even when it means you use up your whole life taking care of others."

Despite these kinds of lectures, the rabbi's talk about "the kingdom" continued to be interpreted, even by these closest companions, as referring to a takeover of the temporal power structure. Even the crucifixion and resurrection didn't change those expectations. Forty days after Easter, right before the ascension, the apostles are still asking him, "Lord, will you at this time restore the kingdom to Israel?"

But at some point during those same forty days, after Salome followed her sons James and John back to Lake Galilee and the family fishing business, Jesus surprised them all by showing up one morning to fix them all breakfast on the beach. When she saw the rabbi cooking over the campfire, did she make the connection with what he'd said that day on the road to Jerusalem about feeding people? "Feed my sheep," he repeated three times to Peter that morning on the beach.

Whether she understood or not, I believe Salome followed her sons James and John back to Jerusalem again after that breakfast and was there at Pentecost in that upstairs room. No doubt she saw Peter and her son John preach in the Temple and heal a crippled man. Certainly she was there when John was arrested and taken off to jail. By then they were all beginning to learn the truth about power.

Did Salome get what she asked for? Her sons indeed became leaders in the new sect later known as Christians. But James was, according to Luke's history of the early church, beheaded by Herod Agrippa, the first apostle to suffer martyrdom. And John, by legend, was exiled to the island of Patmos. Would Salome have made her request on the road that day if she had foreseen the martyrdom it brought? That's a question no mother would want to answer.

What eventually happened to Salome herself we have no way of knowing. But I wonder if she didn't think it was a big mistake when the group's leaders, her sons among them, decided to stop distributing food to the widows so they could devote themselves to supposedly more important work. If no one else, surely Salome would remember what Jesus had said that day on the road to Jerusalem: The people who make sure everyone gets fed—they're the ones with the really important jobs. Even though that work uses up your whole life.

Chapter 12

Imprisoned Mind:
Meeting with a Madman

*J*esus *went* places in order to meet people. He didn't have a call-in show or open a clinic and wait for the sick and damaged to come to him; he traveled to the towns where they lived. In the first chapter of Mark he explains to his apprentices what his plan is: to preach and perform exorcisms in the village synagogues of Galilee. "That is why I have come," he says. Soon he begins to heal people of diseases like leprosy and paralysis as well. Inevitably, this attracts large crowds. The crowds grow so large, in fact, that the synagogues can't hold them anymore, and he is forced to move outdoors.

At this early point in his ministry, when the constant clamor of the crowds begins to take its toll, Jesus instructs his helpers to keep a boat waiting on the inland Sea of Galilee. From there he can speak to the crowds—sound carries better over water anyway—without being crushed by them. Also, should they threaten to mob him, he can use the boat to make his escape.

When this story opens, Jesus has just made such an escape, crossing over a five-mile stretch of the lake with his disciples to what Mark calls "the country of the Gerasenes." On the east side of the lake is a loose confederation of first-century Roman communities called the Decapolis, or Ten Towns. The gentiles who live there won't have much interest in a roving Jewish rabbi. Jesus arrives unannounced and incognito. He obviously isn't interested in whipping up business for an evangelistic crusade, but simply hopes to get a break from the constant demands made on him by the curious and desperate.

The Decapolis is alien territory for Jesus' recently recruited band of Jewish followers, the same kind of place he will later use as the setting for the parable of the prodigal son, who ran off to a "far country" in an effort to break free of his family, but ended up feeding pigs for a gentile farmer and eating slop instead.

As Jesus' little band step out of the boat, they already feel uneasy. The limestone cliffs looming along the shoreline are pocked with caves which serve as tombs. Contact with dead bodies is taboo for Jews anyway, and who knows what heathen spirits might haunt a gentile cemetery? Sure enough, no sooner have they tied up than a wild man comes hurtling down from the cliffs toward them, naked and shrieking. He is covered with cuts and sores from self-inflicted wounds and dragging lengths of clanking chain from the iron shackles on his hands and feet.

He is a creature out of nightmare, a spectacle far worse than the prodigal at his lowest point. The boy in the parable ran wild in more conventional ways, squandering his inheritance on wine and wild women. However low he sank, he eventually "came to himself" and went home again, where his father welcomed him with open arms. In contrast, this man is hardly human. He's like a savage beast, a danger to himself and others.

No doubt his family has long since given up on him. No one waits at home for his return. Most people in the Bible are named by their family relationships. For example, Mary is called the mother of Jesus. David is the son of Jesse; Miriam, the sister of Moses. But this man is known to us only as the "Gerasene demoniac," a sign that he has been cast off by his family. Like Mary of Magdala, the madman is identified only by his hometown. He is the "village idiot," only worse, because his dementia makes him violent, self-destructive, out of control—too wild and dangerous to keep at home. To protect themselves, the villagers have tried to restrain the wild man by chaining him up like a dog, but in his violent rages he wrenches free of his confinement.

Now, coated with filth and festering wounds, he runs, limping and dragging his broken chains, toward Jesus. And suddenly stops. Instead of attacking, the madman falls on the ground at Jesus' feet, howling up at him. The words that issue from his throat are strangely ambivalent. Though he can't possibly know the stranger who has just landed on his shore, he calls him by name. Still, his greeting is shaded with fear and suspicion.

"What do you want with me, Jesus, Son of the Most High God? Swear to God that you won't torture me!"

Though the words come from the Gerasene's mouth, it's the spirits that have invaded him who call out the name and title.

Nevertheless, beneath the whines and howls of the demons, Jesus can hear the stifled pleas of the madman himself, mutely begging for release. Jesus speaks first to the malevolent spirits, ordering them to come out of the man. Then he speaks directly to the man himself, focusing on his true identity by asking for his name.

The demons, however, prevent the man from answering; access to the man's name will give Jesus even more power over their host body. Instead, they reply for the man. "The name is Legion," they say, making a macabre joke, "for we are many."

Apparently, some kind of parasitic connection between spirit and matter must be maintained in order for these spirits to exert their influence. Without the mediation of some physical, sentient agent, they cannot act in the material world. They realize that the jig is up now, however, that they're about to be dislodged from their present host. So they shift their strategy to finding another toehold in the material realm. They beg Jesus for permission to stay in the area. "Please, please, please," they cry, "let us at least go into that herd of pigs rooting around on the hillside!"

We should note that it is the demons, not Jesus, who suggest this scheme. Jesus does not coax them out of the man and trick them into invading the pigs. He only allows the demons their will. But the pigs lack even the puny defense of human reason to resist their invaders. Completely crazed, they do quickly what the man has been doing more slowly: they self-destruct by stampeding over a cliff.

However sorry we may feel for the pigs, imagine how the man felt, suddenly free of his demons. To anyone who has labored under the oppression of mental illness, two thousand pigs would be a small price to pay for restored sanity. Once again the man can use his voice to speak his *own* mind rather than his invaders'. He can have clear, consecutive thoughts that correspond to the perception of his senses. His inner violence stills. The swirling chaos he has inhabited settles into recognizable patterns. The darkened world lights up again. Perhaps best of all, he no longer has uncontrollable impulses to tear off his clothes, cut himself with stones, attack other people. He can take a bath, comb his hair, get dressed. Perform once again the simple, human tasks of caring for his body which the demons had not allowed.

It is, in fact, the stupid, senseless malice of demons that makes them so frightening to us. People who claim to be "mediums," who allow some spirit, presumably that of a dead person, to enter them and speak through the medium's voice, report a terrible exhaustion afterward. Demons appear to "possess" people for their own, often inscrutable reasons, yet they treat the bodies they inhabit with either indifference or horrific cruelty, compelling them to inflict terrible tortures on themselves. If it's true that demons need a physical channel to operate in the material world, you'd think they would treat their hosts in a more kindly manner. But even their own self-interest appears secondary to their spite.

The herdsmen in charge of the pigs hurry off into town to spread the news. The townspeople stream out of Gerasa to find Jesus and the man, now "in his right mind," wearing clothes and calmly seated on the hillside. This sight—not the news of the pigs' fate, as is often assumed—frightens the villagers at first. Their distress is often interpreted as a mercenary concern for the farmer's loss of profit, but that is reading our own twentieth-century values back onto the situation. The pigs are only a secondary concern.

It is the sight of the restored madman that strikes fear into them. He is living proof of this Jewish exorcist's supernatural power—a power that comes from an alien god. In their pantheon, the gods wield raw power, often arbitrarily; the spiritual realm has little or nothing to do with virtuous behavior. The gods act with little regard for morality or human need and must be constantly placated to guard against disaster. The pigs' fate merely confirms their fear that the Jewish holy man will bring down on them the wrath of that

shadowy spirit-filled realm. So they beg Jesus to leave the area—
not because he has disrupted the economic climate, but because
they dread divine reprisals.

And Jesus acquiesces, leaving without protest. He shows no
sign of feeling rebuffed for his good deed, nor does he seem disturbed by their ungrateful gentile ignorance. After all, he hadn't
come to the Decapolis to attempt a cultural or religious reform. He
hasn't even preached the kingdom of God there. Perhaps he realizes the concept would be meaningless to that audience, require
too big a cultural leap. He has only responded to the one person
who asked for his help—the madman.

As Jesus is climbing back in the boat, the now sane Gerasene
begs to come with him. Understand that Jesus has provided no
theological analysis of the event, has not even explained his own
identity to the man. The Gerasene only knows that this stranger has
freed him from the living hell that imprisoned him. He has neither
been instructed in the Torah, nor agreed to circumcision, nor sworn
off bacon. So far, he's only progressed to the stage of dressing
himself. But he knows that Jesus is responsible for his new freedom. It makes sense that he would want to stay near his deliverer,
the only one he is certain can keep his demons at bay. (Jesus himself notes in another place that demons commonly return to their
former host and take up residence there again.)

Why should the man want to stay in Gerasa anyway? People
there won't soon get over their fear of his violent history. They'll
continue to watch him with suspicion and dread. His estranged
family may or may not want him back again. He'll spend the rest
of his life living down his past in the village. Why not leave and
start over again with the man who has released him from torment?

But Jesus turns him down. No, he says, you can't come with me.
Why?

Remember that the man is a gentile. If he follows Jesus to
Galilee, he will no doubt suffer culture shock, trying to understand
and fit into a system of structured laws and requirements foreign to
him—a system that Jesus himself is challenging. Also, Jesus' band
of Jewish followers, jealous of their own individual prerogatives,

already show signs of developing a pecking order. An alien would undoubtedly find himself at the bottom of that heap.

But Jesus is not simply brushing him off. His refusal doesn't mean the man has no purpose, no mission. The Gerasene, after all, shows a willingness to follow Jesus, even without an invitation such as the disciples received. And so Jesus honors the man's devotion in another way.

You belong here, Jesus tells him, in your own hometown. Go on back to your family. Tell them what the Lord has done for you, how he's had mercy on you.

So the man watches as the boat carrying his deliverer sails away. But that is not the last we see of the Gerasene. The record tells us that he turns back toward the land and does exactly what Jesus told him to.

He must have continued to gather strength as the days went by, strength that kept him free of the demons that formerly oppressed him. The last we see of the Gerasene, he is traveling throughout the region of the Ten Towns, telling and retelling the story of his encounter with Jesus. Apparently he's very effective, since he amazes the crowds wherever he turns up. Paul is usually given the title "Apostle to the Gentiles." But maybe the first one was actually this nameless man who knew, more than most of us, how to value his sanity.

Chapter 13

A Way Out:
A Different Map

*I*n America, we tend to think of power in economic terms—purchasing power, leveraged buyouts, financial clout. Maybe the Marxist challenge to democracy in this century brought about this narrow focus. Fearing that the have-nots of the world would, as predicted, rise up and take over from the well-padded bourgeoisie, we've worked hard to bring everyone into the middle class. Despite the fact that our efforts haven't been completely successful, we still believe that economic power is the solution to practically all human problems.

I was surprised, then, to find that no one in the gospels ever comes to Jesus and asks him to make them rich. One man does ask if Jesus will make his brother share his inheritance with him (a request Jesus turns down), but sibling rivalry, rather than poverty, appears to have fueled that dispute. There were certainly rich people among the Palestinian Jews. But in the first century (and probably in most centuries), the lower classes didn't want to abolish the upper class; they just wanted to join it.

Palestinian Jews felt powerless for a number of other reasons having nothing to do with money. Women, for instance, lacked what we consider basic rights, as well as any social control, outside of supervising minor children and slaves. Thus, when the mother of James and John envisions escaping her powerless position, it never occurs to her to ask for her own post in the new kingdom. Her dreams, she feels, can only be fulfilled vicariously, through her sons.

Interestingly, biblical commentators across the board dismiss

Salome's appearance in Matthew's version of this story, preferring Mark's account in which the brothers make the request themselves. One even surmises that Matthew "shifts the responsibility to their mother" because he wants to "spare the apostles." But when they get rid of the mother, I believe the commentators miss an important aspect in the dynamics of power. The powerless will often settle for merely identifying with the powerful. If you can't be a ruler yourself—or a doctor or lawyer—make sure your son is.

Parents, of course, actually have a great deal of power over their children, though after a certain point that authority must be wielded indirectly. Jesus was already familiar with his own mother's attempt to retain her control over him. She had cajoled him into performing his first miracle, albeit reluctantly. Enlisting the aid of his brothers, she had tried to have him certified insane in Capernaum so that he would come back home and settle down. Unlike the biblical commentators, Jesus does not ignore his disciples' mother. He asks her directly what she wants. But when she cloaks her own ambition in a request for her sons' preferment, he switches his attention to the sons themselves. Those who don't ask for themselves have to settle for proxy gratification.

What does he have to say to these men who would be rulers? Essentially, that they don't know what they're asking for. First of all, they don't know what kind of kingdom he's been teaching them to pray for. Second, they don't know how much a throne in his kingdom will cost them. Since we have the advantage of hindsight, we feel a little smug, knowing how those untutored fishermen and their mother missed the point. However, our own knowledge of that curious kingdom of God is mostly indirect. We know what Jesus *didn't* mean—that he had no plans to overthrow the Romans. But any precise definition of that state of being he called the kingdom still eludes us. For one thing, he always described it in analogies—seeds, a pearl, a sheepfold. And the analogies themselves seem chosen to emphasize our impotence either to find or to build such a place. The seed sprouts unseen, the pearl is unexpectedly found, the sheep have to be herded into the fold. *Wait* and *watch* appear to be the only relevant verbs.

This passivity is pushed a step farther when we see how Jesus reacts to people who already have some degree of power—the Pharisees and Herodians. As a party, the Pharisees had a good deal of influence with the masses because of their unpretentious way of living and their commendable concern for the poor. The Herodians, on the other hand, who ate at the tetrarch's trough, had no influence with the people but did have the ear of their master. In both cases, each faction knew to the ounce how much its own influence weighed in the delicate Palestinian power scales. And neither thought it was enough. They wanted more.

Yet Jesus treats their concern about taxes with supreme indifference. While they see the issue as a power struggle between the religious and the political establishments, he defuses the claims of both. If you're going to use the government's money, you have to live by the government's rules. After all, there appears to be no way of living in society without somebody making the rules—and charging us for the privilege. Pay your taxes, but don't take it too seriously, he implies. It's God's kingdom that counts. You're looking for a way out of Caesar's, but you want into God's. Just remember that the tribute you owe there requires everything, your very self.

That's why oppression of the spirit is the one tyranny Jesus takes seriously. Lack of economic clout, cultural position, or political influence are as nothing compared to the loss of one's very self to a power that can subjugate the human will to its own ends. Even prisoners and martyrs can still say "no" in their hearts and minds, but a person defeated by the invisible forces of hostile spirits has lost even that option.

The modern world, we like to think, has outgrown the ancient world's superstitious belief in demons, but that claim would apply only to what we like to call the "developed" nations of the world. The truth is that a majority of people alive on the planet today still believe in demons, malevolent forces that can move in and take over a person's body like an occupying enemy army.

People who have been disinfected of such beliefs prefer to talk about such psychological aberrations in terms of dementia or multiple personality disorder. But a change in vocabulary didn't save Virginia Woolf, the British novelist, who reported hearing voices commanding her to throw herself out of windows. She eventually waded into a river, her pockets loaded with rocks, and drowned herself, "to stop the voices," she wrote in her suicide note. Nor are Christians immune from such attacks. The eighteenth-century poet William Cowper, who wrote a number of hymns for the evangelical movement in England, all his life fought against attacks from similar pernicious voices counseling suicide.

Despite the new vocabulary we have invented to give ourselves a sense of control over self-destructive tendencies, such irrational urges remain as resistant to treatment as the Gerasene's were before he met Jesus. And we have our own oblique ways of acknowledging the chaotic forces that overcome most of us from time to time, in some cases permanently. We enshrine this malevolent power in cultural imagery, calling it "the dark force" of Star Wars or its victims "the living dead" in vampire movies. In any case, whether demon possession or clinically diagnosed aberrations, it's the personhood of the individuals that is at stake. The identity of such sufferers is suffocated, squeezed till they are forced "out" of their minds. This seems to me the worst oppression possible, exceeding any economic, cultural, or political dispossession.

And it is the only one that Jesus did anything about. He never preached anything to the poor other than good news about the kingdom, telling them they were already in it. (This is probably what we find most offensive about the gospels today, when we're convinced that poverty is the one problem we can fix.) He called Herod an old "fox" once, but otherwise showed little interest in politics, as if it were less important than bird-watching and nature walks. He was not unaware of the factional infighting that racked Palestine in his day. In fact, he predicted what its outcome would be several decades before the leveling of Jerusalem by the Romans. Yet every time he encounters a person whose spirit—that essential and mysterious identity we sometimes call personality has been submerged under the chaos of destruction, Jesus acts.

This is his turf, the kingdom within. And they have invaded it. The spirits recognize him, even when ordinary mortals don't. He calls them forth with the ease that accompanies true authority. Interestingly, however, we don't see him fly into a rage with these unclean spirits, nor berate them. No magic bullets, silver swords, angelic armies. This is spiritual statecraft rather than spiritual warfare. He merely speaks to them and they must obey.

Since Jesus chose to take action only in this spiritual realm, does that mean he disdained other provinces of power? Is he interested only in the spiritual? Does matter not matter to him? No one who remembers that he also healed the sick and restored the deformed, deaf, and blind can believe he despised the ordinary physical world. His healings proved both his compassion for and his authority over creation.

Nor did he deny the existence of poverty, political oppression, and other inequities and injustices. The Galileans he mentions sympathetically in Luke, "whose blood Pilate had mingled with their sacrifices," were Zealots, and he included members of that political activist group in his inner circle. Indeed, though he has harsh words at some point for other Jewish factions—the Pharisees, the Sadducees, the Herodians—nowhere does he directly criticize the Zealots. But while he doesn't condemn their fervor for liberty, neither does he want his kingdom identified with their partisan agenda. Thus he refuses ever to name himself as Messiah, knowing the political overtones the title carries.

I don't believe Jesus steered clear of political reform because he considered oppression unimportant. The melee he caused in the Temple showed his anger at the abuse of religious and economic power. But I think he knew any solution to problems of power— whether it involves throwing out the Romans or the Republicans— is only a stopgap measure without the will for justice and mercy. Having already rejected Satan's offer to hand over "the kingdoms of the world" and having refused to turn stones into bread, he sticks to his rejection of the demon of power. He declares his authority but will not assert it over people against their will. (As for those whose will had been taken away, however, those oppressed in their spirit, "driven out" of their minds, he does not hesitate to act on their behalf.

If we go looking for Jesus to show us a way out of our perceived prisons we may be disappointed—unless we're willing to accept his means of deliverance. And those means may sometimes make us martyrs rather than militiamen. Are we then to submit to oppression rather than rebel? Such a condition goes against our cultural grain and natural instincts. I immediately find myself thinking of all the contingencies that would make such a position untenable—protecting the innocent from the violent abuse of power, for instance. At the same time, we must remember that Jesus never backed off from a confrontation with power. He did refuse, though, to resort to the ordinary methods by which the powerful exert their will in the world—coercion and force. But while he declined to exert his supernatural powers to protect himself, he also refused to recant his claims to his identity—even when it cost him his life.

The standard that Jesus set thus cuts both ways. If you take him as your spiritual model, you can neither impose your will on others nor can you stop speaking the truth that your adversary may well find threatening. This is not a comfortable position to be in. In fact, it lost Jesus many of his disciples, John tells us, who "went back, and walked no more with him."

PART IV

LOOKING FOR A WAY IN

People who looked to Jesus to endorse their nationalistic platform were generally dissatisfied with him and his unworldly kingdom. Those who were looking for neighbors, however, were not disappointed.

First-century Palestine was much more ethnically diverse than we usually picture it. The province of Judea had the largest concentration of Jews, especially in and around its capital Jerusalem. The upper classes had settled there after returning from their long captivity in Babylon. The city had remained the New York of Palestine, the cultural hub for all Jews, and, like New Yorkers today, Jerusalemites tended to gauge other's worth by their proximity to that city.

Galilee, a prosperous agricultural region about sixty miles to the north of Jerusalem, was the most densely populated of the Palestinian provinces. By the time Jesus began his mission there, Galilee had a population of about 350,000, many of whom were slaves. About a hundred years earlier, wealthy gentiles had bought up large farms and settled in the province. Though Jews still made up the largest single cultural class—about a third of the population—Jesus was certainly exposed to a more diverse society in Galilee than if he had grown up in Judea.

Between Galilee and Judea lay Samaria, a region that shared a political umbrella with Judea. Their common civil government, imposed by Rome, pleased neither the Samaritans nor the Jews. Centuries earlier, Assyrian kings had settled some of their own

people in Samaria and, despite their eventual assimilation and conversion to Israel's God, the Jews still looked on them as mongrels
who had perverted proper worship, worse than pagans.

In the other provinces of Palestine, Jews were less numerous.
Along the Mediterranean coast, descendants of Israel's old enemies, the Philistines, still predominated. In fact, the term Palestine
means "land of the Philistines." Seafaring raiders in earlier centuries, under Roman rule they continued to make their living as
maritime merchants. Inland, the Transjordan region known as the
Decapolis was inhabited primarily by Greek-speaking gentiles. In
general, because the region between the Jordan and the Mediterranean had been invaded so many times and immigrants sometimes forcibly resettled there, it contained a smorgasbord of
cultures. None of the three rulers who governed the region was
Jewish. Many Palestinian cities—Sepphoris, only four miles from
Nazareth, for example—had pagan temples as well as synagogues.
Within a narrow corridor about 150 miles long and between
twenty-eight and fifty-four miles wide lived millions of people
who coexisted with about the same level of mutual esteem and co-
operation one finds in the same region today.

And, as today, religion proved the sharpest instrument for dividing people. Pagans, of course, were used to living cheek by jowl
with devotees of deities other than their own. Generally, this
caused them no more alarm than a Green Bay Packer fan feels living next door to a Denver Bronco supporter.

Polytheism provided many social advantages to the state. The
gods of the ancient world were by and large local products whose
format could be redesigned for export to other regions. A kind of
ecumenism operated among pagans, wherein a nature goddess
who appeared in North Africa under the name of Isis could emerge
as Ishtar in Babylon, become Astarte in Syria, and in Greece wear
the guise of Demeter. Under Rome, the world had become so cosmopolitan that no one made any more of these adaptations than a
Methodist might today on moving to a new town and deciding to
attend the local Lutheran church. This easygoing approach to theology suited the Roman Empire just fine. As long as a province

was willing to add just one more deity—the emperor—to its local pantheon of gods, Rome didn't much care whom or how its subjects worshiped.

The exception, of course, was the Jews. Alone of all Rome's subjects, they were absolutely intransigent on the religion question. Not only did they insist on only one God, but they allowed no images of their deity to be made. Worst of all, they steadfastly refused to admit even the imperial insignia inside the bounds of their Temple, claiming that it was, in effect, an idol. The farthest they were prepared to go was offering daily sacrifices to their God on behalf of the emperor.

Hellenized Jews like the historian Josephus, who either by choice or circumstance lived outside Palestine, were touchy about comparisons between their culture and religion and that of the Greeks, who still set the intellectual standard in the Roman Empire. Mathematics and philosophy are all very well and good, Josephus said, but only the Law of Moses can tell you how to live everyday life in accordance with divine will. "What form of government then can be more holy than this? What more worthy kind of worship can be paid to God than we pay, where the entire body of the people are prepared for religion?" he asks rhetorically, noting that the Jews teach their laws even to women and slaves. Other peoples, he says, may have remained true to their religion while they enjoyed their liberty, but the Jews "have never betrayed our laws under the most pressing distresses we have been in."

Such fidelity was indeed a heritage to be proud of. That the Jews still maintained their cultural identity, sticking to the Torah, its history and prescriptions, after more than a millennium, was nothing short of miraculous. Not only did they adhere to Torah, they added to it. By the first century, the original Ten Commandments given to Moses had been augmented by over six hundred ancillary laws covering all aspects of human life. Because these laws applied to everyone, the Jews had probably the most ethical, conscientious, and humane society in the known world. Everyone, at every level of society, was afforded some degree of responsibility and protection. The Jews may have had no philosophers to brag about, no mathematicians or inventors, no sculptors or world conquerors, but they felt they had something far more precious: Torah, God's Law for Living.

So impressive was the morality of the Jews that their religion attracted a number of gentile proselytes weary of negotiating the Empire's moral sewers. However, complete conversion to Judaism required male circumcision, not a ritual many were willing to undergo. Therefore, a large number of respectful gentiles stopped at the God-fearer stage, living by the rules that governed ordinary life but stopping short of circumcision. The outer courtyard of the Temple in Jerusalem, its thirty-five acres comprising about two thirds of the stone platform on which the Temple proper rested, was called the Court of the Gentiles. Uncircumcised proselytes were welcome there but could not pass the barrier known as the Warning Wall. To intrude further meant death. That's how seriously the Jews took their religion.

Jesus never left Palestine during his ministry. Few Jews did, unless compelled by external circumstances. Why should they? One ancient Jewish commentary declares there are ten degrees of holiness, and that "the Land of Israel is holier than all other lands." Nevertheless, Jesus had plenty of exposure to gentiles in his travels from one end of the region to the other. Following his baptism by John in the Jordan River, he went on a retreat in the desert south of Judea, after which he returned to Galilee to gather his followers. He then circulated for a time among the Galilean towns and villages, visiting synagogues and healing until the crowds became too large. At least once he went to the coastal city of Tyre and eventually farther north to the Roman city of Caesarea Philippi. On other occasions, he sailed across the Lake of Galilee (also known as Gennesaret) to Bethsaida or over to the Decapolis region. At least once he traveled through the province of Samaria. Thus his travels took him up and down the entire length of Palestine as well as west to the sea and east to the Transjordan.

These journeys exposed him to the whole spectrum of Middle Eastern life—Jews, Greeks, Romans, Phoenicians, and other assorted gentiles. Men, women, and children. Sick and well, rich and poor, kings and outcasts. Farmers, fishermen, tax men, priests, lawyers, soldiers, housewives. Married, single, widowed, and promiscuous. Because of his exposure to such diversity (which would have been impossible had he settled down to a job and family), we have a chance to see how Jesus relates to all classes and conditions of people.

In many ways, he operated like one of the religious teachers called rabbis, though the generic term did not actually become a title until after the destruction of the Temple in A.D. 70. But while most religious teachers and holy men usually addressed audiences limited to Jewish laymen devoted to Torah studies, Jesus attracted a much broader spectrum of listeners, including gentiles, women, and reprobate Jews considered outcasts from their religious community. In fact, these social contacts were what made him initially unsavory to the very religious scholars he most resembled. To them, he was like a Sunday school teacher who insisted on hanging out at the local biker bar.

But what about the regulars at the bar? How did they see him? What did they expect from this unlikely instructor? I think we have to be careful not to sentimentalize the situation. Our modern tendency is to people the bar with stock characters who have a few endearing foibles but are all basically good at heart—the whore with the heart of gold, the hard-drinking hell-raiser who delivers toys to kids anonymously on Christmas Eve. In this fantasy scenario, Jesus establishes an easy camaraderie with these social outcasts, they all have a few drinks and laughs together, he speaks some encouraging, affirming words and leaves them all feeling better about themselves. Jesus—just one of the guys.

But such a scenario diminishes the desperate condition of the outsiders whose stories we read in the gospels. Jewish society, as with most social groups, defined certain conditions—particular diseases, menstruation, outlawed occupations—which excluded one at least temporarily from fellowship in the community. And, of course, gentiles by definition were outside the pale unless they converted. Jesus had an unusual degree of contact with these people considered off-limits by anyone professing to be a teacher

of Torah. Gentiles were often looking for healing, either for themselves or someone else. Suffering made them put away any fears
of rebuff they may have had.

Women were a special case. Respectable matrons were not ordinarily included in Jewish social occasions, but Jesus defended
Mary of Bethany when she insisted on listening to his table talk.
And other women with no reputation to lose likewise found he
spoke up on their behalf when others would have evicted them. Because he spoke and dealt with them directly, women were often
willing to finance his preaching missions and accompany him on
his travels, something no other itinerant rabbi is known to have
countenanced.

But it was his association with secularized Jews that earned him
the reputation for eating and drinking with sinners. These defec-
tors had given up any pretense of observing the rules. Worse than
gentiles, they betrayed their own people by going to work for the
enemy. Whatever they had gained financially from the arrange-
ment, they had lost in respect and standing in their own community. What they wanted from Jesus was a way back in.

Chapter 14

Powerful Outsider:

The Centurion and His Servant

By the time Jesus came on the scene, Rome had been in control of Palestine for about a hundred years. The Roman Empire was by then an ungainly assemblage of thirty-two provinces managed by a hodgepodge of different types of government. Whenever possible, Rome preferred to keep local rulers in place, as long as they could guarantee the peace and collect their quota of taxes for the Empire. However, Rome did keep a military force stationed in districts like Galilee, known to be politically unstable or with a history of revolutionary tendencies.

Being a soldier in an occupied country is not an enviable position. George Orwell, in his essay "Shooting an Elephant," describes his ordeal as a British policeman in colonial India. Despite his sympathy for the desperately poor, as a representative of a foreign nation his best, most humane intentions were always defeated. American troops stationed in alien outposts around the world today know what it's like to be hailed as liberators one day, then despised as intruders and oppressors a few weeks later. Roman soldiers no doubt felt the native Galileans' animosity just as keenly.

One of those Roman soldiers, a midlevel officer in command of a hundred infantrymen, is stationed in Capernaum, the town that served as Jesus' headquarters during his early career. The officer is a thoughtful person, inclined to philosophical and ethical reflection. He has explored the religion of the people he is there to police. The centurion is attracted, as a surprising number of gentiles were, to the moral vision of the Jews. They worship only one God, who they believe created the world and its orderly functioning. Unlike the Roman pantheon of gods, theirs does not engage in the wanton escapades that mirror the depraved society of imperial Rome. At their best, the centurion finds the Jews and their God concerned for justice and harmony within human society.

The Roman officer may have even gone so far as to become an official God-fearer, a quasi proselyte who vows to abide by certain rules supposedly established with Noah, one of the Jews' distant ancestors. This covenant sets a kind of international minimum standard of conduct for Jews and gentiles alike. After pledging themselves to this covenant, gentiles are allowed to participate in the synagogue prayers and listen to the rabbis' teaching. His status as God-fearer would make the centurion something of an oddity among his fellow Romans in the garrison, however, some of whom would suspect he has "gone native."

There is something sad about the centurion's plight. We have no idea where the man actually came from. Rome had amalgamated many diverse cultures, making the Empire unusually cosmopolitan, exceeding even the diversity we experience today. If you had a yen to see the world, all you had to do was join the imperial army. Still, he is an outsider in Palestine, physically uprooted, culturally adrift, a man with enviable citizenship but a rejected heritage.

Of course, the centurion may also have made the alliance with the Capernaum Jews out of prudence. It has been to his benefit to make friends with the local leaders of the community. He has even paid for the construction of a new synagogue for the town—a gesture that also made his job easier. That, after all, had been Herod's motivation for building the new Temple in Jerusalem. Synagogues, however, form the heart of the village's identity, serving not only as a house for daily prayer, but as a Torah school for boys, the courthouse where disputes are settled, and a general community hall. But while Herod's Temple, no matter how splendid, did not endear him to his Jewish subjects, the Capernaum elders, able to observe the centurion at closer range, are convinced of the man's sincerity.

He also shows genuine concern for the people in his household. When one of the centurion's slaves falls ill—a man he particularly values, perhaps the steward of his household or an old tutor who has served as his surrogate parent—the Roman tries every avenue he knows to find a cure. Nevertheless, the slave's condition worsens, and the centurion begins to despair of his recovery.

It is at this crisis stage that the centurion recalls hearing of a young rabbi, no longer welcome in his own synagogue in Nazareth, who has recently moved to Capernaum. He has taken up speaking at Sabbath services in the synagogue, and an exorcism he performed there has set the whole town talking. This feat was followed by reports that the rabbi healed a fisherman's mother-in-law in her own home.

Most people in the ancient world were familiar with wonder-workers who claimed to cure diseases. Josephus wrote that incantations supposedly handed down from King Solomon cured distemper. Even educated Romans resorted to auguries and other magical practices. So, having tried all other alternatives, the centurion decides to appeal to the miracle-working rabbi to heal his slave.

But he hesitates to approach the rabbi directly. Having listened to the Torah debates at the synagogue, he is well aware that there are two different schools of thought among rabbis regarding foreigners. One interpretation, attributed to Rabbi Simeon ben Yohai, says that Israelites are commanded to love strangers even more than natural-born Jews. But the opposing school of Rabbi Eliezer holds that the Torah's many injunctions regarding "strangers" means that foreigners are a threat to orthodoxy and good Jews should steer clear of them. Which school does this new rabbi follow? Maybe the natives of Capernaum trust him, the centurion reasons, but the visiting rabbi may have qualms about helping a Roman officer. Thus, he asks the synagogue elders to act as his intermediaries.

Jesus, meanwhile, has just completed a long teaching session outside of town. The young rabbi is returning to Capernaum when the elders of the synagogue find him. They explain the slave's condition to him, adding, "This centurion is a really good guy, a true friend of us Jews, not like most of his kind. His heart's in the right place. And we owe him. After all, he built the very synagogue you've been teaching in. He deserves your help." (Note that they base their appeal on the merits of the centurion, not the slave who is dying. We never find out any details about the slave.) Jesus consents to go with the synagogue board members, no doubt accompanied by a number of curious onlookers.

Meanwhile, back at his villa the centurion is having second thoughts. He is, after all, only a God-fearer. Most observant Jews won't even come inside a gentile house, no matter how upscale or powerful its owner. If they do, they must go through a time-consuming purification rite afterward. Also, the rabbi is not from Capernaum. Maybe the reputation the Roman has built up here won't count for much with him. And if the rabbi turns out to be from the xenophobic school that thinks all Romans are scum, he might cause a scene. This encounter could turn out to be embarrassing for everyone. Worse than embarrassing for him. A representative of Rome can't afford to be publicly humiliated by an itinerant miracle worker. Perhaps, the centurion thinks, he's been too hasty. Maybe he should leave the rabbi an out, some way for both of them to save face.

So the centurion dispatches some of his friends to intercept the rabbi. The friends manage to head the party off just in time, right before they reach the villa. In fact, the centurion can observe the encounter in the street below from his rooftop. The message he has sent with his friends is a paragon of diplomacy.

"Master," his friends address the rabbi, "please don't bother yourself any further. The centurion says to tell you he knows you may not want to enter his house. That would be asking you to violate your laws just for his benefit."

Everyone stops and waits for the messengers to continue.

"However," the friends go on, "he is sure that you, a man who can perform miracles and command the very spirits, will understand his position. He too is a man in authority. He needs to maintain control over his troops. He has to be able to say to his soldiers,

'You do this,' or 'You go there,' knowing he can count on their obedience. Surely you, as a holy man with spiritual authority, can do the same. It will take only a word from you to heal this dying man. Why not just give the command here?"

Up on the rooftop, the centurion holds his breath. Will the young rabbi understand the intent of his message? Will he be sympathetic with his dilemma? Will he understand the need for discretion?

The rabbi pauses a moment, then nods. "Fine," he says. Then he throws his hands up and turns back to quiet the crowd. "Listen to this," the rabbi announces, raising his voice so everyone can hear. "Here's a man—a Roman—who can muster the kind of faith it takes to heal someone. And he doesn't expect magic tricks either. He just trusts that I can do what I say. Where else can I find that kind of faith? Nowhere else in this country." He laughs. "Certainly not where I come from."

People in the crowd look at one another knowingly, remembering how the rabbi's been run out of his hometown of Nazareth.

The centurion's friends, eager to relay the rabbi's response, hurry inside the house, where they find the slave already sitting up, looking around, asking for something to eat. In a matter of minutes, word of the man's improved condition spreads to the street. The crowd outside begins to buzz with the news. Nazareth's loss is Capernaum's gain. This is going to put their town on the map.

From the roof, the centurion is watching the rabbi, followed by his band of bodyguards, as he disappears down the road. The two men have not spoken, have not even exchanged a look. But the officer's petition has been granted. In one stroke, this holy man has not only healed the slave, but averted a skirmish in the culture wars between Rome and the Jews. He has, in fact, strengthened the centurion's bond with the Jewish community.

So what exactly did the centurion's faith consist of? Did he believe this rabbi was the Messiah the Jews expected to free them from Rome? That would put him in an awkward position indeed. Did he believe the holy man was—as the Roman emperors claimed to be—divine? Who can say? Those questions remain unanswered in the gospels.

As the Roman watched the figures receding in the distance, perhaps he was only grateful, both for his restored slave and for the delicacy of feeling the healer showed in performing this feat in absentia. But maybe he also felt a little disappointed that he'd missed his chance to meet, face to face, this man who, across all the distances that separated them, could read his heart.

Chapter 15

A Dog's Life:
The Syro-Phoenician Woman

*T*here are two stories I would prefer had not been included in the gospel accounts of Jesus: the one in which he curses the fig tree and this one. Both of these stories offend my sense of propriety. I can let the fig-tree story pass as perhaps having some underlying prophetic import in the first century that is now lost to us. But Jesus' seeming indifference to a Palestinian mother's plight doesn't fit with our picture of him as a compassionate healer who never turned anyone away.

Jesus rarely left the Jewish areas of Palestine, and when he did, the trip was never undertaken as a missionary expedition. This story takes place in a town on the Mediterranean coast and precedes the earlier account of the deaf and dumb man's healing. Jesus, you may remember, has left Galilee to escape Herod's suspicious scrutiny and to let the dust settle over his disagreements with certain religious factions. He hopes to keep a low profile in this gentile seaside town. Just as he showed no particular eagerness to hobnob with the Roman centurion in Capernaum, neither does he ever seek out gentiles on his travels outside Galilee. Whatever encounters he has in these more distant regions are always instigated by one of the natives, never by Jesus himself.

He has just arrived in the suburbs of Tyre, a city on the Mediterranean coast of Syria, populated primarily by descendants of the Jews' ancient enemies, the Philistines. Travel arrangements have obviously been made in advance, since he disappears into a house, no doubt one owned by a Jew, as soon as he arrives. If there is a synagogue in Tyre, he doesn't go there, but stays indoors, hoping to keep his presence a secret.

Yet his reputation for healing has spread even to this pagan city. When a native of the area, a woman, learns he's in town, she finds a way to enter the house, perhaps slipping into the courtyard where she discovers Jesus resting. Courtyards were considered semipublic space, almost like the stretch of sidewalk in front of a house in the suburbs today.

The woman has not sought out the mysterious visiting Jew merely from curiosity, however. Her need is more urgent. She has a daughter at home who shows all the signs of demon possession. Mark's gospel calls the girl a "young daughter," probably meaning she was prepubescent. The girl's condition, like the madman's of Gerasa, may have made her wild, causing her to inflict wounds on herself, or perhaps she was growing violent with other family members. The mother knows what future lies ahead for this child if she cannot be cured. She will be vulnerable to all kinds of exploitation, including from those who manipulate people with "psychic" gifts for profit. Women in particular were used as mediums, the spirits of the dead supposedly speaking to the living through them. A scene in the sixteenth chapter of Acts shows a young girl exploited by a pagan magician in this way. Unless the girl is cured, she has nothing but nightmare ahead of her.

The mother has heard of the wonders this Jewish magician has worked among his own people, and that he is especially effective as an exorcist. That the man is a Jew is of no consequence; the religious controversies he's embroiled in at home mean nothing to this woman. In Tyre there's a different shrine on every street corner. The mother will, of course, already have tried all the remedies the local gods offer before approaching the Jewish magician: augurers who examine chicken entrails for clues to diseases, shamans prescribing various potions, prayers, and incantations— not to mention monetary offerings. So far, nothing has worked.

The Jews, she knows, think they're special, that having only one god makes them somehow superior to the rest of the human race. They tend to keep to themselves, won't eat the same kind of food other people do, are afraid for you to even touch them. But she's used to coexisting with strange customs and she realizes from the outset that the Jewish magician may simply rebuff her. However, the mother is determined. If the magician can do the kinds of things she's heard about, she doesn't intend to let him leave Tyre without doing something about her daughter.

Historians and other modern scholars often point out how little human life was valued in the ancient world, how slaves, for example, were treated as no more than farm implements or construction machinery. Thus, it comes as something of a surprise when we discover a gentler sort of family feeling, not only in the gospels but in other ancient documents as well. However brutalized by work and warfare these people were, they remained by and large devoted to their children, willing to make enormous sacrifices on their behalf. And the sacrifice this woman makes is her self-respect.

She approaches Jesus there in the courtyard, falling on her knees in the typical posture of a petitioner and making her plea for him to cast the demon out of her daughter. Then she waits for the magician's response.

At first, according to Matthew's account, there is none. This man in the courtyard simply ignores her. Okay, she thinks, I'll make sure you hear me. So she repeats her request, not once, but over and over, each time louder, in a ululating cry.

The men who attend the magician begin to get nervous. "Do something," they tell him, "anything to shut her up. She's raising such a ruckus the whole neighborhood will know you're here."

Finally, the magician puts down his first-century equivalent of the newspaper and looks at her. "Look," he tells her; "I didn't come here on your account. People like you aren't included in my mission statement. I can't waste my time and energy on you. My own people take everything I've got. Helping you would be like taking food out of the children's mouths and feeding it to the dogs. You can't expect me to do that."

His comparison of the pagan woman to a dog would brand him today as culturally insensitive. Yet we must resist extracting Jesus from his own cultural context and forcing him into ours. Rabbis often made scathing remarks to their questioners. In arguments,

they were absolutely ruthless. No one expected them to perform
like modern-day therapists. Jesus' occasional display of tender-
ness is exceptional for the period.

Besides that, the woman appears well equipped to deal with this
retort. People who live with cultural diversity learn to survive by
growing a thick skin. The woman has probably heard worse than
this before, and she seems perfectly capable of handling the situation now that she's got his attention. She neither flounces off in a
huff nor shrinks back like a bruised violet. Instead, she speaks right
up. "True enough," she says, "but even the dogs get to clean up the
crumbs that fall under the table."

Her words are perfectly chosen. She knows this man sees her as
an outsider. He's made that clear. Like most Jews, he cares only
about his own kind. That's no surprise. By acknowledging her in-
ferior position, she effectively undercuts his argument. And what
does he know about children anyway? She's the mother here, and
she's just as fierce about seeing to her child's needs as this Jewish
magician is for his people.

Who knows—maybe the Jews are right about their god. Maybe
they do know more about that mysterious force that runs things behind the scenes. She's willing to grant him that. She could care less
about having the right answers. What she cares about is having that
force act on behalf of her daughter. She keeps her eyes on the magician's face. Has her smart remark put him off?

After a moment, he begins to nod thoughtfully. "You know," he
says, "I think you're onto something here. Go on home now.
Everything's all right there. Your daughter's going to be fine."

She hurries out of the courtyard and heads for home, forgetting
his harsh words. She rushes into the house, the scene of the child's
violent antics. Her little girl is lying in bed, sleeping peacefully.

We don't know that this woman ever saw the Jewish magician
again. Without at least an elementary knowledge of Judaism, she
would have understood the term "messiah" even less than the Roman centurion did. All she knows about Jews is their claim to have
a special connection with God. For her, the divine is a mysterious
force, and seeking its help is always a stab in the dark. Hard as it

would be for her to separate the idea of magic from her daughter's release, however, she would have noticed that the Jew recited no incantations, performed no magic rite.

Where, she might later have wondered, did his power come from? She had not been "evangelized," preached to, instructed, or asked to adopt a new code of living and become a Jew herself. She knew she was not one of "the children" the rabbi had spoken of, nor would she ever be. So why had the Jew decided to help an outsider like her? What had made the difference?

Chapter 16

Breaking the Cultural Barrier:

The Samaritan Woman

I grew up in the American South when drinking fountains and public restrooms were still marked "white" and "colored." Because the South was also the Bible Belt, many white people felt compelled to justify these distinctions as they would their religious conviction—with biblical texts. Meanwhile, the people they excluded from their schools, restaurants, and churches used the words of that same Bible to sustain their own hopes of a better world. Even as a child, I knew there was something terribly wrong with our singing about Jesus' loving all the children of the world, "red and yellow, black and white," while refusing to eat or drink or worship with those same beloved children.

Religion, instead of reconciling racial or ethnic resentment, has often been the spark that sets it aflame. Azerbaijanis and Armenians, Hutus and Tutsis, Palestinians and Jews, Catholics and Reformers—we all stoke our corporate hatreds with the fuel of religious differences. And sometimes our most brutal wars are with those who share our religious lineage. The cross burned by the Ku Klux Klan was the same emblem of salvation claimed by the people they persecuted.

I rehearse these painful bits of history to provide a cultural context for the confrontation between Jesus and a woman from Samaria, a district that lay between his own native Galilee and the southern province of Judea. Though Samaria was governed by the same imperial deputy who ruled Judea, Jews considered that intervening territory defiled and its inhabitants lower than gentiles. During Israel's heyday, Samaria had been part of David's kingdom. But after the death of David's son Solomon, this northern section of the kingdom had split off. Though this section retained the name of Israel, the southern kingdom, Judah, kept the former capital city, Jerusalem, and with it the Temple.

Eventually, Assyria, the new Mesopotamian powerhouse, overran the Northern Kingdom and deported its leading citizens, resettling alien conquered peoples in their place. These immigrants brought their own gods along with them to the new land. Over the centuries, the Jewish peasants who had been allowed to remain in their homeland married these pagan settlers. Like most embattled people cut off from the headwaters of their past, the Samaritans clung to whatever scraps of their heritage they were able to preserve—in this case, the five Books of Moses. But over time they also assimilated certain pagan customs of their foreign husbands or wives.

Their cousins to the south in Judah were eventually hauled off to Babylon as exiles themselves. These southern Jews managed to maintain their culture intact, however. Finally allowed to return to their homeland, one of their first goals was to rebuild the ruined Temple in Jerusalem. When Jews from Samaria came down to help with this project, their offer of assistance was refused. Stung by this rebuff, the Samaritans set about building their own rival temple on Mount Gerizim. Thus began a feud that would last for centuries.

Along with their new temple, the Samaritans supported shrines to a panoply of pagan deities their immigrant kin worshiped. At one point they even allowed the Mount Gerizim temple to be dedicated to Zeus. Thus in the eyes of the Judeans, as well as the Galileans and those exiled Jews dispersed throughout the Empire, the Samaritans were no better than quislings, apostates, heretics. A disgrace to all those Jews who had struggled and often died to maintain the purity of their religion.

Each group considered itself the true Jews. The Samaritans thought themselves the children of Abraham, equal to their southern cousins. Censure from other Jews stung as only slander from one's own family can. Didn't they all share a common heritage,

follow the same Law of Moses? Hadn't the Jews in Samaria suffered from invasion as much as other Jews had from exile? So why
had the Maccabees, the southern Jewish freedom fighters, destroyed the Samaritans' new temple during their rebellion against
Rome?

The other Jews, however, had a different take on the conflict.
They refused to acknowledge any essential kinship with the Samaritans, whom they considered at best half-breeds. Only grudgingly
did they admit that Samaritans were part of the human race, much
less acknowledge the ties of blood and history that bound them together. Like the signs above the water fountains and restroom doors
in the South prohibiting their use by blacks in the pre-1960 South,
prohibitions against eating and drinking with Samaritans were the
orthodox Jews' only way of maintaining the separation necessary
to keep them from defilement.

Nor did it help to ease the ethnic tensions when Rome lumped
the two regions together into one political unit. Shortly thereafter,
a gang of Samaritans vandalized the Jerusalem Temple during
Passover. The Jews saw Rome much the way my kinfolks regarded
Washington, D.C. — as the far-off federal government imposing its
will in local matters it didn't understand.

Most Jews who had occasion to travel between the northern
province of Galilee and Judea to the south avoided the most direct
route through Samaria. Instead, they took a longer and more circuitous route, crossing to the east side of the Jordan River and traveling down through the gentile regions of the Decapolis and
Peraea, then recrossing the Jordan, an itinerary that considerably
lengthened the trip. Their willingness to quite literally go out of
their way to avoid Samaria shows that the animosity between the
two groups was as deep and complicated as the racial tensions that
tore apart both the American South and the Black Muslims in the
1960s.

At noon one day a woman in the Samaritan village of Sychar
goes to draw water from a well a half mile outside of town. Both
the time and the place are significant. The time because most
women, the wives and daughters of respectable households, cus-

tomarily drew their day's supply of water early in the morning while it was still cool. That this woman should wait till midday probably means one of two things: either she had slovenly housekeeping habits or she had reason to avoid the other women of her village. In this case, perhaps both were true.

The site is important because the well was famous, a historical monument of which the Samaritans are justly proud. Located at a fork in the road from Jerusalem, it reputedly was dug by Jacob, the Jewish patriarch, who had passed it down to his son Joseph, the one sold by his brothers into slavery in Egypt. Long after Joseph died in Egypt, his bones were carried back to Palestine and buried in a field near the well. So despite the Jews' scorn of Samaria, it contained some important sites central to their history, such as this well.

Not that this woman is a particular devotee of religious shrines. In fact, if pious Jews ever needed an illustration of how slipshod religion leads to lax morals, this woman would fit the stereotype exactly. She has had a whole string of men in her life—five of them husbands. Now she's stopped even bothering with marriage. This is why she comes to the well at noon—to avoid the housewives of Sychar. Even Samaritan women have some standards.

It's important not to romanticize this woman's situation though. She is no Elizabeth Taylor, taking on husbands she then discards as easily as out-of-fashion clothes. Women in the first century didn't have that kind of personal independence. It's not clear whether this woman left her previous husbands or if they dumped her. In any case, her options were quite limited. In order to live alone securely, a woman had to possess a fair amount of independent wealth, along with an inviolable reputation. Lacking those, she had to live with a male protector. Without this safety net, just like poor women today, she would be vulnerable to indignities, assaults, and destitution. This woman, having passed from hand to hand, is now living outside all the social boundaries that might provide her physical and financial shelter.

As she approaches the well this day, she sees a strange man slumped beside the well. Though she can tell he's tired and dusty

from the road, she ignores him and lets down her bucket into the
well as if he weren't there.

"Let me have some of that water, will you?" the man asks as she
begins to haul up the filled bucket.

As soon as he opens his mouth, she can tell the man is a Galilean
Jew. You can always tell by their accent. What's he doing here,
anyway? She answers him with a smirk. "Right. Like a Jew would
ask a favor of a Samaritan. I know what you're after, buster."

She had expected, maybe, a little lascivious banter—she knows
what Jews think of Samaritan women. He wouldn't have spoken
to her at all unless he thought she was a pushover.

Instead, he looks up at her thoughtfully. "If you knew who
you're talking to, you wouldn't act so flippant," he says. "You
don't realize it, but God wants to give you something you've always wanted. And I'm the one he's sent to deliver it. If you knew
who I am, you'd be asking *me* for a drink, and not the other way
around. The water I supply is not like any you've had before. It's
full of Life itself."

Great. The guy's a religious nut too. The woman gives a skep-
tical snort. "Okay, Mr. Jew, just where do you expect to get this
Wonder Water? This is a deep well, and you don't have a bucket.
But then I guess you think you're greater than our ancestor Jacob.
Believe it or not, he gave us this well. He even drank out of it him-
self. It supplied his entire operation with good water. And now it's
ours." There, she thinks—feeling she's scored a point for Samaria.
Now maybe he'll go on his way and leave her in peace.

But the man merely smiles and shakes his head. "You don't understand," he says, pushing the point. "Whoever drinks from this
well gets thirsty again. But the water I have keeps on living inside
you. It's like a spring that never runs dry."

"Fine," she says. "I tell you what. Why don't you just give me
some of this magic water that never runs out? It'll save me a lot of
time and effort, not having to make this well run every day."

There's a long pause as the man studies her carefully. The
woman's about to pick up her bucket and leave when he says,
"Why don't you go get your husband and come back?"

Husband? That stops her cold. "You can forget that," she says testily, "because I don't have a husband."

The man begins to nod as if he'd expected the answer. "You're right," he says. "You've already had five of them, even if you're not married to the man you're living with now."

She suppresses a little gasp of surprise, then covers her consternation with a joke. "Wow. I can see I've got a prophet on my hands here." She sits down beside him on the well curbing. "So, Mr. Prophet," she asks, "what do you think? Which is the real temple—the one here on Mount Gerizim or yours down in Jerusalem?"

Of course, she knows what he's going to say, being a Jew. But he surprises her by brushing the question aside. "Forget that, lady," he says, shaking his head. "Jerusalem or Gerizim—the place just doesn't matter that much."

She sits back, startled. And this guy calls himself a Jew?

"What matters is who you're worshiping," he continues. "It's true that you Samaritans have gotten muddled up about God. At least the Jews haven't mixed up the true God with all those other fantasy gods. But things are about to change anyway. From now on, anyone who's really looking for God will realize he's not limited by time and space. He transcends those boundaries. God lives in another realm altogether—that's where you have to go if you want to find him."

This is getting a little deep for her, she thinks. Maybe she'd better bring the conversation back down to earth. "I suppose you're talking about the Messiah," she says. "We Samaritans have heard about him too, you know. But I don't worry about that kind of thing." She gives a little wave of her hand, as if dismissing the issue. "I figure when he comes, he'll explain everything anyway." She slaps her thighs and starts to stand up. "I'll just wait till he shows up and ask him."

"Wait," he says, "listen to me. I'm trying to tell you something here. The one you're waiting for to explain everything—the Messiah—you're talking to him right now."

The woman frowns at him, and not just because of the outrageous claim he's just made. It is dawning on her that for some time now he's been talking to her as seriously as he would to a man. From what she's heard, a Jew would rather burn the Torah than talk to a woman about Moses and the Law. And why would he be making his crazy claim to her, of all people?

But before she can respond, they are interrupted by the man's friends, returning from Sychar with groceries. When the other men see her, they mutter to one another, glaring at her suspiciously. She can tell they're dying to ask their friend why he's talking to her. But she also notices that none of them dares to challenge him directly. Maybe he really is someone important.

Slipping out of the cluster of men milling around the mystery man, she hurries back into town, leaving her bucket behind in her confusion. She goes immediately to the marketplace, hurrying from stall to stall. "You've got to come see this," she tells the people lounging there in the shade of the canopies. "I met this guy out by Jacob's Well, and you wouldn't believe what he said."

The good people of Sychar are more than a little skeptical of the woman's news. Her head's easily turned, they know. She's always getting excited about some new man. "Really?" they say. "Like what?"

She throws up her hands. "He's some kind of prophet, I guess."

They shake their heads. "A prophet? In Sychar? Sure." They begin to laugh.

"I'm telling you, it's the truth."

"Honey, you'll believe any line a man hands you. Go on. Get outta here."

"I can prove it," she cries, desperate for them to believe her.

"Yeah? How?"

"Well. He told me things he couldn't have known unless he's a prophet."

"Like what?"

"Like, well, the things I've done." She pauses. "All of it."

One of the vendors smirks. "That's not hard. Everyone around here knows about you, sweetheart."

"He's not from around here," she blurts out. "He's a Jew. A Galilean."

That gets their attention.

"Maybe he's like—you know—the Messiah. The one who's supposed to save us?"

At first they look at one another and shake their heads. But then they look at the woman again. "A Jew, you say?"

She nods.

"And he knew about. . . . " And they start to tick off the names.

She keeps nodding through the entire litany of her past lovers, looking them straight in the eye, not wavering.

Finally they shrug. "Okay," they say to one another, ignoring her now, "we may as well go see."

So they shut down their stalls and trek out to the well, attracting a crowd of curious followers as they go. And the woman tags along, eager to be vindicated, hoping the man and his band of followers haven't already moved on.

The men who had scowled at her before are still lounging in the shade around their leader, eating their lunch and drinking from the bucket of water she left behind. He's not eating himself, but making sweeping gestures as he talks, as if he were scattering seed.

The group of Samaritans approach the well cautiously, listening as the man finishes what he's telling his band of followers. The woman watches all the faces. The man's friends have a certain hangdog look, as if they've just gotten a scolding. The suspicion on the faces of the Samaritan men is gradually replaced by curious attention. There, she thinks to herself, didn't I tell you so?

The man at the center of this circle spends the rest of the day there by the well, surrounded by the growing crowd from Sychar. When evening comes, someone invites the man and his friends home.

Who would that have been? The mayor? The chairman of the Sychar Chamber of Commerce? Or the person we know only as the Samaritan woman? The gospel does not say.

But the people of Sychar are careful not to give her too much credit. "Sure, you told us about him," they say to her after Jesus has spent two days among them, "but it wasn't until we heard him for ourselves that we were convinced he really is who he claims to be." Samaritans aren't that different from Jews when it comes to women, especially women like her.

In fact, I wouldn't be surprised if this woman from Sychar, evidently the impulsive sort, didn't up and leave town, becoming one of those "certain women" who attended Jesus on his travels throughout Palestine. She was, after all, like the man she'd met at the well, an outsider even in her own hometown.

Chapter 17

The Hospitality of Sinners:
Dinner with Zacchaeus

Zacchaeus was a wee little man," we used to sing in vacation Bible school, "and a wee little man was he." It was a great song for eight-year-olds, especially since it had accompanying hand motions, the closest Baptists got to dancing in those days. Identifying people by physical characteristics has since become a mortal sin in our culture, but Zacchaeus's squatty stature was exactly why we kids appreciated the little guy; it made him like us. That, and the fact that he was smart. He figured out a way to overcome his vertical disadvantage and outwit the Big People. Just as we hoped to.

But once you become an adult, you're supposed to put away childish things. Or so says St. Paul. And because Zacchaeus was linked in my mind with the silly children's chorus, I tended to discount the fellow. After all, he appears only in Luke's gospel, the one farthest from an original source according to most scholars. Yet in the end, it is Zacchaeus's size that saved his story for me. It's one of those peculiar details, thrown in for no apparent reason, which make a narrative convincing.

In general, the New Testament is short on descriptions. About the only color mentioned in the gospels is white, an adjective attached most often to "raiment," that all-purpose outfit worn by biblical characters. But you will look in vain for anyone's eye or hair color. And nowhere else do the gospels remark on anyone's height—or lack of it. Since Zacchaeus, a tax collector, was easily identified by his occupation, this seemingly superfluous physical detail lends verisimilitude to Luke's story.

Zacchaeus's story, in fact, serves as almost comic relief from the tragedy that is just beginning to unfold. In the previous chapter, Jesus and his band are on their final approach to Jerusalem, where arrest, torture, and execution await him. Jesus has tried to tell his companions this, but as usual they are either too dense or in denial. They just don't get it.

To reach Jerusalem, they must go through the town of Jericho, a choice location for a tax collector like Zacchaeus. Situated in the Jordan Valley, Jericho's prosperous farms flourished from an irrigation system fed by spring waters. Several trade routes intersected at Jericho also, making the city a prime location for Roman tax-farmers.

The Roman IRS worked this way: The imperial government took bids on local tax concessions from Roman citizens who, in turn, farmed them out to native collection agents. As a "chief tax collector," Zacchaeus was in charge of yet another tier of collection agents, each of whom dealt only with a particular tax category—agricultural taxes, import and export duties, real estate taxes, assessments for public buildings. On the local level, the system operated more like an extortion racket than an official bureaucracy. Only the Roman citizen holding the tax franchise was a bona fide government official, and he took no responsibility for the conduct of the subcontractors who actually did the collecting. All the emperor cared about was that the tax money eventually made its way to Rome, not the methods used to collect it.

Since the government provided no salaries for the concessionaires, each level of this pyramid scheme had to finance its own operations. With no governmental guidelines regulating them, the collectors extracted as much from the people as they could get away with. Obviously, the more menacing the means, the bigger the take. On the lower rungs of the tax ladder, the collectors operated as gangsters rather than bureaucrats, often resorting to torture, especially in rural areas, in order to squeeze every last shekel from their victims.

Their fellow Jews, of course, saw these native tax collectors as collaborators with the army of occupation, traitors to their own people. One rabbinic treatise on ritual purity declares that a house is more defiled by a tax collector than a robber. Only those places in a house where a robber actually set his foot had to be purified, whereas the entire contents of a house were contaminated by the tax collector's visit. The treatise reasons that a robber would only touch what he was stealing, whereas the tax man would handle every item in the house to assess its value.

Jews who worked the tax racket were, of course, excluded from ordinary community affairs. This meant they could not read from the Torah scrolls in the synagogue, their sons would have no bar mitzvahs, nor their daughters receive marriage proposals from Jews. The only friends they had were other racketeers and gentiles. Like drug dealing nowadays, tax collecting could indeed be a profitable business, but it came with a heavy social price.

Our own cultural tendency today is to romanticize any "outsider." "Inclusiveness" is one of our primary moral virtues. But once we're the victim of a mugging or when our own neighborhood is terrorized by street gangs, that attitude often changes. As for understanding what it's like to live under foreign occupation, only the true Native Americans among us have had that experience. The Jews hadn't maintained the integrity of their culture for centuries by blurring the boundaries between themselves and their foreign conquerors. Only by running a tight ship, keeping the lines absolutely clear, had they survived invasion, deportation, and occupation. Conscious of being a people set apart, called out for a special purpose in human history, the Jews knew that dissolving the barriers that separated them from the rest of the world could defeat that purpose.

The orthodox Jewish community in Jericho thus despises Zacchaeus for his role as the town's head tax collector. As the Romans' henchman overseeing the tariff operation for personal and commercial taxes, his hand has been in every pocket in town. There isn't a business or a household where he is welcome. No doubt his own digs are palatial by Jericho standards, but who can he show them off to? His own hired goons? The floozies he drinks with at the tavern?

But Zacchaeus has an excuse for his disloyalty. When the other

boys started having growth spurts, right about the time of their bar
mitzvah, he'd been left behind. People began calling him Shorty
or Half-Pint. What other vocational choice did he have, he asks
himself. He's always been pushed aside, treated like an outsider.
And now he's making the town pay for it—in cold, hard cash.

Who knows what prompts him to join the crowd forming along
Jericho's Main Street the day Jesus comes through with his band
of followers. Word must have reached him about old Bartimaeus,
the blind man who waits every day on the north end of town, shaking his cup and hoping to hit up travelers. Supposedly this touring
rabbi has gotten Blind Bart's sight back for him. And collected a
crowd for himself. Maybe that's what got Zacchaeus's attention.
Because where there's a crowd, there's bound to be money. People will be setting up lemonade stands, selling pita sandwiches.
Maybe the rabbi and his men will be taking up a collection. And
no one does business in Jericho without Zacchaeus getting his cut.

But there's another possibility. Zacchaeus has heard that one of
the rabbi's right-hand men is a tax collector. Or was, until he took
up with the rabbi. It's hard to believe that someone in the tax racket
would suddenly get religion. But intriguing.

So Zacchaeus locks up his office and heads down to Main
Street. The crowd has swelled to such proportions by then that he
can see he's going to miss the main attraction. Everyone's dragging sick kin downtown, hoping for a cure. Workers are leaning
on their shovels, watching the action. Housewives have come out
of the courtyards to stare. Kids are darting in and out among the
close-packed crowd. Zacchaeus knows he'll have to find a spot
with more elevation if he expects to see the action.

After climbing the steps of several public buildings and failing
to catch more than a distant glimpse of the famous rabbi, Zacchaeus has a new idea. Up ahead at the edge of town, right before the
road forks off toward Jerusalem, stands a sycamore-fig tree, a
landmark because of its size. Its branches, thickly blanketed with
new leaves, arch over the roadway. The rabbi and his bodyguards
are moving like molasses through the crush of people clogging
Main Street. Zacchaeus should be able to reach the tree before this

slow-moving parade and hide up among the leafy branches. He'll have a ringside seat—or a bird's-eye view anyway—for the rabbi and his entourage.

Zacchaeus has shinnied up the tree and inched out along a limb overhanging the Jerusalem fork when he sees the crowd approaching. They are still several yards away when the rabbi pauses and the whole party comes to a halt.

The rabbi levels his hand over his forehead, shading his eyes as he peers up into the branches of the tree. He frowns slightly, then tilts his head as if trying to get a better focus. Zacchaeus flattens himself along the limb and holds his breath.

The rabbi takes a few steps forward. When he's right under the tree, he points directly up at Zacchaeus. "Hey!" he calls out. "You up there—is that Zacchaeus?"

By now everyone is staring up into the tree branches. At the sound of his name, someone spits into the dust of the road. Zacchaeus doesn't move. Is this guy trying to publicly humiliate him? This is turning into his worst nightmare.

People begin to point. "See? There he is. No, a little to the left."

"Hey, Zacchaeus," the rabbi yells again, "didn't you hear me? Come on down here out of that tree. My friends and I need someplace to stay tonight. I don't think we're going to make it to Jerusalem today. Do you think you could put us up at your place?"

Slowly, Zacchaeus sits upright on the limb. Then he begins to edge back down the trunk. Gripping it with his knees, like a child, he slides to the ground, dusts off his clothes, and hurries over to Jesus, wiping his hands automatically on his robe before extending them to the rabbi.

"Glad to meet you, rabbi," he says, looking around at the crowd. "Sure. I've got a nice big villa. Plenty of room for you and your friends too. Come on. I'll show you the way."

And the entire entourage moves off toward the bluffs overlooking Jericho where Zacchaeus has built his gangster mansion, complete with a swimming pool and sauna.

The crowd that has collected on Main Street, however, does not follow. They wouldn't set foot inside the walls of Zacchaeus's compound for all the gold in Caesar's coffers. And they're more than a little disappointed in the rabbi as well, despite his having helped Blind Bart. What does he mean, staying with a cheat and a thief? How can he stand to eat with the man?

In the end, however, their curiosity gets the better of some, who slip into the courtyard to watch the dinner party in progress there that evening. Wealthy hosts often opened the gates of their compounds when they threw a big party so that uninvited onlookers could at least enjoy the spectacle, and the people who venture inside to watch tonight will later be glad they went. They will get to tell the rest of Jericho what happened that night in Zacchaeus's villa.

Right in the middle of the meal—between the couscous and the roast lamb—Zacchaeus stands up and raises his goblet. "I want to propose a toast," he says. "To Rabbi Jesus."

"To Jesus!" the rabbi's band of roughnecks shout. They drain their glasses and hold them out for the servants to fill again.

"And I have an announcement to make as well." Zacchaeus lowers his goblet before he speaks again. "I know what I've been doing is wrong," he said. "I haven't been living like a good Jew. I should be helping the people of Jericho, not wringing every shekel I could from their miserable hides. I admit it. I was wrong."

Then the little man takes a deep breath, lifts his head, and looks around the courtyard, his gaze penetrating well back into the shadows. "But talk is cheap. Anybody can say they're sorry as long as they can go on living the high life. All good Jews know what Torah requires. If you cheat somebody you're supposed to pay them back double. Well, I haven't been a good Jew for a long time. So to make up for it, I'm going to do more than that. If I've inflated anyone's tax bill, I'm going to return the excess, not just double, but fourfold."

The rabbi doesn't say a word, though he appears to be listening intently to his host.

Zacchaeus takes another big breath before he goes on. "I've dealt with hundreds of people during my tenure as tax collector. Some of them are probably already dead. Others have been forced off their farms. Maybe some have even turned to crime to make a living. There's no way I can find all those people and return what I owe to them personally. Now I've heard that in such cases, one school of rabbis recommends making reparations by contributing to the town's public utilities—for upkeep of the wells and irrigation ditches. They say that benefits the entire community."

The people in the shadows look at one another, raising their eyebrows. But Zacchaeus isn't finished.

"I've decided instead," he says, "this very evening, to give away half my assets—bank account, real estate, everything—directly to the relief of the poor. Maybe some of that will eventually find its way to the people I've harmed and their families."

He looks around at his assembled guests and at the people staring at him along the courtyard wall. "I want to be a Jew again," he says before he sits down, "a real Jew."

When Zacchaeus has settled on his bench at the table again, and the murmurs from the shadows have subsided, the rabbi holds up his hand and speaks. "I want to propose a toast as well," he says. "Today this man has found his way back into the household of Israel. His house is no longer unclean. A son of Abraham lives here. For that we should rejoice tonight." He raises his goblet. "To Zacchaeus!"

Chapter 18

A Way In:
Or Inside Out?

*I*t's ironic that outsiders should look to Jesus for help, since he was an outsider himself. His hometown of Nazareth rejected him; he rejected his family. Indifferent to politics, he wasn't nationalistic enough for the Zealots, yet Herod and Pilate considered him a political threat. He provoked his own exclusion from the one circle he seemed to care about—the Jewish religious establishment.

To gentiles, of course, Jesus' religious credentials meant little. Though the centurion recognized him as a rabbi, neither he nor the Syro-Phoenician woman cared which faction of Judaism Jesus belonged to. They left the finer theological quarrels to the experts. Like some cancer patients today, so desperate for a cure they are willing to follow any new regimen or travel to a foreign country to find one, these two gentiles risked public embarrassment, even humiliation, by asking for Jesus' help. They sought him out simply because he was the most effective wonder-worker around. They weren't interested in learning from him. All they wanted was results.

Christians caught up in their own sectarian strife are often surprised at how little outsiders care about the issues that divide believers. The "unchurched," like these two gentiles, often turn to a person they figure has a direct pipeline to the supernatural when the chips are down and they've exhausted other sources of help. They don't want to listen to arguments for the existence of God or explanations about sanctification or predictions for the millennium. They want a miracle. They'll worry about theology later.

Jesus responded to that kind of desperation-driven concern more willingly than his church often does. He demanded no theological litmus test before agreeing to heal people or free them from demons. Though he sometimes made a healing or exorcism the occasion for instructing others, he never made conversion a condition for relieving a tormented mind or body.

Christian evangelism sees its primary mission as saving souls. And indeed Jesus tells the people at Zacchaeus's dinner party that his ultimate purpose for coming into the world was "to seek and to save that which was lost." But at some point the church began to connect Jesus' command to heal the sick with its mission to make disciples. Healing, medicine, food, all kinds of physical assistance are sometimes seen as bait in a spiritual fishing expedition. Contributors to mission projects often want reassurance that their money will provide a good dose of theology along with the antibiotics.

There's a certain stinginess or even mean-spiritedness in that attitude, one that doesn't fit with the generosity of a God who makes the rain to fall on the just and the unjust. The faith of the centurion and the gentile mother was merely in Jesus' miraculous powers, not in a creed declaring his identity as Messiah, Son of God, Savior of the world, or any other title or tenets.

Jesus' primary goal was rather narrowly defined—to challenge his own people, not to convert the heathen to Judaism. His trips outside the Jewish regions of Palestine were temporary escapes from the pressures or dangers of his ministry, not missionary journeys like the apostle Paul's. Matthew's gospel records his sending his disciples to "the lost sheep of the house of Israel," and instructing them to avoid the cities of the gentiles and Samaritans. Matthew may have had his own reasons for putting these words in Jesus' mouth, but, in all four gospels his primary audience for teaching about the kingdom of God is his fellow Jews.

If Jesus had any residual cultural contempt for gentiles, he had it knocked out of him by his confrontation in Tyre with the mother of the sick child. He himself attributes this change of heart to the woman's spirited response that even outsiders may benefit from the overflow of love's largesse. *Because of your reply,* he says, the demon has been driven from her daughter. Jesus returns from this incognito seaside junket still convinced that his primary mission lies within his own native sphere, but his encounter with the gentile mother has made the circumference of that orb more permeable to gentiles.

As for the centurion's story, I believe it illustrates how strong even the most tenuous threads of faith can be—and how tactfully those spidery connections should be handled. If believers want to model themselves after the person they believe in, they do well to consider their ties to outsiders, even people they perceive as cultural or political enemies. The centurion was no doubt proud of his Roman citizenship, which, like being an American today, conferred a privileged international status. On the other hand, the centurion admires and honors the monotheism and morality of the Jews.

The centurion's spirituality may have been as nebulous as most people's today—a vague sense of a Higher Power in the universe to which one attributes the foundations of natural law or basic morality. One can roll along quite comfortably through life with that relatively undemanding, impersonal system. Until some calamity occurs. Then suddenly a system isn't enough. You want not something, but someone—a presence who can answer your cries for help.

Jesus not only responds to the centurion's request to heal his servant, but he also handles the centurion's delicate political position with tact and magnanimity. Luke shrewdly does not tell us what happens later with the centurion. We don't know if he became a Jewish convert following this episode, or if he made a contribution to Jesus' travel expenses, nor even if he freed his slave. But if we knew that the healing had somehow paid off in any of these ways, that would undermine the story's point—how to treat an outsider. Whoever asks should receive, even Romans.

So much for gentiles and Jesus. What about the Samaritan woman and Zacchaeus, one a quasi Jew, the other a lapsed insider?

From the beginning, sexuality had been blamed for the feud between "thoroughbred" Jews and their half-breed cousins, the Samaritans. Orthodox Jews in the south believed the deviant Samaritan cult was the result of their northern cousins' succumbing to the wiles of foreign women. And the woman Jesus meets at the well outside Sychar is a Jewish mother's worst nightmare—the kind of "strange woman" described in Proverbs who waits to entrap the simple sons of Israel.

Yet this meeting occurs by happenstance, not by design. Contrary to stereotype, the woman does not accost Jesus at the well; he addresses her first. As a woman, she couldn't maintain her dignity and initiate a conversation with a man. As a Samaritan, she would have been as touchy about talking to a strange Jew as any Palestinian today. By initiating the conversation, he avoids a challenge to her dignity and puts himself in the vulnerable position.

On the other hand, Jesus is not overcome with guilt about the fact that he's a Jew, a member of a group who, on the whole, despise her kind. He shows none of the awkward agony of the well-intentioned.

Nor does he cut the woman much slack about her present living arrangements. He lets her know that he sees through her not-quite-truthful representation of herself as unmarried. But he does this in a startlingly matter-of-fact way. While he does not pronounce judgment or predict doom, he offers no false sympathy either. He doesn't confer victimhood. Instead, he takes the promiscuous woman seriously in every way, treating her as a moral agent, responsible for her actions. At the same time, he considers her intellect capable of serious theological inquiry. He goes beyond simply treating her as well as he would a Jewish woman; he treats her as a human being.

Compare that to how we might handle the "Samaritan problem"—any social or ethnic class issue—today. First, we're careful to put ourselves in the role of patrons, the ones in control. Then we hire people to be the go-betweens, the social workers, the relief force, the shelter supervisor—people who actually have to deal with outsiders. In our heart of hearts, we're afraid to set foot on their turf—to go through Samaria—ourselves. It's too dangerous. And no matter how earnest our desire to help, we're struck dumb if we ever stumble on a social pariah. What do you say to a hooker or an illegal alien anyway?

Jesus began the conversation with his own thirst. But it soon swung toward the woman's needs. Here he was absolutely forth-right too. He made no bones about the fact that he had what she needs. Again, no apologies, no shame. All because, I believe, he never really saw her as an outsider. Unlike the mother from Tyre, this Samaritan shares a common heritage and history with him. Despite the historical disputes that have separated the children of Abraham, Jesus can draw on that common heritage to explain wor-shiping "in spirit and in truth."

Establishing our kinship with spiritual cousins—those who share our heritage but in a form we consider deviant—is probably more difficult for us than dealing with out-and-out heathens. Christians may find it harder to talk to a Mormon than a Hindu. Or a Russian Orthodox than a Rastafarian. Those who do manage to connect with their outlandish cousins often get as little support for their efforts as the disciples gave Jesus that day at the Sychar well.

Not that making those connections is an easy job, or one to be undertaken with sentimentality. It requires walking a fine line, a tightrope, a razor's edge. It demands both total openness, which never closes the door, and unremitting honesty, which doesn't hesi-tate to pose hard questions.

And what about those other circles we must negotiate, the ones that demarcate the righteous from the backsliders inside our own communities, our own congregations. They tell us who's in, and who, like Zacchaeus, is out.

Again, let me emphasize that differences are real. Ignoring frac-tures in the circle doesn't make it, in fact, unbroken. Zacchaeus was a man who broke faith with his people. Jesus does not pity the tax collector because of his status as a rejected outsider. He doesn't of-fer him sentimental goodwill. Instead, he brings him to repentance, a feat that could not be achieved by ignoring him. The rabbi had to get physically close enough to him to gain his confidence.

As a stranger to Jericho himself, Jesus is in a position to be-friend the rascal. If he had been a member of the town council or the synagogue president, gaining entry to Zacchaeus's home and heart would have been more problematic. The last person in the world to successfully convince us of our sins is a member of our own family. Jesus admits that he himself was ineffective in Nazareth and failed to convince his own family members of his mission. Which may have been why he chose to have no home, no community, other than the portable one he carried with him. He needed to be the Stranger to everyone in order to arrest their attention.

Zacchaeus felt himself utterly *known* by this Lone Ranger who rides into town and calls him by name. Known, found out, exposed. But also valued. By going to Zacchaeus's house, Jesus draws a curtain of privacy around the tax collector, which allows him to repent. Public humiliation would have been an obstacle to change. Yet what Zacchaeus repents in private, he requites in public. Only repentance—and restitution—can integrate a sinner like Zacchaeus into the community again.

And here, I think, our identification with Jesus must come to an end. That he "consorted with sinners" is often used to justify cultivating associations that are, frankly, just more interesting and entertaining than those sometimes found in church. Really, what we all want is to be taken in ourselves, into the camaraderie of the glamorous or even just the lively. Like it or not, we are all part of the communion of sinners, the widest circle of all. As such, we are unlikely to convince or convict a fellow member of greed or betrayal or malice. Only the Ultimate Outsider can do that.

PART V

LOOKING FOR ANSWERS

Last summer I lectured at a Canadian college on the subject of memoirs, those records of personal memories written by people trying to salvage time, to preserve their lives on paper. I claimed that this impulse springs from the human desire to discover meaning in our lives, to sort all the disparate bits of events into a pattern that makes some kind of sense beyond mere sequence. At root, I said, this impulse is essentially religious—just another bit of evidence that we fear our lives are futile, no more than cosmic accidents, and that we yearn, along with the rest of creation, to be reclaimed, salvaged, from that fate.

During the question-and-answer period, one woman objected to my claim. Not everyone searches for meaning in life, she said. Only the affluent and educated indulge in such metaphysical extravagance; the poor and overworked can't afford such luxuries, and the ignorant lack the skills to wonder about where they came from, where they're going, or what it all might signify. And why did I call such an enterprise religious anyway? Maybe writing memoirs was no more than a survival mechanism, a coping device, a means of protecting ourselves from the awful truth that we matter not one whit to any lurking cosmic consciousness.

I gave her the old routine about the etymology of the word *religious,* and how the root meant tying things up, putting all the pieces together, but I could tell that answer didn't really satisfy her. I'm no good at thinking fast on my feet. I usually have to be lying down. So it was four o'clock the next morning before I began to formulate a decent answer to the woman's question. I couldn't see how the quest for meaning could be anything other than religious—not until I recalled certain difficult periods in my own life when I'd posed the same question to myself.

When I had been particularly depressed and desperate, questions about meaning had a way of turning back on themselves, feeding into an endless, recursive loop that made me suspicious of the workings of the mind itself. *Do I want to believe the universe has meaning and that there's a point to my life just so I'll feel better and be able to carry on? Am I just kidding myself, inventing meaning in order to pacify my fears?* My brain would turn into the snake eating its own tail.

At such a point people can put their heads in ovens or jump off bridges. But doesn't such a radical response itself prove something about us, I argued in those predawn hours. Why think: if life has no meaning I'm going to end it? Why get worked up about meaninglessness? If the universe or its creator doesn't care, why should we? Isn't suicide an act of anger directed against a power one perceives to be unknowing and uncaring? Why strike out against someone or something you've decided isn't there? Isn't our anger—or our melancholia, if we can't face suicide—a way of scratching that stubborn itch for the intentional, for deliberate design, a premeditated plan? Though I could offer the woman in the now-dispersed audience no proof of purpose, neither could she demonstrate its absence.

The rest of her question—whether circumstances prevent some people's search for meaning—I found easier to deal with. Yes, I had agreed, people can indeed be brutalized by conditions that reduce them to their basic survival instincts. I've read enough concentration-camp memoirs to know this. And I too have been so bone-tired I didn't care about questions of ultimate significance. But the fact that human beings can be reduced to a quivering mass of nerve endings doesn't mean they're incapable of reflective thought. Ashes don't define a forest, even though it can be burned to smoldering stumps. We, as well as all creation, are more than the sum of our chemical components. And at times the gruesomest of circumstances can produce prodigious monuments to meaning. The same concentration camps that reduced prisoners to skin and bones also yielded books like Viktor Frankl's *Man's Search for Meaning* and righteous champions like Elie Wiesel.

The gospels themselves provide plenty of evidence that the quest for meaning is not limited by social class or economic condition. A wide array of people during the first century—educated and illiterate, rich and poor—inquired into the meaning of their lives. The disciples, after all, were for the most part blue-collar workers. Yet they were sufficiently intrigued by ultimate questions that they left their livelihoods behind to follow a man who promised them answers. I don't know many scholars with that kind of dedication to searching for truth. It was Pilate, a man of position with the benefit of a classical education, who gave up on the search, asking with a rhetorical sneer, "What is truth?" Those crowds who followed Jesus into the wilderness weren't interested solely in bread or healing. Many of them also hungered for answers to their questions about their worth and destiny. And in Matthew and Luke's gospels, Jesus thanks his heavenly father for hiding the answer to Pilate's question from "the wise and prudent" while revealing it "unto babes"—that mass of humanity we name the "multitudes."

Not that Jesus was ideologically an anti-intellectual. He also spent hours discussing questions put to him by Torah scholars and Pharisees. Jesus gives his attention to the rich young ruler and the powerful Nicodemus as readily as he does to the proletarian crowd. As a young adolescent he was so intrigued by the deliberations of the Temple academics that he stayed behind in Jerusalem for three days, listening to the debates and asking questions. (This scene might have been taken from his bar mitzvah, except, of course, that his parents weren't present. They had been searching for their twelve-year-old son rather than the meaning of life.) He obviously found the Temple's scholarly environment congenial, since "all that heard him were astonished at his understanding and answers."

Jesus doesn't hesitate to discuss serious matters with women either, a radical departure from the practice of most rabbis who did not usually admit them to such discussions. We've already seen how he debated with the woman at the Sychar well. Jesus also replied to questions put to him by John the Baptist's devotees when that prophet's arrest and execution had shaken their expectations. Jesus even answered his mother and brothers when they followed him to Capernaum and demanded to know what in the world he thought he was doing. Unfortunately, they were in no mood at that point to listen to his answer.

If you asked Jesus a serious question, you got a serious answer. Unless, of course, you already assumed that neither he nor anyone else had an answer. As far as I can see, the only question he ever refused to answer was Pilate's.

Jesus, it is clear, took the life of the mind seriously. He also took seriously the institutions of his day that were dedicated to intellectual inquiry—synagogues, the Temple, Torah schools, and local conclaves of rabbis and Pharisees. He recognized their place of leadership and responsibility in the cultural and religious life of the people. Whenever he reprimanded those individuals who held such positions, it was not because of their questions, but because they had allowed power rather than wisdom to become their pursuit. He took questions of ultimate meaning too seriously to make them the special province of only a privileged few. Either such questions were important to everyone, carved on each human heart, or they weren't significant at all.

Still, not everyone who brought questions to Jesus was capable of hearing the answers. Sometimes other issues in people's lives jammed the communications conduit. Money, sex, and power, for instance. Sometimes family ties. Those interferences had to be dealt with first, the line cleared of static, so that his interrogators could hear what he was saying. Sometimes he accomplished this by asking them questions in return:

> *Why do you call me good?*
> *Who do men say that I am?*
> *How can the guests of the bridegroom fast while he is with*
> *them?*

In fact, at the Jerusalem Temple during Passover, Jesus makes his reply to the chief priests' question about his authority contingent on their first answering his: "I will ask you one question. Answer me, and I will tell you by what authority I am doing these things. John's baptism—was it from heaven or from men?"

Infuriating as this tactic must have been to his opponents, another kind of answer Jesus gave to questions—the parables—was equally disturbing. His questioners usually wanted answers to what they considered binary problems—a simple yes or a no would do. Thumbs up or down. Instead they often got analogues. Parables. Little stories that had to be chewed on awhile before one could decode their message. Sometimes more than one. *The kingdom of God is like a mustard seed?* What kind of answer is that?

Just this: the kind that can be carried around inside a person because, being a picture, it's not easily forgotten. The kind that doesn't allow you to simply check another item off your list of cosmic mysteries. The kind that gradually pervades your imagination and soaks into your bloodstream and becomes part of your very tissue and bones. The kind you can live with for days, months, years, while it sprouts and may one day even bear fruit.

Chapter 19

How Dumb Can You Get?
The Dense Disciples

*W*e actually know very little about most of the twelve disciples, other than their Jewish ancestry and their names—and a couple of those are even in question. Bartholomew and Thaddeus—who were these men mentioned only once in the list of Twelve? At least four in the group made their living as fishermen. The one called Matthew, or sometimes Levi, was a tax collector. Another was a member of the radical sect of Zealots, as the traitor Judas may also have been. Philip, like Peter and Andrew, was from Bethsaida, a town on the northeastern shore of Lake Galilee.

Certain details in the text allow us to infer a few more bits of information. For instance, since Jesus healed Peter's mother-in-law in Capernaum, we know that disciple was married. Also, according to church tradition, Peter's memories provided the material for the gospel of Mark. A number of scholars link John's gospel to the disciple of the same name, citing the early church father Irenaeus as their authority.

But who were these men who followed Jesus first around Galilee and later down to Jerusalem and death? We don't even know their ages. Were they all thirtysomething, like Jesus? Did they have families to support? Were they an ancient version of Robin Hood's Merry Men, social malcontents who hoped to profit one day from their allegiance to a man who promised a new kingdom? Like most biblical narrative, the gospels sacrifice description for plot. Event rules. What we know about the characters, their backgrounds and motivations, comes to us through dialogue and action. Which means, of course, that our picture of Peter, at once the mouthiest and the most impulsive of the lot, is the most complete.

But did these men we call the disciples go looking for Jesus, or did he in fact seek them out?

In the usual impression of that initial meeting, instilled by Bible movies and sermons based on Mark's gospel, Jesus, after his baptism by John the Baptist in the Jordan, strolls along the lakeshore till he comes across Simon and his brother Andrew net-fishing. Jesus tells them to follow him and he'll set them to catching men rather than fish. Immediately, they drop everything and follow. A little farther down the beach he comes on another couple of brothers, James and John, who, with their father Zebedee, are mending fishing nets in their boat. They too respond to his call, leaving their father behind, no doubt stunned and horrified, with only the hired hands. The details of this scene, characteristically sparse yet precise—two different kinds of nets are mentioned—strike us as authentic.

What possessed these four fishermen to do such a thing?

I first heard this story at an early age from Mrs. Batcher, my Sunday school teacher, whose hushed tones implied that Jesus' eyes could drill holes in people from twenty paces. His presence was so compelling, his manner so magnetic, that he well-nigh hypnotized these simple fishermen and drew them after him in some kind of spiritual enchantment. Since Mark's gospel mentions no previous meeting with Jesus nor gives any reason for the men's instantaneous attraction, Mrs. Batcher's inference was not wholly unjustified.

John's gospel, however, gives us quite a different picture of their initial encounter with Jesus, one that occurred earlier and does indeed show the disciples seeking Jesus out. In this version, two protégés of John the Baptizer listen as the famous prophet proclaims that Jesus, whom he's just dunked in the Jordan, is more important than himself. That he is, in fact, "the Son of God." Obviously intrigued, the Baptizer's two erstwhile disciples follow Jesus along the road to the nearby town of Bethany, though they are either too shy or too fainthearted to introduce themselves or question him. After all, what do you say to someone who's just been labeled "the Son of God" by your own religious guru?

After a while, the mystery man stops in the middle of the road, turns, and asks, "What are you fellows looking for?"

What can they say? "Are you really the Son of God? Are you really more important than the Baptizer?" How would that sound? Instead, they ask, "Whereabouts are you staying?"

The man motions with his arm, "Come on and you'll see." And they do.

In a rare burst of specificity, the gospel places this encounter at four o'clock in the afternoon. Their conversation must have continued into the night, however, because the men are still with Jesus the next morning, convinced by then that this person is everything the Baptizer claimed. In fact, one of them, whom the gospel only now reveals is Andrew, hunts up his brother Simon, supposedly still back in the Baptizer's camp. "Come on," he tells Simon, "we've found the Messiah!"

Only twice in the four Gospels is that specific term applied to Jesus, here and by the Samaritan woman in a later chapter. For Jews—and Samaritans—of that age, "Messiah" was shorthand for Deliverer, an apocalyptic David, who would set the world to rights. And he would start by freeing the children of Abraham from their foreign oppressors.

Andrew returns to the place where Jesus is staying, with his brother Simon in tow. "I know you," Jesus says. "You're Simon, Jona's son. But I'm giving you a new name. I'm going to call you Rocky." Which is roughly what our Latin translation of Peter means.

But what about that second disciple, the one who, with Andrew, had abandoned the Baptizer and followed Jesus from the Jordan to Bethany? What was his name, and what had he been doing all this time? Throughout the fourth gospel, nothing more is ever said of him. Mysteriously missing is also any mention of the two brothers, James and John, who play such a prominent part in the other three gospels. In Matthew, Mark, and Luke, the brothers James and John are always paired with Peter and Andrew. In fact, Luke claims the four were business partners. But John's gospel never names them. It does, however, refer repeatedly to "the disciple whom Jesus loved" or "the beloved disciple." This is the man I believe was that second disciple of the Baptizer who left him for a bigger Fish.

After Andrew's brother has joined this nucleus group, they all head north with their new leader. Peter and Andrew, we're told, are from Bethsaida. When they reach their hometown, they add Philip to their party; he then recruits his friend Nathanael. Jesus' little band of volunteers has now grown to six.

A few days later, Jesus performs his first miracle—turning water into wine at the wedding in the nearby town of Cana. It is this demonstration of his power, John's gospel records, which cements their devotion to Jesus. Still, their new leader has given them no indication of what shape his future will take. Will he be a prophet like John the Baptist? A revolutionary like Simon the Zealot? A teacher like the rabbis who roamed the countryside? While they are waiting for Jesus to give them further instructions, the two sets of brothers return to their fishing business. This is the point at which Mark's gospel probably takes up the story. His skeletal account of the brothers leaving their livelihood and father emphasizes how much they forfeited in order to follow Jesus. John's version explains why they did it.

The fourth gospel also shows that these men were not so "simple" as our sentimentality often depicts them. Obviously, they were dissatisfied with their life in Galilee before they met Jesus or they wouldn't have been drawn to the Jordan to investigate what that wild man, the Baptizer, had to offer. They were already seeking someone who could answer their questions, could show them how to make sense of life. That their search had initially taken them so far from home meant they were either dissatisfied or disillusioned with their local religious scholars and Pharisees. Would they have switched their loyalty to a virtual unknown without some sign of his miraculous power? Probably not, at least in the beginning. But once they tasted the water he had turned to wine at Cana, they figured they'd found the real thing.

Were these men originally motivated by politics? Were they the sort of malcontents who today would join a militia group and stockpile weapons? Again, probably not—initially. After all, the original four (or their families) owned their own businesses, which did well enough for them to employ other workers. And their early attachment to the Baptizer, who counseled tax collectors to be honest and soldiers to be content with their wages, suggests they were searching for a kind of practical spirituality—how best to live their lives—and not finding adequate answers at their local synagogue.

Yet to Jews in first-century Palestine, indeed to just about anyone during that era, religion and politics were inseparable. We all too easily read back onto the ancient world (and even onto other cultures today) our own attitudes about the dividing line between church and state. But the Roman emperors would never have insisted on being worshiped as gods if they had seen government and religion as separate domains that could afford to ignore each other.

So while the Baptizer preached repentance rather than rebellion, he also expected the advent of the promised Messiah to radically alter the entire world, including who was in charge. In fact, Herod later arrests John for condemning his marriage to his sister-in-law, considering the prophet's accusations a political threat. Like the Roman emperors, he realized that reality can't be compartmentalized, that his crumbling moral image with the people would affect their willingness to acknowledge his political authority. Meanwhile the Baptizer, languishing in Herod's dungeon, finds his certainty of Jesus' identity as the Son of God growing shaky. He sends two of his own followers to the man he'd dubbed Messiah with this most poignant question: "Are you the one who was to come, or should we look for another?"

It was a question that would haunt the Twelve during those long months tramping around Galilee at the heels of a man who talked to them in riddles. Without the miracles, who knows if any of them would have stuck with Jesus. But once they see the Leader can turn water into wine and put a chicken—or at least bread and fish—in every pot, not to mention heal the sick, they feel sure they've picked a winner. At first Jesus tries to keep the miracles a secret. But no way can you feed thousands of people and keep it quiet. This man, the disciples feel, is unstoppable now. He not only makes campaign promises to the multitudes, he actually delivers the goods.

At some point, the disciples begin to see these miracles—especially the mass meals—as a means to an end. This becomes clear in the scenes immediately following the feedings of thousands. After the first feast, Jesus sends the disciples off in a boat, saying he'll catch up with them later. They've reached the middle of the lake when they spot him coming toward them—walking across the waves. Naturally, they're all scared witless. Mark's gospel says that the disciples were afraid because "they did not understand about the loaves, but their hearts were hardened." To them, the miraculous meal was merely a way to increase the Leader's clout with the masses.

After Jesus provides a second free meal, the disciples are again in the boat—this time the Leader is with them—when they begin to worry because no one remembered to pack a lunch.

"What is your problem?" Jesus demands, obviously exasperated. "Have you already forgotten that five thousand people were just fed with only five loaves? And how much was left over?"

"Twelve basketfuls," they mumble.

"And you're worried about food? You guys just don't get it, do you?"

Of course they didn't get it. They were fixated on food as power. That Jesus fed people out of compassion goes right over their heads. They are beginning to see that his ability to work wonders means that he could take over the country. Isn't he always talking about the new "kingdom of God"? Even his healing they see as a way of enhancing his growing reputation. And they begin to see themselves as bodyguards, an elite corps of escorts whose job is to protect the Leader from the masses. Several times they try to fend off his petitioners or drive off the street urchins pursuing him through town.

From their perspective, it's unfortunate that the Leader spends so much time sitting around arguing petty points of the law with rabbis, scholars, and Pharisees. Who needs to worry about religious rules when you're the special forces for a wonder-worker? After they get caught picking grain from a farmer's field on the Sabbath, the local Pharisees immediately complain to Jesus. But the Leader defends his men, comparing them to David's band of guerrillas who, with a bounty on their heads, took consecrated bread from a priest's altar. His justification of their act inflames the disciples' imaginations as much as it offends their accusers. If Jesus is like David, they think, then that makes them his army. True patriots of Israel on a mission too important to worry with niggling little rules. Let the stay-at-home scholars and the compromising Pharisees argue over how and when to wash their hands. As the Leader told them at the outset, they've got bigger fish to fry.

Such grandiose visions come naturally to the disciples, as they would to anyone chosen to be in on the ground floor of a movement to change the status quo. Everything they know about the promised Messiah, the deliverer of Israel, encourages their ambitions. True, other Galilean rebels have failed in the past, but then none of them could heal the sick or walk on water. And the Leader is already talking about a coming confrontation with the authorities in Jerusalem.

Sometimes, however, what he says about this showdown sounds a little unsettling, as if he doesn't expect to come out on top. Peter has even taken him aside and tried to reason with him about this negative thinking. Sure, no one expects the big shots in Jerusalem to give up without a fight, he tells Jesus, but after all, he's the chosen one of God, isn't he?

At that, the Leader blows up, calling Peter "Satan" and other choice names. But then, he often loses his temper with his troops, calling them dimwits, telling them they don't understand what he's all about. But what can you expect from a guy who's under the kind of pressure he is? People always pushing and shoving to get close enough to touch him. Everybody wants a piece of the Leader. He has trouble just finding time to eat or sleep, much less to do all that praying he thinks is so important.

Up to now, they have spent most of their time in Galilee, rallying the home team, solidifying their backing among the common people, from the disciples' point of view. Then one spring day the Leader decides it's finally time to head for Jerusalem. As usual, he chooses exactly the right moment to make his move—Passover week. Jews from all over the world will be packing the streets for the holiday that commemorates the Exodus and their people's supernatural deliverance from slavery in Egypt. No one will miss the parallel with the Jews' current domination by Rome. The crowds' national pride and solidarity will be at its highest pitch. The timing is a stroke of genius on the Leader's part. Even Thomas, the gloomiest of the group, agrees to go.

Of course, now that the crisis is upon them, the climax to all their hopes and dreams, the disciples are a little nervous. Especially when the Leader keeps bringing up the possibility of arrest and crosses. No need to remind them that crucifixion is the Romans' favorite method for getting rid of rebels. The Leader talks about "rising from the dead" too, and they are not so sure they understand what he's getting at. But then he's always telling strange little stories and expecting them to figure out the meaning. Maybe "rising from the dead" is his code language for going underground if there's trouble in Jerusalem. Then, when the establishment has been lulled into a false sense of security, he'll emerge again at the strategic moment to take control.

So certain are the disciples of their Leader's intention to take control that on the march to Jerusalem they begin wrangling among themselves about who will get the top spots in the new regime. The Leader, however, stops and looks back at them. "You all are no better than the Romans you want to get rid of, you know that? I don't know why, but I expected more than that from you. You're here to serve the people, not boss them around. Isn't that what you've seen me doing? Haven't you caught on to that yet?"

Unfortunately, though, the disciples do not catch on. Not yet, anyway. And who can blame them? Doesn't Jesus admit, at least in private, that he's the Messiah, deliverer of the Jews? Sure, they worry about not having any weapons or even a battle plan, but then Jesus has told them several times that it's just not time yet. When they get to Jerusalem, no doubt then he'll let them in on the plan. And, they remind themselves, the Leader has supernatural powers. He can call armies of angels to his defense when the crisis comes.

When they reach Jerusalem, their hopes soar. The victory parade into the city is everything they've dreamed of. Their fears about the lack of planning melt away when the Leader sends two of them to pick up a colt he's arranged to have waiting for his grand entrance. This must mean he has a whole network of supporters already planted in the city. And when the crowds see him, they go crazy, just as the Twelve knew they would. During the next several days, the Leader spends a good bit of time giving speeches in the Temple. The disciples can see this is part of the plan too. He needs to get the Passover crowd solidly behind him for the final coup d'état.

Still, the disciples can feel the resistance from the establishment building. The Temple big shots keep trying to lay a trap for him, but the Leader outwits them every time, just as they knew he would. Several times his Galilean followers quiz him about his strategy, want to know when the big moment is scheduled, how they should get ready for it. His original cadre, the two pairs of brothers who have been with him the longest, confer with him privately, asking him to reveal the secret sign that will set the whole conflagration off. All they get out of him, though, is a command to be on their guard, constantly on the lookout. That and more obscure poeticizing about earthquakes and falling stars.

The band spends the week before Passover in suburban Jerusalem at the house of friends, who throw a big party for him. Everyone's feeling good now. After months on the road, camping out, scraping by, the hard part is just about over. The next few days will tell the tale.

The night of the Passover meal the Leader announces they'll stay in the city; he's made preparations there for the festival banquet. Once more his followers are reassured that the Leader has things under control. Sure enough, everything's already set up when they arrive at the large upstairs guest room. The celebration is going fine—they're smacking their lips over all the traditional dishes and lots of wine—when the Leader drops a bomb into the middle of the revelry.

"One of you is going to betray me," he says, looking slowly around the room. "Someone at this very table."

If that doesn't put a damper on the party! They all fall silent, looking uneasily at one another. They know the accusation, plainly spoken for once, is entirely possible. Probably several of them have already been approached by agents from the Temple offering to buy information that might convict the Leader of some actionable charge. But each one protests it couldn't be him.

This momentary break in their fellowship seems to be repaired, however, when the Leader passes around the last ceremonial cup of wine, insisting that they all drink up. He even makes a speech about solidarity, calling the wine his blood and the bread they're eating his body. More of his poeticizing, they think. He concludes the celebration on an upbeat note for once, promising again what they've all hoped from the beginning.

"The next time I drink," he says, lifting the cup, "it will be in the new kingdom."

A shout goes up. The new kingdom! It's close now, they think, very close.

So close, in fact, they don't even return to the house in the suburbs that night. Instead they sleep in a cave in a nearby olive orchard. The Leader seems suddenly distraught, but then who wouldn't on the eve of an impending battle? His followers have eaten too well and drunk too much to worry about it tonight. They stretch out and fall asleep.

A few hours later, they awake to the sound of angry voices and swords rattling. They shake the grogginess from their heads. Torchlight is searching the shadows. By the time they've struggled to their feet, their hearts racing now, it has indeed finally begun—the moment they've waited for, hoped for, given up everything for.

Except—the moment is over before it's even begun.

They see Judas, his face lighted by torches, step forward and kiss the Leader, then drop back into the shadows again. Just as they're all realizing they're surrounded by Temple guards and Roman soldiers, they see the Leader drop his head, surrendering to the commander.

They stare at one another. What about the secret reinforcements? The army of angels?

Peter, determined to defend his hero, pulls out a sword and strikes one of the men. But the Leader speaks sharply to Peter, tells him to put the sword away, then touches the side of the man's head where he's bleeding. The next thing they know, the guards are leading Jesus away. This is not the beginning, but the end.

The Twelve melt away into the night. The Baptizer's question comes back to them then: *Are you the one?*

And now they know the answer.

But the tragedy isn't over yet. They must spend the next few days hiding out in that room where they'd last eaten with the Leader, terrified they'll be discovered and executed as rebels too. Confusion reigns. They thought they had found their answer in Jesus, but now they see the last three years have all been a tragic mistake.

Still, the shame of having abandoned him like cowards adds to their despair. They had not even helped the women in their party take his body off the cross to bury it. Nor do they visit the grave later. When the women come back from the tomb with word that the corpse is missing, some of them decide it's too dangerous to remain in Jerusalem any longer and decide to make a break for it.

Two of these are making their way west out of the city, heading for the village of Emmaus, when a stranger joins them on the road. Incredibly, he seems to be unaware of the recent turmoil in the city, and they find themselves pouring out their disappointment to the stranger, telling him how their dreams had died with the Leader. Their tale ends plaintively. "We had hoped he was the one who would redeem Israel."

"Is that what you expected?" the stranger asks. "Maybe we should talk about this."

And so he starts over again from the beginning, explaining himself, just as he had during that long night back in Bethany with those first two disciples, answering the questions they don't even know how to ask.

Chapter 20

Good Enough?
The Rich Young Ruler

*M*aybe the disciples wanted Jesus to lead an army of dissidents to power in Jerusalem, but not all Jews were interested in joining an underground resistance movement. Rich ones, for instance. In fact, outside his circle of close companions, most people classified Jesus as an itinerant, even charismatic, rabbi—up until his final week in Jerusalem. And it is on this final march to Jerusalem that a figure traditionally identified as "the rich young ruler" comes looking for Jesus.

The title is a conglomerate one; Mark's gospel first calls him rich, Matthew describes him as young, and Luke adds the term ruler, though a more precise translation is "magistrate." The word may also have meant something like "aristocrat" or "from one of the leading families." Since the encounter takes place in the Judean hill country, the man is probably from the landed gentry, his wealth likely a product of the vineyards or agricultural estates Jesus often used as settings for his parables. In our day he could have been one of the Gallo brothers or an heir to a big cattle ranch. But this young man is not particularly interested in the family business.

Unlike the disciples who frequently worry about where their next meal is coming from and often quarrel over the choice seats on Jesus' cabinet, this fellow is not consumed with petty anxiety about the things of this world. He is, in fact, an amateur Torah scholar. Given his background, he could spend his days frittering away his fortune at the races or else become so absorbed in business that he has no time for religious questions. Instead, his mind and means are devoted to serious study of Hebrew scripture.

Indeed, he has been pondering one of the chief religious controversies of his day, one involving time, destiny, the future. On the one hand, the Pharisees claim that resurrection from the dead can be inferred from scripture. The second of the Eighteen Benedictions of the daily Jewish liturgy praises God for "bringing the dead to life" and not abandoning "those who sleep in the dust." On the other hand, another religious party, the Sadducees, maintains that the scriptures show no support for a doctrine of resurrection. To further confuse matters, in Alexandria, the intellectual center of the Empire, the Jewish philosopher Philo employs Greek notions of the soul's immortality to explain a kind of nebulous spiritual afterlife. Yet literature produced by the ascetic Essene communities speaks of a coming age in which the righteous will be vindicated and rewarded.

In any case, people in first-century Palestine did not think of "going to heaven" in the way we do today. They had a whole menu of options to choose from in answer to the question "what comes next?" And the resurrection option meant something earthier than our visions of ethereal family reunions. For one thing, people didn't measure time in centuries but in "kingdoms," periods of political power—such as Egyptian, Assyrian, Persian, Roman. The new science of history was beginning to make it clear that no kingdom lasted forever. Thus, the Jews looked back with longing to the glorious age of King David's reign and even farther back to the stories of their deliverance from the Evil Empire of Egypt. But many also looked forward to a coming age when God would establish his everlasting kingdom, using the Jews, purified by suffering, as his chosen administrators.

Others, especially those influenced by the pervasive Greek culture that surrounded them, understood the prophecies in sacred texts to have a more spiritual meaning. To think of the Ruler of the Universe in terms of power politics went against their finer grain. Many educated Jews preferred the Platonic realm of the abstract Ideal to Adam's old original dust. The young aristocrat is uncertain how to locate himself on this doctrinal spectrum. After studying the subject thoroughly, he can't believe that this life is all there is. He expects something more. But where and when? And, most importantly, how? Whatever it turns out to be, he doesn't want to miss out on it.

Therefore, when he hears that a celebrated new rabbi is passing through his region, he goes out to wait for him along the road-side—face-to-face encounters with experts being the only alternative in an age without call-in shows or e-mail. When the teacher's entourage comes into view, the rabbi is surrounded by people the young aristocrat wouldn't like to meet in a dark alley—beggars, squealing children, women carrying cooking pots. Yet he knows this may be his only chance to get the rabbi's attention, so he rushes into the road and literally throws himself at the rabbi's feet—an uncommon display of humility for a wealthy, respected pillar of the community.

"Good Teacher," he blurts out with no preamble, "what must I do to inherit eternal life?"

Not, notice, how can I be a good Jew, follow the rules, fulfill my religious obligations. He knows the answer to those relatively simple questions. He makes sure the new rabbi knows he's not your ordinary synagogue-on-the-Sabbath type, but a seeker with serious questions, probing the profounder depths of the spirit.

Using one of his characteristic ploys, the rabbi eyes him closely, then answers with his own question: "Why are you calling me good? God is the only one who deserves that name."

The young man sits back on his heels. This wasn't exactly the response he was expecting, either to his exuberant greeting or his challenging query.

The rabbi continues: "Besides, you already know the answer to your question. The commandments are clear to everyone. Surely you know them: Don't commit adultery. Don't murder. Don't lie, cheat, and steal. Honor your father and mother."

The young man gets to his feet, alarmed that perhaps the rabbi isn't taking him very seriously. The way the rabbi has rattled off the easy rules makes him feel foolish. Any child knows this stuff. The rabbi didn't even mention the first and really hard commandment, the one that allows room for discussion and interpretation *Thou shalt have no other gods before me.*

"Wait," the young man protests, "you don't understand. I know all that. I've kept all those rules since I was a little kid." Eternal life is a difficult and hotly debated topic, after all. It's got to be more complicated than that.

This isn't the first time someone has asked Jesus this question. A professional religion scholar back in Galilee also wanted to know about "eternal life." Jesus answered him similarly: "What is written in the Torah? How do you interpret it?" The scholar had replied with the two commandments Jesus himself says are the most important: Love God with your whole being and love your neighbor as yourself. Jesus commended him for this answer, adding, "Do that, and you'll live." But the scholar, not content with that, then insisted Jesus define "neighbor." And got a story about a Samaritan in response.

Perhaps at this point, however, the rabbi senses that the young man's interest is more serious than the Galilean scholar's. After all, he is not a professional, not a member of the academic elite. Also, the subject of eternal life — or to render the Greek in more literal English, "age-lasting life" — is one dear to Jesus' heart. It is, in fact, the gift he claims to bring to the world. And to give the young man credit, he hasn't been put off by a rather curt response. Maybe too, after listening to his disciples snarl at one another over power slots, it's a relief to find someone who's at least asking the right questions. Someone who is thoroughly educated in scripture. Someone earnest, sincere, with a little spiritual depth, who can see past the cheap trappings of political perks and prerogatives. What a comfort to have a person like him on the team he's training.

So the rabbi looks him over carefully. He takes in the fine linen clothes, the hands more used to holding scrolls than hoes or fishnets, the face so open and intent.

The young aristocrat waits expectantly, hopeful that he's about to hear the secret of life itself from the rabbi's lips. Will the teacher give him a reading list? A special set of religious exercises, demand he fast, require a pilgrimage?

"Okay," the rabbi finally says. "You've kept the rules. That's good. But there's one more thing you need to do. Go back home and settle your affairs. By that I mean you should sell off all your assets, lock, stock, and barrel, and turn over the proceeds to the poor. That way you won't be tied down anymore. In fact, think of it as an investment. You're transferring your account from the temporal world to the one that truly outlasts the ages—the eternal kingdom. Now, when you've taken care of that business, then come and join me. But you should know, it won't be easy. This is a dangerous job. In fact, it could cost you your life."

The young man looks stunned at first, as if he's just received a paralyzing blow. This doesn't make any sense. If the rabbi wanted him to become one of his students, to wander about listening to his wisdom, he would do that. In fact, with all his money he can underwrite a whole school of students for the rabbi. They wouldn't have to travel around then, living off handouts. They could set up an institute, build dormitories, lecture halls. Students could come from all over the empire to study with the rabbi. But sell off all his property? His family estate? This just doesn't make sense, not when it could be put to good use. Turning it over to the poor— well, does it really help impoverished people to just give them money with no strings attached? If the rabbi would tell him to set up a free clinic, hire a legal defense team to represent peasants who get thrown off their land for unpaid taxes, that might make sense. But giving money to the poor is like throwing it away. So many *good* projects could be funded with his wealth. Surely the rabbi will listen to reason?

But before he can even open his mouth, the rabbi is shaking his head.

From the look in his eyes, the young aristocrat can already tell it's no use. The rabbi has anticipated his objections and rejected them.

The young man heaves a sigh and turns away, his arms and legs unaccountably heavy. So much for the new rabbi and his unreasonable reply. The land's been in his family forever—it's his God-given inheritance. Getting rid of it so cavalierly would dishonor his parents. Maybe it was a dumb question to begin with. Maybe he's silly to think there are such things as answers. At any rate, there's no point in worrying about it anymore. He'll just have to get on with his life.

So why does he feel as if something has died, as if he's carrying a corpse around inside?

As he starts back down the road to his estate, he hears the rabbi saying to his scruffy friends, "You know, it's hard to be rich—especially if you're looking for something better. The wealthy have a hard time imagining anything better. Even heaven." He doesn't say this in an angry voice. He doesn't even sound offended or rejected. But he does sound sad, almost as if someone has died.

Chapter 21

Secret Admirer:

Nicodemus

*T*he story of Nicodemus and his encounter with Jesus contains perhaps the most famous verse from the entire New Testament. It's the one you see noted on a hand-lettered signboard at almost every nationally televised professional football game. The same one my Sunday school teachers made sure I memorized before I could say the alphabet. The one that begins "For God so loved the world . . . " At church we were told that, by learning this single verse, we'd always have the "plan of salvation" at our fingertips, like a spiritual first-aid kit. Here, reduced to one pithy sentence any child could understand, was all the information you needed to make it to heaven.

Originally, these words weren't spoken to a child, however. Nor were they intended as a clause in a spiritual insurance plan. They were dialogue in a drama enacted on a shadowy stage between a young man just launching his public career and a seasoned veteran of Temple politics who comes with understandable trepidation to seek his counsel.

Nicodemus is a member of the Sanhedrin, the board that governs not only Temple operations but all the intertwined religious and civil affairs in the city. In some ways the Sanhedrin operated like a city council, except that its link to the imperial government was more complicated than the relationship between local and federal governments today. If we think of the Romans as a United Nations peacekeeping force (one that doesn't hesitate to exercise its muscle), then the Sanhedrin might compare to the indigenous rulers of some politically explosive protectorate. Though the Sanhedrin's executive and military powers are limited, it has free rein, legislatively and judicially. It can make laws pertaining to Jews and hear cases concerning infractions of those laws, but to enforce its rulings, it must rely on Roman officials.

Membership in the Sanhedrin puts one in a powerful, though at times dangerous, position. For example, Herod the Great, displeased with the Sanhedrin's performance, once executed over half its seventy members and replaced them with his own handpicked men. This slaughter, a generation before our story, unexpectedly benefited the Jews, however. Till then, the Sadducees, a minority party made up primarily of families from the priestly nobility, had controlled the Sanhedrin. During their long dominance, the Sadducees feathered their nests with interpretations of the Torah that favored their own priestly privileges and increased their wealth. Herod's decimation of the old Sanhedrin opened it up for the first time to Pharisees, the reform party to which Nicodemus belongs.

The *chaburah,* or brotherhood of Pharisees, was never large— only a few thousand at most—and these were scattered throughout Palestine. Members were required to follow hundreds of ritual laws to the letter, a life too stringent for ordinary folk. Yet despite their own elite status, the Pharisees operated as spokesmen for the middle class and the laboring poor. They were also committed to the peasant class, defending them against oppression from both the Roman government and the Jerusalem priesthood. The party saw itself as the conscience of the nation, the yeast that leavens the lump, its moral leadership. Yet they only maintained their position on the Sanhedrin by making certain concessions to both their Roman and their priestly opponents.

Nicodemus has heard about the young rabbi from Galilee, a region famous for both its charismatic holy men and its rebels. Though barely in his thirties, the rabbi has already gained notoriety for his innovative teaching and miraculous healings. Those deeds pale, however, beside the pandemonium he recently created in the Temple, attacking the concession selling sacrificial animals inside the Temple precincts. (Though John reports that this event happened early in Jesus' public career, the other gospels place it, or a similar event, immediately preceding his crucifixion in Jerusalem.) When called to account for his actions, the young fellow reportedly made some veiled comment about destroying the Temple and rebuilding it again in three days. To the Temple officials, that sounded like a terrorist threat. And now the Galilean has dropped out of sight.

So when Nicodemus goes looking for Jesus, it's under cover of darkness. But why would a respectable Pharisee, one of the leading citizens of Jerusalem, seek out a nobody from the provinces anyway? Perhaps he has Jesus pegged as one of the Hasidic rabbis, a charismatic enthusiast whose fervor can cause trouble for the entire city. Yet the powerful Pharisee comes alone, obviously with no intention of arresting Jesus. Is he coming to warn the young troublemaker then? Or to reason with him about his revolutionary agenda? Debate religious issues? Whatever Nicodemus expects from the interview, he knows the meeting could potentially damage his reputation. Thus the darkness.

I picture Nicodemus as an older man, tall though stooped, whose outer cloak has the prescribed knotted fringes that mark devout Jews. He has the slightly bemused expression of melancholy one often sees on the faces of well-intentioned politicians. He takes the responsibilities of his office seriously, yet experience has taught him to compromise if he expects to achieve any of his laudable goals. And, like most politicians, he's used to being criticized, even vilified, by the very people whose lives he works to safeguard.

"Rabbi," he says, addressing the younger man with wary respect, "we realize your teachings must have God's approval since no one could perform the miracles you do unless God was working through him." A good opening, he feels. Plenty of approbation and no accusation.

But if Nicodemus is expecting an initial exchange of cautious pleasantries, he's thrown off guard by the Galilean's response. The young rabbi accepts Nicodemus's praise with no hint of false modesty, but fails to return the compliment—or even to acknowledge the Pharisee's official position.

"True enough," Jesus agrees, and, instead of inquiring politely into the reason for the great man's visit, launches into one of his famous non sequiturs. "No one can see the kingdom of God unless he starts all over again from the beginning—and I mean the *very* beginning. From birth, in fact."

"I beg your pardon," Nicodemus stammers uncertainly. "I'm not sure I'm following you here." He wasn't expecting—or asking—to be instructed in theology by this youngster. He hasn't risked his reputation to spend the night untangling poetic metaphors. But then young people are always wanting to reinvent the wheel. They think nothing of throwing out two thousand years of tradition meticulously accumulated and preserved by their ancestors.

"Can a person really start over again from the beginning?" Nicodemus asks. "I'm not sure you realize what that would entail—trying to wipe the slate clean and start all over from scratch. You may as well expect to climb back into your mother's womb. How can these things be?" The Pharisee looks at the younger man, so earnest and confident, and shakes his head. "Take an old man like me. I've spent a lifetime learning, studying, working to get where I am. Surely you're not suggesting I'd be better off scrapping all our heritage and starting over again?"

"It depends if you want to live in God's kingdom," the young rabbi retorts, undaunted by the older man's years and experience. "That's the essential question. Scholarship doesn't get you an entrance ticket. And the only reward for following the rules is a reputation for respectability. If that's enough for you, then fine. But if you want to live with God—in his kingdom—then you have to undergo a radical restructuring, as drastic as being formed again in your mother's womb. But first you have to give up the old life. That's what the ritual water is for—to wash away the old you."

Nicodemus strokes his wispy beard. Baptism—this is a concept he's familiar with. When a gentile converts to Judaism, he has to make certain prescribed sacrifices at the Temple, but he also must undergo a ritual bath. After that, he's considered an entirely new person, freshly born into the Jewish inheritance. Nicodemus gives a provisional nod and waits to see where the young rabbi is going with this.

"Just as your body grows gradually—and without your direction—inside your mother's womb, your spirit must take shape within God's spirit. When you are born into that kingdom, then you're living God's own life, breathing God's own breath. It becomes your very heartbeat."

Now Nicodemus sits back and frowns, shaking his head. *God's own breath* —What can this young fellow possibly know about the Spirit of the Eternal One? God's life isn't like human life. Far from it. The kingdom of the Eternal will arrive on this earth when people learn to do their duty, not when rash enthusiasts try to turn the system topsy-turvy. Wait till this youngster has lived in this troubled world a little longer. He'll find out what life is really like—a long chain, each link forged by hard work and difficult compromise. What would become of God's people if it weren't for men like himself who work to make the weight of that chain bearable?

The young rabbi, as if discerning Nicodemus's objections, holds up a hand. "Don't be put off by my talk about being born a second time. I know it sounds wild—scary even. Especially if you've dedicated your life to judicious management, diplomatic mediation. But life comes from God's spirit, and that's outside our control. Living in God's kingdom means getting blown about by his spirit. You never know what direction that wind will come from next. It's totally unpredictable. Its power comes from something we can't even see. An invisible force fuels the new life I'm talking about. You can't hope to corner it or fence it in. You simply surrender to it."

Nicodemus blows out his own heavy breath. He recognizes the hidden challenge in the young rabbi's soliloquy. It calls the Pharisee's entire career into question. "So okay. Just how does this work then?" he asks. "You just let this mystical wind blow you about willy-nilly, I suppose."

But the young rabbi is not intimidated by the ridicule. "What? You're one of the nation's intellectual elite and you don't know this?" he says, returning the sarcasm. "You think I'm unrealistic, that what I have to say doesn't apply to everyday life. But I've had plenty to say about how to live in this world, and nobody listens.

Why should I expect you to understand when I talk about life in God's own kingdom?"

How much longer this conversation goes on and what its final result is, we don't know. At this point, it appears that the gospel writer himself can't resist getting in on this discussion. It becomes impossible from this point on to untangle the rabbi's words from the author's amplifications, since ancient manuscripts don't supply quotation marks. Nicodemus never speaks again, though.

In fact, the Pharisee disappears altogether at this point, though he must have continued to mull over his strange conversation with the young rabbi. After that night visit, Nicodemus follows the career of the Galilean from a distance, with guarded but growing interest. When the young man is later executed—a regrettable if inevitable outcome—Nicodemus and Joseph, a wealthy Jew from the town of Arimathea, petition the Roman procurator for permission to remove the body to a tomb Joseph owns.

Fortunately, the sepulchre is near the crucifixion site, within the Pharisee's legal limits of a Sabbath's day journey, for Nicodemus is still on the Sanhedrin and has not given up his strict observance of Sabbatarian laws. But he is also generous and supplies the necessary ointments and spices for embalming the young rabbi's corpse—a risky act of charity. Both the Roman officials and his colleagues on the Sanhedrin could easily accuse him of being a secret supporter of the young radical from Galilee.

But for some reason, both the expense and the risk seem worth it. The night Nicodemus asked the young rabbi his question—*How can these things be?*—he'd felt old and disillusioned. Convinced he'd never feel the wind in his sails again. And now look at him. Risking a lifetime's reputation for a flash-in-the-pan Galilean fanatic. He can't imagine what's got into him.

Chapter 22

Answers:

The Right One to the Wrong Questions

Are you the one?"

"What must I do?"

"How can these things be?"

All excellent questions. In fact, the very questions we would like to put to the elusive hero of the gospels ourselves if we could track him down today. Even baptized believers still pose these same questions, like Nicodemus, in the darkened privacy of their midnight hearts. Of course, they may alter the wording slightly. For instance, they ask:

"Am I fooling myself?"

"Am I doing it right? Am I doing enough?"

"Start over *again*? How can I?"

Strangely enough, no one in all the gospel accounts ever asked Jesus the question he was dying to answer. The one he repeatedly insisted on answering whether or not anyone asked. When no one came forward with this essential query, he posed it for them: "What is the kingdom of God like?"

Probably people didn't ask because they thought they already knew the answer. But Jesus knew they didn't. Not even those he took into his confidence, who were closest to him.

For three years he tried to show the disciples what the kingdom of God was like. If you are on a spiritual quest, it helps to have an idea of what you're looking for. But the paradoxes of the parables frequently seem to overwhelm the disciples' comprehension. You die in order to live? You give up everything you have in order to get what you've always wanted? The latecomers get the same rewards as the ones who signed up early? That didn't sound like any kingdom they had ever heard of.

It is perhaps too easy to dismiss the disciples as thickheaded yahoos, but the only precedent they had for a messiah was David, that historic figure during whose reign their people had prospered. Yet Jesus refused to be recast as a renegade chieftain, massing his guerrilla forces in the Galilean hills, waiting for the strategic moment to make his grab for power. The kingdom of God, he tried to tell them, would not be inaugurated by a People's March on Jerusalem. But when Jesus tried to make clear that Jerusalem would bring humiliation and death, his warning fell on deaf ears.

Are you the one? This was the question constantly eating away at the disciples. Have I thrown in my lot with the right candidate for messiah? Is he the real McCoy? Am I on the winning team? The answer depends on what you expect "the one" to look like. Unfortunately, the disciples had a messiah-shaped template already built into their heads, one that Jesus' didn't fit. They stuck with him for three years only because his flesh-and-blood presence was able to overwhelm their programed expectations.

Even so, many of his disciples outside the inner circle did turn back when they heard his talk of dying. When Jesus saw his once-large followings begin to dwindle, he asked the Twelve if they were going to desert him as well. Peter's answer was poignant: "Lord, to whom shall we go? You have the words of eternal life." He was simply the only show in town.

Still, the process of reeducating the disciples' expectations was to take years. It would not even be complete by the time of the crucifixion. In fact, the resurrection itself did not instantly answer that all-important question, "Are you the one?" Although the disciples had already heard reports that Jesus had disappeared from his tomb, Cleopas tells the mysterious figure on the road to Emmaus how shattered Jesus' supporters were since they "had hoped that he was the one to redeem Israel." Indeed, it would take fire from heaven to consume their faulty concepts and a wild wind to blow away the ashes of their assumptions.

Nevertheless, not everyone's hopes for Jesus were as crassly

self-serving as his closest companions'. More intellectual types
were willing to accept him as an uncommonly enlightened spiritual master—a role he did not reject. For these thinkers, the important question was procedural: *What must I do?* What's the
proper system, method, righteousness routine? For a culture like
ours, absorbed in process, in management techniques and seminars
for success, such a question seems not only natural but necessary.
Nor does Jesus try to deflect it. If you're asking this question, at
least you have the right goal in mind—eternal life, life in the kingdom he likes to talk about so much.

Jesus answers this question straightforwardly. No beating
around the bush, not even the metaphorical shrubbery. Start with the
easy stuff, he says. The Ten Commandments. Surely you can avoid
killing people and sleeping with your neighbor's wife. And naturally you'll want to take care of your aging parents. Following
these practices doesn't take a spiritual giant. They're merely the
blueprint for a functioning human community. (Though a society
of spiritual dwarves like our present one finds even these simple
rules difficult.)

It's the second level of difficulty that stuns us. "Sell everything
you own and give it to the poor," he tells the wealthy young magistrate of Judea. But that's not all. After you've had your garage
sale, leave home and follow him down the road that could lead
anywhere.

The rich young ruler could see—and probably smell—the ple-
beians surrounding the rabbi on the road that day. He had a clear
image of what following this teacher would mean. But where
would that road lead us today? To Mother Teresa's lepers in Cal-
cutta? To become a Peace Corps worker? A Little League coach?
It's all a little hazy. And somehow we feel that, until we figure out
that second instruction to sell our belongings and follow him, we
can forgo the first injunction—obeying the Ten Commandments.
We heave a sigh of regret and relief, then ponder our options. We
may not exactly turn away like the young Judean magistrate, who
at least was honest about his failure of nerve, but like a previous
scholar who had put the same question to Jesus, we keep asking for

more information, more definition of terms, anything that will delay our making a decision.

My personal instincts say it is better to be the disciples on the road with the wrong answer than the rich young ruler who knows the right answer but still turns back to the same old life in the villa. If you stick with the one whose words, as Peter said, generate life, those words may eventually penetrate even the thickest skull or hardest heart. Living with the answer, even when you don't understand it, turns out to be better than knowing but rejecting it.

Then there's Nicodemus. The young Judean aristocrat was tangled up in his wealth, but the ties that bind Nicodemus are nobler—his responsibility to his nation. Honor fastens him firmly to that power structure which has conferred the position of trust and authority he holds. He carries out his duties from a sense of moral obligation. And, so far as we know, he never cut those ties.

But notice too that Jesus never tells Nicodemus to resign from the Sanhedrin. This time he does not demand that the powerful Pharisee sell all his property and take off for a life on the road. He has a different answer tailored for Nicodemus. When Nicodemus describes the Galilean rabbi as "a teacher come from God," a miracle worker with divine credentials, Jesus accepts this role and demands no further concessions from the Pharisee. Nor does he rebuke Nicodemus's cautious approach. But he does tell him the truth about the kingdom of God—that neither knowledge nor power will get you there, that Nicodemus needs to start over again.

Yet a man with a long and honorable career in public service doesn't like to think about starting over again. Retirement, maybe, where he can look back at his accomplishments with satisfaction. But not beginning a new life, undergoing a complete transformation. Such a metamorphosis would require even more effort than carrying his current wearisome load. He's an old man, not a child.

Nevertheless, Jesus is adamant. Nicodemus must give up his illusion of control—belief that earthly Israel depends on his steady hand at the helm. God's breath will blow the ship of state wherever it pleases, no matter if Nicodemus is there with his counsel or not.

No overachiever likes to hear this message. People with weighty responsibilities find it hard to take them—or themselves—lightly.

Publicans and sinners have it easy in the gospels. They know what's keeping them out of the kingdom. They don't even have to ask many questions. They are the sick who know they need a doctor. Often they're eager for a chance to start over. (Compare, for instance, the thieving tax collector Zacchaeus, who willingly surrenders his wealth and begins again, to the rich young ruler, who finds it too much to ask.)

It's the good people in the gospels who have it hard. Say you've got a good job, a powerful position, the respect of your community, weighty responsibilities, a good education. Starting over from scratch isn't going to look so good. Your very identity depends on those accoutrements.

And that's not all. You sell your stocks, and they're gone. You sign over your house, and there's no going back. You follow Jesus then because, as Peter said, you have nowhere else to go. That's clear enough. But what if there are people who *depend* on you? What if you're a congressman, a teacher, a pastor, a mother? Then you find the Spirit's birth canal a tight fit for your important obligations.

In our heart of hearts—which is a child's heart—we all long for freedom and lightness of being. We seek all our lives for that secret. Some of us dream of flying. But when we hear the answer, it seems impossible. Become a child—a helpless newborn? At that point, we echo Nicodemus's question: *How can these things be?* Then we go back home, take up our weighty lives, and continue to think it over.

PART VI

LOOKING FOR A FIGHT

Jesus was not the only Palestinian renegade executed by Rome during the first century. During Jesus' early childhood, Judas the Galilean died for leading a tax rebellion. His father had earlier been executed by Herod for leading anti-Rome riots, and Judas's two sons were crucified a decade after Jesus for following in their father's footsteps. John the Baptist, hailed by the people as a prophet, was beheaded in Galilee by Herod Antipas. Jesus' crucifixion as "King of the Jews" was followed a few years later by that of Theudas, a messianic pretender who plagued Pilate's successor. Finally, when Zealots initiated yet another insurrection in A.D. 70, Rome finally leveled Jerusalem and dissolved the Judean state altogether.

In other words, there was as much fighting in first-century Palestine as there is today. The battles Jesus fought, however, were always verbal. And his opponents were always fellow Jews. He never took up the sword, and he never argued with gentiles about religion. But then, so far as we know, devotees of Zeus or Astarte did not come with spiritual questions. Thus, his dealings with gentiles were not contentious. He healed them and their kin, freed them from demons, no doubt fed some among the crowds who followed him. But the Gospels record only two gentiles who ever questioned Jesus. One was the Syro-Phoenician mother who demanded his attention for her child. The other was Pontius Pilate.

Jesus' battles, though verbal, were nevertheless frequent and fierce, and they make up a surprisingly large proportion of the gospels. Many take place in various Galilean towns, sometimes in synagogues or in courtyards of private homes, otherwise in the street or some other public setting. A number occur during visits to Jerusalem. None, however, can be fully understood outside the context of the combined political and religious tensions in Palestine at the time.

While the Sadducees and Pharisees, the two major parties controlling the Sanhedrin, struggled to maintain a balance of power in order to ensure peace in the region, a third group called the Essenes refused to recognize as legitimate the Temple's current high priest, handpicked by Rome. Instead of accepting this unpleasant if inevitable political reality, as the Pharisees had, the Essenes withdrew to the desert to set up a religious commune, where they awaited an apocalypse they believed was fast approaching. At that time a mysterious figure called "the Teacher of Righteousness" would arise to vindicate the faithful. Denouncing the Jerusalem Temple as politically corrupt and sacramentally compromised, the Essenes instituted their own sacrificial rites, a heresy roughly equivalent to disgruntled Catholics setting up a new Vatican in Arizona, and one that led to all Essenes being officially barred from entering the Temple precincts.

Strangely enough, the Essenes are never mentioned in the New Testament, though both Josephus and the Jewish philosopher Philo refer to them with admiration. In 1948, remnants of the Essene commune's library were discovered in a cave in the cliffs above the Dead Sea. These scrolls provided physical evidence of the part the sectarians played in ancient Palestine.

According to Josephus, the Essenes claimed over four thousand members, a surprisingly large number. The much more influential Pharisees claimed only six thousand card-carrying members among the two million Jews inhabiting Palestine at the time. Besides those Essenes living in the isolated desert community, other lay members lived in enclaves scattered throughout Palestine. We never see Jesus engaged in debate with Essenes, however. After the discovery of the

Dead Sea Scrolls, a few scholars speculated that Jesus himself may have been an Essene, though most have since discounted that theory. His remark about those who make themselves "eunuchs for the kingdom of heaven's sake" may refer to the Essenes' vow of celibacy, a custom otherwise uncommon among Jews. Though the Essenes went further than even the Pharisees in their stringent ritual observances, their most distinctive characteristic was their communal sharing of wealth and property, much as the young Christian church would later do.

The Zealots comprised what Josephus calls "the fourth philosophy" among Palestinian Jews. Their roots were firmly planted in Galilee's soil. (Josephus credits Judas the Galilean, the one who led the unsuccessful uprising during Jesus' childhood, with founding the Zealots.) Though the Sadducees and Pharisees considered them extremists, the Zealots had considerable influence among the common people, championing their complaints against oppressive Roman taxes. Indeed, their movement was based on the belief that only God was ruler of Israel and that political submission to Rome and its henchmen was tantamount to religious heresy. Josephus, in the pay of Rome himself, accuses the Zealots of being no better than bandits, since they sometimes assassinated Jews they suspected of collaborating with Rome. After the destruction of the Temple in A.D. 70, the Zealots retreated to the mountain fortress of Masada and held out there against the Roman legions for another three years before eventually committing mass suicide.

Needless to say, the Zealots, like the Essenes, held no seats on the Sanhedrin. However, Jesus, who drew his supporters largely from those who suffered most under Roman domination, picked at least one of these radicals for his band of apostles, Simon the Zealot. Some scholars believe Judas may also have been a Zealot, his betrayal a result of disillusionment over his leader's failure to provoke an uprising against Rome. Clearly, all the disciples expected Jesus to take political action, judging by their interest in the top spots in his new regime. Nevertheless, we never see any open debate between an avowed Zealot and Jesus, though some of the questions he answered dealt with issues high on the Zealots' agenda—whether to pay taxes to Caesar, for instance. And anyone listening to his public lectures and debates would have been well aware that Zealots and their sympathizers were in the audience.

But what about that audience, the silent onlookers to these verbal contests? The biggest part was made up of the *am ha-eretz,* literally, the "people of the land," a term used by the educated caste to designate the peasant class, the multitudes, the masses. The lower, and thus largest, segment of any society. Like most blue-collar workers, these people generally left politics to people with time and money to spend on it; their own energies went into surviving. Once in a while some of them, fed up with their hard lot, would fall under the influence of an insurrectionist and stake their lives on a doomed rebellion. But the politically powerful Sadducees had nothing but contempt for farmers, fishermen, and day laborers, and the Pharisees saw the working class mostly as raw material for their theological reforms. Many of the *am ha-eretz* attended their local synagogue, observed the major festivals, and tried to follow Torah law as best they could. For others, the only distinguishing mark of their religious heritage was circumcision.

Though Jesus healed many of these people, none of them would have dared engage him in theological debate. Nevertheless, like the hundreds of millions of Americans who sit in front of their television sets every evening, absorbing the ideas of our culture's media elite, the "people of the land" came to listen to these debates for their entertainment value if nothing else. Jesus may not actually have expected to change the minds of his opponents, but he must have hoped his answers would fall like seed into the open ears of the common people.

His adversaries in these contests were equally aware of their audience. They didn't pick fights with Jesus simply to exercise their rhetorical skills or to change one rabbi's mind. They knew these polemical contests could have far-reaching consequences. The Pharisees had most at stake in these confrontations. Their political clout depended on maintaining their influence over the very people who crowded into courtyards and public squares to hear the controversial new teacher. Their rivals, the Sadducees, didn't much concern themselves with what happened outside Jerusalem, and thus did not enter the fray until late in Jesus' career. For their part, the Zealots kept a low public profile, and the Essenes by and large practiced withdrawal from public life.

Thus the Pharisees, well aware that their broad base of support came from the unruly multitudes, saw this unpredictable itinerant rabbi as a threat. Only by promising to keep the people in the provinces peaceful had they won their seats on the Sanhedrin council. Thus it was essential that this loose cannon, Jesus of Nazareth, be contained.

Of course, as in most political or religious factions, internal divisions existed within the Pharisee party itself. The more conservative branch followed the tradition of Shammai, one of a pair of leading scholars who had died during Jesus' childhood. The school of Shammai generally interpreted the Torah injunctions more strictly than their liberal counterparts, the school of Hillel, who promoted a kinder, gentler Judaism. In fact, some of Jesus' teachings recorded in the gospels echo precepts taught earlier by Rabbi Hillel. For example, Hillel had said, "What is distasteful to yourself, do not do to your neighbor; that is the whole Law, the rest is but commentary." Jesus restates this almost exactly in the Sermon on the Mount: "In everything, do to others what you would have them do to you, for this sums up the Law and the Prophets." Probably Nicodemus was a student of Hillel, as was Gamaliel, the Pharisee who later saves Peter and his fellow apostles when they are arrested and brought before the Sanhedrin for preaching in Jerusalem.

Other important antagonists in these debates were the professional clique of scribes, men who, from copying scrolls of scriptural texts, were considered experts in Mosaic law. Their historical prototype was Ezra, the scribe responsible for reviving the Jewish heritage after the Exile. The Jews had, in fact, survived their captivity in pagan lands as a people only because words were portable: they had carried their history and their laws, embedded in words, with them into exile. Whereas scribes had previously been little more than human copy machines, after the Exile they gained new status as cultural heroes, interpreters of the Torah, authorities familiar with legal precedent. They make up some of Jesus' fiercest adversaries in debate.

We should not automatically assume, however, that Jesus' opponents in these debates were motivated by malice. Ours is an age that prizes consensus, strives to level difference, often by simply acknowledging its inevitability. We tend to terminate arguments with platitudes like, "Well, it's different things to different people." But to stifle controversy by claiming that reality depends on perception alone would have made no sense to Jews. Their culture has maintained its identity by clarifying rather than blurring the distinctions between varying opinions. Whereas we avoid conversations about religion and politics in polite society, Jesus' compatriots considered debating those topics a sacred obligation.

Theological disputation was central to teaching and maintaining Torah. The cultural and religious identity of the Jews rested on the practice of public discourse about the interpretation of scriptural texts. *Aboth,* a collection of rabbinical teachings compiled not long after the destruction of the Temple, lists four steps in this educational process: first, studying the law; second, teaching it to others; third, expanding the law by adding interpretations to cover new situations; and fourth, applying the law to specific cases. By posing and answering questions concerning Torah, Jesus and his challengers were engaging in these steps of the traditional process, as essential to Judaism as sermons are to the Christian church.

These debates could get pretty hot. It didn't pay to have a thin skin. You had to be willing to give as good as you got. Jesus' responses to his opponents could be both ingenious and stinging. He uses sarcasm, ridicule, parody, and exaggeration to score rhetorical points in these contests of wit. Sometimes he makes his point simply by stonewalling. When a delegation from the Temple hierarchy, for example, demands to know what gives him the right to teach, he refuses to answer until they state publicly their views on John the Baptist. A crafty move on his part, since they dare not offend the audience at this debate, who consider John a national martyr. Jesus sometimes even resorts to name-calling, denouncing his adversaries as snakes, hypocrites, a generation of adulterers, and a number of other choice titles that would have made Mrs. Batcher, my old Sunday school teacher, gasp.

She imagined, as she smoothed the little paper doll of Jesus onto the baby-blue flannelgraph, that this contentious rabbi had intended to teach us good behavior. How to make polite conversation. Or at least tactful tête-à-têtes. Nonconfrontational methods of making a point. She never suspected that he would lead us to write letters to the editor, picket the White House, filibuster at school board meetings. Perhaps if she had read the gospels more carefully she would not have asked us so often, "What would Jesus do?"

Chapter 23

Get the Guest:

At the House of Simon the Pharisee

What would you do if Jesus came to your house?"

This was another of Mrs. Batcher's favorite questions for our Sunday school class, one asked in a tone that made us fidget in our metal folding chairs. From her tone, we could tell she was certain none of us would make it through even one meal without upsetting our milk or our parents. She meant us to squirm in shame, remembering our unmade beds and unhung clothes. Jesus, with his X-ray vision, would surely see into the messy closets, read what we'd written in our diaries, shake his head over the sibling squabbles that were sure to erupt.

In the gospels Jesus was invited to a number of homes, and he never looked under anyone's bed, so far as I can tell. His reception varied a good bit from place to place, however. To Simon the Pharisee, this roving rabbi, the latest craze among the common people, was an unknown quantity to check out. As a community leader and expert in the Law, Simon felt obliged to delve into the rabbi's background, to take his theological temperature, especially after supporters of John the Baptizer had raised the question of the rabbi being messiah material.

The Baptizer himself was already a threat to the shaky peace in the region. His purification rituals down at the Jordan River were drawing spectacular crowds of sinners, all eager to wash their sins away in an orgy of repentance. Such mass rallies made Rome extremely nervous. Messiah-talk was even more dangerous.

Simon hadn't been surprised when the crowds rushed off to see a lunatic notorious for dressing like a caveman and eating insects. What the Baptizer offered them was a freak show in the desert.

Every petty thief and cheap hooker in the region was happy to splash into the river, thinking a little muddy water was all it took to wash away their sins. One of the great rabbis of the past had taught that only a single day of repentance by every child of Abraham would be enough to bring on the messiah's arrival.

But Simon knew already how this revival would end. Would all those fishermen and hired hands really give up their old ways? Clean out their cupboards, wash their clothes, resolve to start following the Rules for Right Living?

For about two minutes, maybe. The emotionalism of the Baptizer's preaching would provide no lasting defense against their sins—which were themselves emotion-spawned. The crowd's hunger and lust would outlast their transitory penitence.

Education, training, discipline—that was the road to holiness. Everyone was waiting for a messiah who could deliver them from pagan oppression, but it was that hard road to holiness, not the easy pathway of passion, that would lead to their nation's redemption.

And there was never any lack of messiahs offering to free the people. Identifying the right one was the hard part. Every time you turned around, some new firebrand was claiming God had appointed him as the Jews' deliverer. Simon had grown extremely skeptical about these would-be messiahs. The last time some young rebel from the district had felt the messiah-call, he'd broken into the Roman arsenal at Sepphoris, and two thousand Jews had been crucified to pay for his folly. So any time Simon heard messiah-talk, he knew it was his duty to make a careful investigation.

So far, the rabbi from Nazareth had proved very clever, Simon had to admit. The answer he'd given the Baptizer's envoys was canny, obviously designed to circumvent possible sedition charges by Rome. The rabbi had made no direct messianic claims, only told the Baptizer's men to rely on the evidence of their own senses—to judge by what they had seen and heard: crippled people walking, blind people seeing, encouraging words for the poor.

And the rabbi from Nazareth was trying a completely different tactic than the Baptizer. He was no ascetic like John. Just the opposite, in fact. When he wasn't working the crowds, he hung out in cafés and bars, building up a solid following among the vulgar class, people who didn't even pretend to observe the Law of Moses. People who drank too much, ate too much, didn't keep kosher, and slept with whatever they could buy for the night.

Simon had been in the crowd listening to the new rabbi one day, mentally comparing him to his rival down on the Jordan, when the man, as if reading his mind, had suddenly said, "There's no pleasing you people, is there? You're just like fussy children who can't make up their minds what they want. Some of you think you're too good for John's baptism. You think he's a fanatic, that he's gone overboard. Then you turn around and criticize me because I don't make the same demands he does, saying I'm not strict enough."

The rebuke had made Simon stiffen. He knew exactly the incident the rabbi was referring to. Not long ago Levi, a Jew who'd sold out to the Romans, had thrown a big party for the rabbi—using tax money skimmed from the pockets of his fellow Jews, of course. Simon and the other Pharisees in town had refused to attend, making it clear they wouldn't eat at a table filled from Rome's trough. The Baptizer might be a little kinky, but at least he wasn't a traitor.

Simon had been stung by the rabbi's reproach. It wasn't fair to portray him and his fellow Pharisees as finicky or hard to please. In fact, the Pharisees were the only party in Palestine who cared both about God and about the lower classes. This radical young rabbi would be better off aligning himself with Pharisees than with those hotheaded Zealots. It's the Pharisees who manage to walk that narrow line between principles and pragmatism. If the man expects to survive, he could learn something from the Pharisees. Maybe it's time, in fact, someone taught the teacher a lesson.

Simon strokes his beard thoughtfully as a plan forms in his head. Why not invite the rabbi to dinner, just as that scoundrel Levi had? Hospitality to traveling teachers is, after all, on the official list of meritorious acts. Only this time, the teacher will be the student.

On the evening of Simon's dinner party, the tables are set up in the courtyard, low benches angled around them like petals on a daisy. Since the people in the village are excited about seeing the visiting celebrity, Simon, following the usual custom, arranges space for them inside the courtyard where they can observe the festivities and enjoy the entertainment. In fact, their presence is an essential part of his plan.

As the guests arrive, servants appear with basins of water, ready to wash the road dust from their feet. After washing their hands — all the way to the elbows — and waiting while a servant sprinkles attar of roses on their hair, the dinner guests stretch out on the benches, careful to lean on their left elbows, leaving the prescribed right hand free to reach for food. Such details, they know, are important to their Pharisee host.

When the visiting rabbi arrives, Simon, instead of rising to welcome the supposed guest of honor and greeting him with the traditional kiss of peace, ignores him. But he watches the rabbi stealthily from the corner of his eye to see how his plan will work. The rabbi stands for a moment, looking around at the assembled guests. Eventually he finds an empty spot on a bench where he sits down to take off his sandals. Having been instructed by their master to ignore the rabbi, the servants don't bring a basin of water for his feet or offer to perfume his hair.

Simon smiles to himself. The teacher is famous for his parables, the little stories he invents for instructional purposes. Well, let him enjoy telling this one. Let him call it "The Rabbi Learns Some Manners." The point should be clear to him by now. You don't publicly reprimand the pillars of a community without paying a price.

Simon is feeling more than a little smug about the success of his plan. Without speaking a word, without engaging in acrimonious debate, he has bested this new celebrity rabbi, put him in his place. He smiles and nods affably to his other guests. His little piece of performance art is working well; the rabbi has not dared to protest the lack of customary courtesy. Smart. Calling attention to the slight would only add to his humiliation. The rabbi admonishes his followers to take the lowest place at the table instead of grabbing the best bench. *Wait till the host invites you to move to a better spot,* he teaches. *Then everyone will get to see you being honored.*

Dream on, Simon chuckles to himself. Don't hold your breath, buddy, waiting for me to ask you to take the place of honor. Not at my table.

At this point, however, a small commotion develops just inside the entrance of the courtyard. Simon can't quite make out what it is—the lights from the oil lamps don't reach into the shadows along the walls. Some villager, probably drunk, wanting a closer look at the guests in their finery and the conversation of his betters. Fine, Simon thinks. The more witnesses to the rabbi's humiliation, the better. The people will see for themselves that, for all his cleverness, the teacher from Nazareth is no match for their local Pharisee.

It is only later, when a lone figure detaches itself from the shadows and comes within the circle of lamplight, that Simon grows concerned. The intruder is a woman, one who's no stranger to the assembled company. Her hair is loose around her face, a badge of her occupation—town prostitute.

Simon sits up now, alarmed. Has the clever rabbi planned his own surprise? Maybe he's hired this hooker to embarrass his host. If nothing else, her presence defiles the entire house, including his guests. Simon glances at Jesus, half expecting to see a smile of mocking triumph.

Instead, he sees tears—the woman's. And she's not laughing in derision, but wailing. In fact, she's making a spectacle of herself, sobbing and tossing her long, unbound hair about in an ecstasy of—what? Joy? Grief? Insanity? Is the woman drunk?

She staggers forward and collapses at the foot of the rabbi's bench. Babbling something incomprehensible, she grabs the man's feet and begins to cover them with kisses. Simon flinches in disgust.

The rabbi, however, doesn't move. For a long moment he's absolutely still until the woman's frenzied outburst wears itself out. Finally, she takes a deep, shuddering breath and begins to dab with her unkempt mop hair at the tears and mucus smeared on the rabbi's feet, as if to repair the mess she's made.

Still the rabbi doesn't move.

Then, hardly even daring to glance at him, the woman unstoppers the little vial of perfume she carries on a string around her neck and pours it on his feet.

Simon's eyes are darting around the tables at his other guests. What's going on here? Till now, he has vacillated in his assessment of this new teacher, believing him to be clever, a worthy opponent if nothing else. Now Simon sees he's been a fool. The man obviously is a fraud. It doesn't take a prophet to recognize the woman for what she is—a common whore. And no holy man would allow such degraded scum to fondle his feet in this disgusting manner.

But Simon's cunning does not desert him, not even in this moment of crisis. He controls his initial impulse to call for the servants and have them throw both this religious impostor and his woman out of the house. Doing that would only reveal he'd been duped, made to look like a fool. Now he's doubly glad he's openly snubbed the would-be rabbi. His guests will believe that he saw through the man from the beginning.

But then the guest himself speaks. "Simon," he says, apparently unruffled by the woman's scandalous performance, "let me tell you a story."

What? Simon thinks. You've got to be kidding. But he stifles this. "Go right ahead, rabbi." He gestures as if giving him the floor, and says the title of respect with a note of obvious sarcasm.

"Once upon a time," Jesus begins, "a banker loaned two people some money. One got twice as much as the other. But when the loans came due, neither debtor could pay up. So the banker simply wrote both debts off his books. Just like that. 'Paid in full.' Now then, tell me, Simon, which one of these bankrupt debtors is going to love that banker more?"

One corner of Simon's mouth lifts in a condescending smile as he gives the obvious answer. "My guess would be the debtor who owed him the most."

"Right on the money," the rabbi says. But he's not through. He gestures toward the woman still hunched at his feet. "You see this woman, Simon? When I got to your house this evening, no one offered me any water to wash my feet. This woman is the only one who's done that—and with her own tears. Then she used her hair to dry them. And another thing. No one greeted me with a kiss when I came in either, but she's more than made up for the lack. Look—she hasn't stopped kissing my feet. I got no perfume for my head like the other guests. But she used up her entire flask on me." He holds the vial upside down to demonstrate.

"Now let me tell you something, Simon," the rabbi continues. "She may have racked up a considerable number of sins in her line of work, but because she's also a woman who loves extravagantly, those debts will be wiped off the books for her. I'm not mentioning any names, but some people seem to think the debits to their account with God are minuscule. Those same people usually have a tiny little heart as well, one with very little room for love."

In the silence that suddenly descends upon the dinner party, Jesus turns to the woman at his feet and addresses her directly. "You don't have to worry," he tells her. "Your sins are forgiven."

There is a sharp intake of breath around the table. Who does this guy think he is anyway, the other guests think—God Almighty?

And as if to answer their unspoken reproach, Jesus repeats what he has just told the woman. "Because you believe in me," he says to her, "you're rescued from your fate. You don't have to worry. The slate's wiped clean."

And there, unfortunately, in the gospels' typically truncated fashion, the story ends. It leaves us with the usual unanswered questions. Did the other guests snicker behind their hands at Simon? Did the woman herself become one of the "certain women" who followed Jesus like groupies around Palestine? Did Simon, the host who tried to get the guest, get the point?

Chapter 24

Arguments about Life and Law:
Confrontations with Pharisees

*M*y generation will probably be the last that remembers "blue laws," those now antique attempts to impose Sabbath sanctity on the operation of businesses. Up till the 1960s, practically all stores, at least in my part of the country, were required by law to close on Sundays. Department stores, supermarkets, most service stations, in some places even movie theaters, shut down on that day. At most, a few restaurants in town stayed open in order to accommodate the after-church diners—although some congregations refrained from patronizing such establishments on Sunday, sometimes all week.

But life in general proceeded at a more peaceful pace then. Not only did our town observe the fourth commandment, to "remember the sabbath day, to keep it holy," it didn't have interstate highways punctuated with McDonald's, which would later encourage weekend trips and nonstop Sunday sports marathons. Particularly devout families sometimes had their own peculiar rules about what was and was not acceptable Sabbath behavior. In mine, for instance, no one was allowed to read the comics from the newspaper until after church. This will strike many as quaint or even silly today, but such customs were a way of following the commandment's injunction to "remember."

You never forgot it was Sunday when I was a child. You wore special clothes on that day—your "Sunday best," including your best underwear—and ate special food, usually pot roast or fried chicken. The day made a small blip of celebration in my parents' otherwise flat-line workweek. My father was glad to put aside his paintbrush and ladder, and my mother was grateful the Bible freed her from the wringer washer and clothesline at least one day a week. They were both thankful for their own rest and sympathetic with a like need in waitresses and delivery boys.

Probably only migrant field hands and employees of companies demanding long overtime hours are that physically exhausted today, however. As likely as not, we see Sunday as a chance for exercise, a time for physical exertion at a health club or ball game to make sure our muscles don't atrophy. We use the break to burn off the excess calories our jobs no longer demand. And those averse to exercise want entertainment, not reflection, distraction rather than rest. These days, we want *more* to do on Sundays, not less. For us the Sabbath means forgetting, not remembering.

No single subject was disputed more often between Jesus and the Pharisees than the kinds of activity permissible on the Sabbath. This was not a novel issue for debate then. The boundaries of Sabbath-keeping had been disputed for generations. The Pharisees and Sadducees had argued about whether the golden table in the Temple, where the twelve shewbread loaves were displayed, should be washed on the Sabbath.

Josephus, the historian, records that the Essenes were "stricter than any other of the Jews in resting from their labors on the seventh day." Not only would they not cook on the Sabbath, they wouldn't even pick up a dish. They took Sabbath-keeping to the unnatural extreme of not defecating on that day. But a band of Maccabean revolutionaries provide perhaps the most amazing example of devotion to the Sabbath. Escaping into caves, along with their wives and children, they refused to take up arms when attacked on the Sabbath, preferring to suffer martyrdom by suffocation from the fires set by the Roman soldiers rather than break the fourth commandment by defending themselves.

Most people, however, were willing to settle for following the thirty-nine rules set out in the Mishnah to define the prohibition against work. These included the obvious kinds of farm labor like plowing, reaping, and shearing sheep, but added minute indoor tasks such as separating two threads, tying or loosening a knot, writing two letters, or even erasing in order to write two letters. Later rabbinic writings expanded the list even further.

All religions tend to emphasize customs and practices that contribute to their adherents' visibility and make them distinct from the surrounding culture. One's spiritual devotion may be deep and genuine, but who knows that, if you look or act like everyone else? For outsiders to recognize a religion, it needs some conspicuous way to signal its existence. Who would notice Hare Krishnas, for instance, without their shaved heads and saffron robes? Would Sikhs seem so imposing if they wore baseball caps instead of white turbans? The Amish without their buggies, beards, and flat-brimmed hats would just be farmers. Hasidic Jews even today rely on their long side curls and black hats and coats as identifying marks of their orthodoxy.

For Jews of the first century, Sabbath keeping (along with the physical, though not as visible, sign of circumcision) provided the outward sign that set them apart from the surrounding pagans. Everyone in the Empire knew that Jews would not work or travel on the seventh day of their week. Not everyone, however, appreciated this mark of distinction. Apion, an anti-Semitic writer of the first century, ridiculed the Sabbath by attributing the derivation of the word to the Egyptian term for jock itch; the Jews escaping from Egypt, he claimed, would have grown mighty tender about the privates during the long trek to Canaan. Other gentiles simply saw Sabbath keeping as a Jewish excuse for laziness.

Whatever party they belonged to, most Palestinian Jews were committed to observing the Sabbath, though with varying degrees of rigor. The ordinary working-class Jew, one of the "people of the land," would celebrate the Sabbath meal when the sun went down on the sixth day of the week, recite the Sabbath prayers, take the day off. But he would be less careful than members of the various religious parties about whether he took one stitch or two to mend his tunic.

The Pharisees were probably more liberal than most sects in their interpretation of Sabbath restrictions, despite the way they are pictured in the popular imagination today. Rabbi Hillel and those of his school would have agreed with Rabbi Jesus that healing on the Sabbath was not only within the limits of the law but a fulfillment of it. Nevertheless, when a group of Pharisees see Jesus' companions swaggering through the fields, stripping off the heads of ripe grain as they go, they can hardly ignore such flagrant and public desecration of the day set aside by the Lord for rest. For strangers to "glean" from the fields—gather grain by hand rather than using a sickle—was indeed permissible under Torah law. But never on Sabbath! Such activity obviously constituted work. What were these men doing if not reaping? And more than that, what was rubbing the grain to loosen the husks if not threshing—another of the thirty-nine forbidden Sabbath activities?

From what we can tell, in both Mark's and Matthew's account, this incident takes place relatively early in Jesus' public ministry, either in or near Capernaum. In that town Jesus has already healed Peter's mother-in-law and the paralyzed man let down through the roof. Peter himself may have been a resident, though not a native, of Capernaum. Thus other matters may be at issue here.

First of all, there's the matter of turf. Pharisees were generally looked up to as leaders in their community. A number of Pharisees were present at the healing of the paraplegic who was let down through the roof in Capernaum. While a celebrity like Jesus might bring their town honor, put it on the theological map, the Pharisees must proceed cautiously with their hospitality. If this rabbi goes too far, he could just as easily bring disaster to Capernaum.

Then there's the problem of his growing band of followers. They're all unemployed now, having left their various occupations—some more honorable than others—and are becoming a drain on the area's resources. They're not just flouting religious rules, they're affecting the economics of the area. Is this ragtag band actually the beginnings of a peasants' revolt?

The situation is more complicated than the pared-down text shows on the surface. The disciples are obviously hungry (at least in Matthew's version), yet no one invites them to dinner. Why? For one thing, Sabbath meals differed from our Sunday pot roasts; the Jews ate leftovers. No food could be prepared on that day. And who would have planned for thirteen or more mouths to feed that Sabbath? Maybe Jesus and his band have already exhausted the town's hospitality. Or perhaps, being men and on the road, they have neglected to make arrangements the previous day for their own Sabbath meal. Or do they consider themselves such an elite corps, VIPs, Friends of Jesus, that they can get away not only with breaking the Sabbath but with vandalizing some local farmer's harvest? (Interestingly, none of the disciples are identified as farmers, men tied to the land and less likely to up and leave on a lark.)

Thus the Pharisees, as guardians of their community, confront the rabbi about the incident. While he has not been foraging for food himself, they hold him responsible for his companions' behavior. And they have every right to demand an explanation. Note that they do not form a posse to drive the looters out of the fields, or call 911 as we would do today if someone trespassed on our property. They keep the conflict rational, not physical. Explain yourself, they say. Give us one good reason your pupils should get away with breaking the Sabbath laws.

What do they expect? An apology? Some embarrassed comment about how boys will be boys? An appeal to their sympathy, one that emphasizes the men's hunger and homelessness? Or an ingenious argument based on the seven hermeneutical principles of Hillel? Whatever they expected, it certainly was not what they got—a response even more shocking than the arrogance of the disciples.

The rabbi, innocent himself of any wrongdoing, launches into a defense of his brash band of bodyguards. "Haven't you read the scriptures," he asks disdainfully, "the part about David when he was hiding out from Saul? What did David do when he and his guerrillas were being hunted down out in the wilderness? They were desperate, so they stole into some priest's shrine and ate the twelve loaves kept on the altar there for God. Now, as you know, that was strictly against the law. No one could eat that bread except the priests, and then only after it had lain there a week."

The Pharisees frown at one another. What's this insolent fellow getting at? What's his point? Surely he's not comparing himself to David, the hero of Israel?

But the rabbi is not content to leave it at that. "And surely men as learned as yourselves know that priests performing their duties in the Temple at Jerusalem are expending energy in ways that would qualify as work for ordinary Jews. Do you call the priests Sabbath breakers? Or do you consider them above the law?"

The furrows in the Pharisees' brows deepen. Worse and worse. First he compares himself to David, now to priests. Just who does this guy think he is?

Having led them to this overwhelming question, the rabbi finally presents them with an answer of sorts. "Don't worry," he says, "I'm not claiming to be a priest. I'm even more than a priest. I'm the Temple itself, the place where God lives. What's more, if God truly lived in you, you'd be more like him. You'd have a little mercy and not try to substitute rules for intentions. The Sabbath was invented in order to give human beings a break, remember? Not to make their lives harder."

At this, some of the Pharisees nod thoughtfully, recognizing Jesus' reference to a story about two rabbis arguing over whether it was permissible to save a life on the Sabbath. One of the rabbis appeals to a passage in Exodus that says, "And you shall keep the Sabbath, for it is holy to you." He ends his argument triumphally: "To you the Sabbath is handed over, but you are not handed over to the Sabbath." Now they can peg this rabbi theologically. He belongs to the school that emphasizes that the Sabbath is a gift, rather than a burden.

But just as the local Pharisees are about to recast their arguments, perhaps to make clear there's a difference between gifts and booty, the rabbi from Nazareth throws everything into confusion once more. As if fearing they may not have fully understood his former analogies, he makes one last and even bolder claim: "The Son of man is lord of everything, even the Sabbath."

The Pharisees are stunned into silence. Only the Messiah, when he arrives, will have the right to suspend the rules governing the Sabbath. They watch, speechless, as the young rabbi turns and marches away, not down the road that leads out of town, but straight to the synagogue, as if daring them to follow and see what will come next.

They shake their heads. If this man had only been content to be a liberal. If he had left those veiled analogies about David and the Temple hidden behind a screen of implication. Then they might have thought he was merely being metaphorical, aesthetically audacious. But you can't go around calling yourself Lord of the Sabbath. Not and get away with it. And no two-bit rabbi from Nazareth can expect anyone to think he's the messiah. Not when he can't even control his own followers. No. It's time this guy leaves Capernaum before he causes some real trouble.

Chapter 25

On Trial:

Before Pilate and the Sanhedrin

*I*n the first three gospels, most of Jesus' verbal battles are fought with the Pharisees and scribes of Galilee, a region with a well-developed reputation for theological controversy. Only later, when his fame has grown to alarming proportions, does the religious establishment in Jerusalem take an interest in the rabble-rousing rabbi from Nazareth.

On the other hand, over half of John's gospel takes place in the Jewish capital city. While the three synoptic gospels condense his trips to Jerusalem into one event, the gospel of John describes three separate occasions on which Jesus visited the city. And each of those times there was trouble.

According to John, Jesus drove the money changers and merchants from the Temple not long after beginning his public career. On his second visit to the city, during the autumn Feast of Booths, he did some very confrontational, even inflammatory preaching. At one point the Jerusalem Pharisees were ready to stone him for blasphemy. Only on his third visit does the rabbi from the Galilean backwaters succeed in badgering the allied forces of Rome and Jerusalem into getting rid of him. In this gospel, religious leaders looking for a fight have no trouble finding one when Jesus is around. John's Jesus is neither gentle, meek, nor mild, but caustic, provocative, and incendiary. The kind of troublemaker people in the South called an "outside agitator" during the '60s civil rights struggle.

In the '90s, a decade that glorifies consensus, we like to think improved communication is all that's needed to settle disputes.

But at some point in a controversy the two sides may understand each other perfectly; they simply have diametrically opposing views of reality. At the crossroads of two such irreconcilable paths, the final showdown between the rabbi from Nazareth and his religious and political adversaries begins.

Interestingly, however, Jesus modulates his response to his opponents during their final encounter. Whereas he has formerly been quick with a witty answer or a provocative question of his own, he suddenly subdues his combative tendencies. His enemies are still looking for a fight, but they find less fight in him. Instead, he appears to be engaging in a private war of attrition.

Of the four gospel authors, only the man responsible for John's claims to have been an eyewitness to this final confrontation. He, along with Peter, follows the band of Roman soldiers and Temple police back into the darkened city. The prisoner is taken to the house of Annas, the true power behind the Temple throne. Having been deposed as high priest a decade earlier, Annas subsequently finagled the post for four of his sons; Caiaphas, the current high priest, is his son-in-law.

Our eyewitness, described as "the other disciple," is allowed to enter Annas's palatial residence and observe the proceedings because he "was known to the high priest." Meanwhile, Peter huddles over a fire in the courtyard, fearful of being identified as part of Jesus' cadre.

Annas himself presides over the ecclesiastical examination of the rabbi who, earlier in the week, has ridden into the city on a donkey colt, the crowds greeting him like a king and roaring that here is the long-awaited messiah. Annas realizes the delicacy of the situation and just how much is at stake, both for the Jewish people at large and for him personally. The fortunes of his aristocratic family depend on dealing effectively with this pesky provincial prophet. What Rome hath given, Rome will just as quickly take away if Annas's dynasty fails to keep the unruly Jews under control. And there is an economic component to his distress as well. Annas and Sons own the Temple concession where worshipers buy their animals for sacrifice—the very stalls this radical rabbi emptied earlier. The Galilean rabbi is threatening not only his family's power and prestige with the Romans, but their income as well.

The Romans, of course, only care that the peace is maintained in this unpredictable city, especially now at Passover when patriotic uprisings habitually occur. Annas figures that Pilate, Rome's deputy in Jerusalem, having supplied a sizable military guard to arrest the rabbi, will be committed to seeing this affair through to its conclusion. Annas's role is to get enough information out of the prisoner to prepare a charge sheet and forward it to Pilate. That means the prisoner must be accused of sedition rather than heresy.

Rome, having a completely multicultural policy in all matters theological, refuses to deal with religious conflicts among the Jews, whom it has already granted a special dispensation from its usual rule of displaying the emperor's image in their Temple. Religious controversies being notoriously complicated, and, with all the diverse gods and practices across the Empire, it chooses to leave such matters to local ecclesiastical authorities.

Annas, as a priest, can only investigate the rabbi as a heretic, so he must somehow find a way to somehow link the heresy to sedition. The Sanhedrin may retain the right to have heretics stoned, but that would not be a wise move in this situation. Given the rabbi's current popularity, such a sentence might well lead to riots. If there's going to be trouble, better to let the Romans sentence the man and shift the responsibility to them.

The first questions Annas puts to the rabbi are purely theological. He asks the man to summarize his religious teachings and tell who his pupils are. These names will make up the list of coconspirators Annas will include with the charge.

But the Galilean, instead of answering the question, gives an insolent rejoinder: "I've made my teaching public from the start, both in the provincial synagogues and here in the Temple. The places ordinarily frequented by Jews. It's not like I've been hiding anything. In fact, why ask me? Ask those who've come to hear me speak. They can tell you."

Whap! Provoked by this impertinence, a Temple guard slaps the rabbi. "Who do you think you're talking to here, buster? Watch your mouth."

The rabbi blinks but shows no sign of defending himself. Except verbally, of course. "If you think I'm lying, then prove it. Otherwise, why rely on violence to make your case?" He looks, not at the guard, but at Annas as he adds, "Unless, of course, you think you haven't got a case."

Annas strokes his beard, considering. He had hoped to rely on mere intimidation. Better for any physical damage to the prisoner to occur here in his private quarters than in his son-in-law's official courtroom. But the Galilean rabbi is proving craftier than Annas had given him credit for. If the man had resisted, or even defended himself in a way that could be called resistance, Annas could lock him away until the Passover holiday was over. Now he's going to have to send the troublemaker to his son-in-law to make these proceedings legitimate.

"Take him to Caiaphas," Annas says, then adds, "and tie him up." The prisoner should at least look as if he's dangerous.

Caiaphas's quarters are just across the palace courtyard where Peter still huddles by the fire. The sight of his leader in chains is not reassuring. He glances quickly away.

After the official charge papers have been drawn up and Caiaphas has signed them, the party of armed guards form a phalanx around the prisoner and move on to the northwest corner of the Temple grounds. On this elevated spot overlooking the city sits the Fortress of Antonia, where the Roman judicial halls are located. It is almost dawn by now.

Inside, Pilate's servant shakes his master awake. The Roman deputy is not particularly pleased at being disturbed at this early hour, but he's been half expecting it. Passover is always the most difficult time of his official year. The servant tells him the Temple police are waiting outside, apparently with a prisoner in tow. They have declined to come in, the servant explains, for fear of profaning themselves on their festival day.

Pilate snorts at this, not amused by the quaint fastidiousness of these religious fanatics so early in the morning. He recalls now having supplied a phalanx of Roman soldiers to the Temple police the night before to help with holiday crowd control, but no matter how much you do for these people, he mutters, it's never enough. Give them an inch and they want a mile.

He saunters out onto the portico of his fortress, where the Temple guards are waiting with the prisoner. "Okay, okay," he growls, "what's this all about?" In the growing light he peers at the man in chains. He looks appropriately subdued. "He doesn't look exactly dangerous to me," Pilate says. "What's he done?"

The Temple police, used to being treated with more respect by their own people, answer a little stiffly, "We wouldn't be wasting your time, sir, if he hadn't broken our Law."

Pilate, still muzzy with sleep, rubs his face and then waves dismissively with one arm. "Law, schmaw," he says. "You people have so many laws I can't keep up with them all. Go judge him yourselves. Take him back to Caiaphas. Go on, get out of here."

The chief of police straightens himself, his chest jutting out in offended pride. "It's not the kind of case we're allowed to handle, sir. It's not only a religious matter. And it's a capital offense, besides."

Pilate inhales a long breath of the chill morning air and lets it out slowly while he runs his hand over his chest. Too risky, he decides, to blow this one off. "Okay," he finally says, "bring him on in." He motions to his Roman guards to take charge of the prisoner.

When they bring the rabbi in, Pilate is sitting behind his desk, reading the charge paper the Temple police had given him. He glances up at the man and studies him closely. "It says here that you think you're the king of the Jews," he says. "That right?"

Instead of denying the charge, the prisoner replies with no evident fear or dismay: "Is that your own idea or is that what they told you about me?" A crafty response—answering with a question.

Pilate throws up his arms. "Hey. Do I look like a Jew? What do I care about your religion's crazy ideas? It's your own people, you know, who say you claim to be a king. If that's not the real story, then tell me—what have you done to get them so riled up?"

The prisoner shakes his head as if doubting the governor's ability to grasp the situation. "You don't understand," he says. "If I am a king, it's not the kind you mean. If I were, do you think I'd be standing here in chains? If I'm trying to take over the government, where's my soldiers? If this were a revolution, wouldn't this army of rebels I'm supposed to be leading have risen up by now? Would they have let me get hauled before Caiaphas?" He shakes his head again. "You don't understand. It's not like that at all."

Pilate frowns. "But you haven't denied that you're a king."

The rabbi lifts his head, his old debating tactics taking hold for a moment. "King is your word. You're the one who keeps harping on that. My only intention—the whole reason for my existence—is to make the truth clear, plain as day." He looks at the governor skeptically before he adds, "At least to the ones who care about the truth."

It's Pilate's turn to shake his head now. "Right," he snorts. "And I suppose you've got a foolproof formula for truth."

Then the Roman governor shrugs and goes back out onto the portico, where the Temple police are waiting. But it occurs to him that someone in his position shouldn't have to be scurrying back and forth like this—in and out and back again—carrying messages between some scruffy rabbi and these holier-than-thou Jewish cops. "Okay," he tells them. "I've questioned the prisoner and as far as I can see, the guy's done nothing wrong. Why don't I just let him go? I know it's your big holiday, and I always let somebody free on your feast days. Why not this so-called King of the Jews?"

"But we don't want him," they exclaim. "No. If you're going to let somebody off, let it be Barabbas."

Barabbas? Now this is a surprise, Pilate thinks. The man's a proven rebel, already convicted. What is with these people? And, throwing up his hands in a gesture of aggrieved acquiescence, he goes back inside once again to face the prisoner.

Pilate stares at the man a long moment, pondering. He can't afford to make a mistake here. Maybe the prisoner's just being crafty, trying to get him off track by talking philosophy. Maybe what he needs is a touch of the whip to bring out the real truth. Lots of prisoners confess once they're presented with a little pain. And if that doesn't work, maybe a good whipping will at least placate those obstinate Temple guards.

"Okay,"—he motions to his own guards—"have him flogged." Pilate waits while his soldiers have their fun with the rabbi. For some reason, he's not amused this morning with their mockery, much less their brutality. He's eager to get this business over with. The prisoner is led back in, his back bloody beneath the purple cloak the guards have dressed him in, lampooning him as a king crowned with a twisted wreath of thorns. Pilate nods, then goes out once again onto the portico. The Temple guards have now been joined, he notices, by their masters, Annas and his brood. They give him a suspicious stare, as if hoping to catch him in some bureaucratic slipup.

"All right," he shouts at them in exasperation, "here he is. You can see for yourselves. I've had him flogged, trying to get a confession out of him, but he hasn't made a peep."

At his signal, the Roman guards bring the battered rabbi out onto the porch. Pilate, hoping the delegation from the Temple will yield now that they've seen the state the man is in, takes a more placating tone. "See? I don't really think the man's guilty. Do you?"

"What?" they say. "You've got to be kidding. You know the penalty for insurrection. It's crucifixion, not some piddling little scourging."

Now Pilate is thoroughly exasperated. "Fine!" he cries. "You want him dead, you kill him. I don't want any more to do with him."

"But he's got to die," the crowd at the bottom of the steps shout at him. "He's a blasphemer. He calls himself God! Don't you understand what that means to us? It's our duty to see he dies for that."

So why don't they stone him as a heretic? Pilate wonders. Why insist he be crucified as an enemy of the Empire? Looking down at Annas and his gang, he can tell these people are looking for a fight. He suddenly has an uneasy feeling that, unless they get what they want, the chief priest and his family will find a way to make him look bad in Rome.

Pilate takes Jesus back inside his judicial chambers to think over his options and the consequences of exacerbating his already strained relations with the Temple officials. He'd started out so well in his new assignment. He'd kept these people happy by reconfirming Caiaphas as the ruling high priest. But after that, nothing has gone right. There was the water project fiasco—who could have predicted the Temple bureaucrats would object to a project that would benefit their own operations? That episode had ended in a riot, and the commander he'd sent to quell it had let his soldiers get out of hand. Whatever support Pilate had among the common people was lost after that.

Of course, Passover is just beginning, and he does have Caiaphas's priestly regalia locked up in his own fortress vault. Without his official costume, the high priest can't perform whatever mumbo jumbo he does over there in their Temple. But if Pilate plays that card, he knows he'll have a full-fledged rebellion on his hands. And his one hope of getting out of this godforsaken place lies in keeping the peace. Why won't Caiaphas and his buddies take care of this guy themselves? They wouldn't hesitate to kill anyone who happened to stumble into the wrong room over there in their Temple. And they even stone the odd wife who gets caught in the wrong bed from time to time. So what's the reason they want him to do their dirty work for them? Why do they want to make this into a federal case?

He sighs and looks over at the prisoner. Should he be going to so much trouble for this bedraggled fellow anyway? That's the real question.

"Look," he finally says, "don't you see that your life is in my hands? I can either have you crucified or I can let you go. But you've got to give me something to go on here. Something to tell those folks outside that will satisfy them. And none of that truth crap this time, either."

The rabbi looks at him and shakes his head once again, one side of his face already swelling from the beating he's taken. "No," he says, "you're wrong."

"Wrong? What do you mean? Look, I know these people. If I can throw them a sop—"

"No, that's not what I mean. I mean it's not up to you. This really doesn't even concern you. This fight is between me and the people outside. And they're not going to give up. You're just in the wrong place at the wrong time—you don't have any control here."

Pilate stares at him in disbelief. "Well, if that don't beat all." This is the first time he's ever been lectured by a prisoner whose life was in his hands. "Okay, buddy," he says, taking a long breath, "I'm going out there and give it one more shot. But that's it. After that, I'm done with the whole business. You understand?"

The prisoner looks at him but doesn't speak. And somehow, even before Pilate walks out for the last time onto the portico to make a final appeal, he suddenly sees what the outcome is going to be. Caiaphas will play the Caesar card. He can hear the crowd, grown into a mob now, beginning to chant: "See-zur, See-zur, See-zur." Caiaphas and his henchmen have convinced the people that the rabbi is a political prisoner. Which leaves Pilate no choice.

The fight is over. That much is clear. He just isn't sure who's won.

Chapter 26

A Fight:
Hard Choices

*L*ots of people want to fight with God. Bright young people usually want to fight *about* him, to debate his existence. But when, like Job, we come up against injustice or personal tragedy, we somehow assume God's existence and begin to question his purposes, his motives, or simply his good sense. Even atheists shake their fists at heaven.

But who would want to fight with Jesus, that icon of love, trust, peace, and mercy? He displays all the attributes we don't always credit his Father with having. Even in Mrs. Batcher's scenario—the one where Jesus comes to your house and finds your room a mess—we can imagine Jesus turning his soulful, disappointed gaze on you, not scolding or threatening. Mrs. Batcher's Jesus would probably help you straighten up the mess before your folks got home.

And to give the lady her due, Mrs. Batcher's version of Jesus shares some qualities, at least tangentially, with the man who defended the prostitute washing his feet with her tears. In the Gospels, Jesus is often merciful and compassionate. He frequently speaks up for the underdog, whether sinner, Samaritan, child, or charity case. And, of course, that's the Jesus we would all exploit. Because most of us think of ourselves as underdogs. When Nietzsche called Christianity a religion of slaves, he was thinking of this aspect of human psychology—our invincible belief in our own victimhood.

The people in the gospels who came to Jesus looking for a fight did not, however, think of themselves as underdogs. If anything, they saw themselves as the top dogs, the ones with the answers. Unlike Job, who acknowledged he couldn't win his fight with the Almighty, the Pharisees and law professors who comprised most of Jesus' adversaries fully expected to win their arguments with the Galilean rabbi.

Nor did the rabbi ever back away from these confrontations. I suspect, in fact, he welcomed them since they provided an important public forum for his ideas. Engaging intellectual and moral leaders in debate validated him as a person worth listening to in those communities he toured. And he proved a worthy opponent. He could riposte and parry with the experts in that verbal swordplay for which the Jews were famous. He knew all the vocabulary, the reference points, the rhetorical strategies of the various rabbinical schools. He was aware of the political and theological factions in Palestine and the shifting alliances and enmities among them. And while it would obviously have been expedient for him to make common cause with, say, the Pharisees, whose interests most closely coincided with his, he seemed determined to demarcate clearly his own agenda.

These controversies, in fact, gave him public definition. He used them to show who he was not—a neo-Pharisee, merely improving on the past. In order to say positively who he was, he had to cut his closest ties—the ones to his family and his ecclesiastical party. Fighting free of those deceptive similarities meant fighting hardest against those with whom he had the most in common. And fighting, as Mrs. Batcher often told us, is not nice.

But being nice does not break through ambiguity barriers. By being nice, Jesus could have been accepted as an innovative rabbi and lived a long and productive life. Instead, he chose these defining verbal battles. Because there's just no easy way to tell people you're God. No nice way to put it.

Jewish scholar Jacob Neusner makes precisely this point in his book *A Rabbi Talks with Jesus*. By clarifying his disagreements with Jesus, Neusner proves a more astute apologist for the Christian faith than many Christians who would melt definitions down into a homogenous spiritual goo. Ignoring the differences between

the world's religions is the only way some well-intentioned ecu-
menists can see to foster goodwill and tolerance. Yet Rabbi
Neusner exhibits both these qualities without sacrificing his own
clarity. Imagining himself among the audience at one of Jesus' debates, he allows that "no thoughtful person could have heard such
challenging words and turned away indifferent." But he realizes
that the Galilean iconoclast who allowed his followers to gather
grain on the Sabbath "was not just another reforming rabbi, out to
make life 'easier' for people."

Jesus' claim to authority is at issue, not the more lenient, or less
lenient, character of his rulings on what we do on the holy day. At
issue here as everywhere else is the person of Jesus himself.

Neusner finds Judaism's deepest value in the ways it creates and
sustains a community. Keeping the Sabbath, he would argue, as
with all the other commandments, was made, not for the benefit of
the individual, but for the community. Neusner concludes his
imagined argument with the Galilean rabbi by deciding not to become one of his disciples. "Can I say why in one word?" he says.
"Yes, because for Jesus, 'you' is as often singular as plural. But for
the Torah, from Sinai onward, 'you' is always plural."

Israel is more important to Neusner than individuals. And this
is indeed a defining point that separates the first-century from the
twentieth-century rabbi. And it is also the point of the story about
Simon the Pharisee's dinner party.

As with the debates, the key to this story lies in its public setting.
Without that context, neither Simon's behavior nor the woman's
humiliation would mean much. What these two people want from
Jesus is, however, quite different. Simon's motives for inviting
Jesus to dinner are probably mixed. On the one hand he is curious
about the new rabbi. Such a celebrity could be a feather in his social
cap. On the other hand, the Pharisee is taking a certain risk by
inviting the man to his house. The rabbi has no official sanction by
any ecclesiastical accrediting agency. Simon probably thinks he is
doing Jesus a favor by asking him to his home.

The woman, on the other hand, has nothing to lose. She wouldn't
dream of debating theological issues or scoring telling points with

the new teacher. As a prostitute, she can't sink any lower on the social scale, no matter what kind of fool she makes of herself. She already knows the host and his friends despise her. Her loose hair, her weeping, her extravagant spilling of the perfume—all these are signs of an overwrought sensibility. From the safe distance of twenty centuries, we tend to sentimentalize this woman whom few of us would willingly admit to our own homes. But imagine this emotional display taking place during the "sharing time" of your local church service. Wouldn't we all break out in a cold sweat? The woman calls attention to herself in a way that—if we are honest—shocks our sensibilities. We might even complain that she was putting her individual needs above those of the community.

In our easy sentimentalizing, we often miss Jesus' response to this outburst. He does not, in fact, gather her to his bosom, shush her sobbing, or thank her for dousing him with perfume. Though she may have craved that kind of attention, it's not what she gets. Instead, the prostitute receives what she needs most: forgiveness, assurance, emotional stabilizing. "Go in peace," he tells her.

Did Simon get the fight he was looking for? Did his strategy of shaming his guest succeed? Simon wins round one by inviting the rabbi to his home, thus scoring points for hospitality to a traveling teacher. He also wins round two, ironically, by snubbing his guest. He succeeds in making Jesus look like a mere hanger-on. But Simon loses the third and crucial round when the prostitute's extravagance puts to shame the shabby hospitality the Pharisee has offered the guest of honor. The value of her act would not have been clear, however, without Jesus' story about the two debtors— a clever trap that caught the conscience of the Pharisee. The wily rabbi, who had waited patiently at the lowest seat during dinner, finally outwits Simon by comparing his hospitality unfavorably to the town prostitute's.

Jesus freely chose to participate in these public debates and semipublic dinner parties at which he was the featured after-dinner speaker. At those events, he understood the rules of engagement and manifestly relished his triumphs. A trial, however, is a different kind of fight, one that's not optional. On that night when the soldiers invade the olive grove are his companions are sleeping, the rabbi suddenly becomes the underdog himself. The encounter is no longer a debate, but an arraignment. Instead of questions about Torah, there are accusations against the man. The rules have abruptly changed. Quick wit, skillful stratagems, pithy stories will not work here.

But the issue is still the same; as Neusner saw even in the Sabbath debates, the question is still about Jesus' identity. The rabbi identifies himself to the contingent of arresting officers as "Jesus of Nazareth," not once but twice. When he is arraigned before Annas and Caiaphas, they demand the names of his followers. His refusal earns him his first blow in what now degenerates from a war of words to physical assault. In Pilate's judicial chambers, the matter becomes even clearer. "Are you the king of the Jews?" the Roman governor asks Jesus outright.

Everything hinges on the reply to that question. All the debates, the dinner parties, the open-air sermons, every public utterance of the rabbi have led to this defining moment. *Who are you?* The question tunnels through the existential wormhole of the centuries, afflicting us just as it did Pilate. But as with John the Baptist and his own disciples, Jesus refuses to answer for Pilate. Like beauty in the eye of the beholder, recognition comes only from the heart of the questioner. It's a riddle the rabbi refuses to solve for us.

You've got to feel sorry for Pilate, though. He never actually went looking for Jesus. This rabbi, a native of his enemy Herod's province, was simply thrust under his nose to deal with. Sleep-starved, career-hungry, Pilate lacks the spiritual equipment of Jesus' Jewish adversaries. During periods of rampant anti-Semitism, the high priests have often been given the lion's share of the blame for the crucifixion; in that scenario, the Roman deputy is a mere pagan pawn in an internecine plot. But when Jesus tries to give him a few hints about his identity—"my kingdom is not of this world"—Pilate dismisses all metaphysical inquiry with his famous sardonic reply: "What is truth?" That rhetorical question has served as the slogan for spiritual sloth ever since. Anything I can't define, Pilate insists, doesn't exist. The less I seek to understand, the less I'm responsible for.

If Pilate comes to no decision about his prisoner's identity, Jesus does succeed in planting a seed of doubt in the governor's mind—"You would have no power over me unless it had been given you from above," he tells Pilate before he is sent to his death. By refusing to define himself as a victim, by making it clear that he chooses this death, Jesus uses this last confrontation to intimate his identity.

Thus, even as a prisoner, Jesus appears to have got what he wanted from these fights. But what about his adversaries?

Simon the Inhospitable Host got more than he bargained for—or less, depending on how you look at it. Just as in the Psalms, the proud man is humbled.

But the Capernaum Pharisees who accuse Jesus' disciples of Sabbath breaking—what did they get out of their confrontation? They challenged Jesus directly, and they got an equally straight-forward response. Jesus, to Mrs. Batcher's chagrin, appeared to relish the full-body slams of rabbinic debate as much as his opponents did. He never declined comment; he never let good manners get in the way of a good argument. But he was a canny debater, and if you tried to maneuver him into a hole, he would simply pop up in a different place on the playing field. Some of those Capernaum Pharisees undoubtedly went away mad. Others probably left puzzled. Some may have been convinced. But none were dismissed or patronized.

If your quarrel with the rabbi went deeper, however, and became, like his official interrogators' in Jerusalem, a duel to the death, then that was a different matter. Then he would let you have what you wanted. He would let you kill him.

And if you were caught up like Pilate in the crossfire of circumstances, uncertain of the consequences? If you think truth too obscure, too indefinite to bother with? He might give you a little help, a few hints. But in the end, even though his life depended on it, he would leave the choice to you.

PART VII

LOOKING FOR A REASON TO HOPE

I suffer from no crippling diseases, nor am I blind or deaf. So far as I know, I'm not possessed by a demon. I'm neither politically oppressed nor a social outcast. So I have had to imagine how Jesus looked to people seeking a remedy for those kinds of distress. Nevertheless, despite my privileged and generally healthy state, like all but a small percentage of people blessed with persistently sanguine personalities, I have known moments of despair, when Thomas Hobbes's description of life—"solitary, poor, nasty, brutish, and short"—looked fairly accurate. What I learned in college to call "the human condition" is always tinged with dark knowledge and fear. That we die; that we are futile; that we are alone. And no amount of money, power, or muscle tone can hold back our inevitable fate.

Despair appears to be a cross-cultural phenomenon. No civilization is without its expressions of angst. Though we like to think it's a twentieth-century invention, a psychic infirmity brought on by the industrial revolution or the threat of nuclear holocaust, the truth is that the human race has shown signs of hopelessness ever since it began keeping records. A generation or two before Jesus, the Roman philosopher Lucretius wrote, "Life is one long struggle in the dark." Ecclesiastes, written centuries earlier, states its theme repeatedly: "Vanity of vanities . . . all is vanity." And one of the world's oldest manuscripts, an Egyptian papyrus written two millennia before Jesus, is titled "The Man Who Was Tired of Life."

What accounts for such a persistently bleak outlook on life? Is despair just a part of our physical makeup—a result of insufficient serotonin? Certainly some people are observably more prone to depression than others. Is the cause genetic? Behavioral conditioning? Then why don't children from the same families have matching happiness quotients? Despite modern pharmacology and psychoanalysis, we still have not located the dark and hidden headwaters of despair.

Certainly no one should be deceived with a promise that religious conversion provides a surefire remedy. Some spiritual giants have, in fact, suffered terrible bouts of melancholy. Luther felt personally assailed by the devil. The poet William Cowper, who wrote words to some of the finest hymns in the English language, attempted suicide at least twice. C. S. Lewis spent his last days tormented by grisly, desperate dreams. The phrase "dark night of the soul" was, after all, invented by St. John of the Cross, one of the Doctors of the Church. A highly tuned spirituality may, it seems, actually deepen despair, opening one's eyes to an abyss those with duller vision don't see.

Despair focuses our attention on death, loss, and futility. Unlike the other primates with whom we share certain characteristics, only humans know that we will die. And not only ourselves, but everyone we love. Nothing lasts in this mutable world. Not our best efforts nor our finest moments. What we hold today will slip from our grasp tomorrow. So why struggle to attain even worthy goals? What's the use? Our intelligence, beauty, strength, all we possess will eventually be taken by time. Such a bleak view of existence even has biblical support. The author of Ecclesiastes, purportedly a man enjoying all the comforts the ancient world had to offer, reacts to this universal human fate with bitter simplicity:

> And I thought the dead, who are already dead more fortunate
> than the living who are still alive; but better than both is he
> who has not yet been, and has not seen the evil deeds that are
> done under the sun.

This is despair in extremis—the desire not merely to die but never to have been born. A negation of creation itself.

Job's wife also counsels despair when the couple are faced with the loss of all their possessions, their position, even their children. "Dost thou still retain thine integrity?" she mocks her husband as he sits on his ash heap, covered with boils. "Curse God, and die." Job, however, refuses, clinging to his integrity, insisting on his innocence before God. Unlike their Greek contemporaries in the first century, the Jews did not consider suicide an honorable or heroic death. When King Saul, defeated by David's army, falls on his sword at Gilboa, he becomes the single Jewish suicide in the Hebrew scriptures.

Judas is the single case of suicide in the New Testament. According to Matthew's gospel, his remorse over his betrayal of Jesus was greater than his ability to believe in his victim's forgiveness. Here, then, is yet another cause for despair—a preoccupation not with what has been done to you, but with what you have done to someone else. Such shame is deepened by the knowledge that the deed cannot be undone, that no amends are possible. What if you backed out of your driveway, felt a muffled thud, and discovered you had run over your child? Or if you mistakenly gave someone a fatal dose of the wrong medicine? But those are accidents, not involving purpose or will. Now suppose that in a momentary fit of pique or spite or frustration you did something that destroyed a person you cherish. Wouldn't you spend the rest of your life running that film backward, anguished by the impossibility of undoing what you'd done? Not being able to live with yourself leads inevitably to the suicide's conclusion.

Undoing the past, bearing the present, anticipating the future. When these seem impossible, beyond our abilities, despair is our only option. Our vision narrows, first to a tunnel, then to a pinprick, ultimately to darkness. Nor is this darkness merely metaphoric. People in extreme states of depression literally cannot perceive color; the world becomes a wash of gray. The body's physiological processes simply begin to shut down under the psychological pressure of despair.

No doubt this is why Gregory the Great, one of the Doctors of the Church, linked despair with sloth when he drew up his list of the Seven Deadly Sins. Generally speaking, if you cannot lift up your heart, you usually can't lift your hand to comb your hair or wash your face either, much less go to work or pay the bills. Instead you crawl in bed and turn your face to the wall. Infants abandoned in their cribs with no one to hold or touch them become lethargic and unresponsive to stimuli. Obviously, you don't need to name this malaise to suffer its effects.

Tradition calls Jesus' last words from the cross—"My God, my God, why hast thou forsaken me?"—the cry of dereliction. Did Jesus himself despair? Was he a derelict, an emotional vagrant, cut loose from his moorings to the Father he was always talking about? Did he, like Judas, give up hope? Was it necessary for him to hit the same bottom his betrayer had in order to justify the claim that he was "as we are in every respect tempted"?

Hope, which St. Paul lists as one of the theological virtues, is probably the most neglected of the three. Hope seems trifling when compared to love, which the apostle declared greatest. It even comes off a poor second to faith, that sustaining hardtack on which the righteous are said to live. Yet even the unrighteous can hope. Not only can, but must. Peter, despite his denial of Jesus, still hoped for forgiveness. That proved the difference between him and Judas. And David sinned as much and as grievously as his predecessor, Saul. But after mourning the death of his child as just punishment for his sins, David astonished his court by washing his face, getting dressed, and beginning to live again. Hope made the difference.

Hope makes life possible. It's as necessary to the high rollers as to the homeless. People can live without a lot of things—air-conditioning, television, automobiles. Even, for a time, food. But no one can live without hope.

Chapter 27

Where Is He When You Need Him?
Martha of Bethany

*I*t's evident in the gospels that women were attracted to Jesus. In fact, the number of women featured in these stories is yet another way they deviate from historical narratives of their period. Josephus, Tacitus, and Pliny include few women in their accounts, and those usually from the aristocracy. Yet the gospels are filled with women, most of whom are at best middle class.

About half the people Jesus healed were women. He has some of his longest conversations with them. And they form the economic backbone of his traveling band. Yet the men who wrote the gospels were not exactly feminists. With the possible exception of Luke, they probably made no conscious effort to impose a gender quota on their historical narratives. Still, the number of women drawn to this charismatic rabbi was simply so large and the role they played so crucial that to chronicle his life without including them would have been impossible.

Our age, reflecting its own preoccupations, has attempted to make the rabbi's appeal sexual. Nikos Kazantzakis, the Greek novelist, explored this interesting possibility in his novel *The Last Temptation of Christ*. While hormones and romantic fantasy no doubt accounted for a goodly number of groupies pursuing Jesus, only someone with limited understanding of women would claim that his primary appeal for them was sexual. Jesus' appearance is never described in the gospels—we don't know if he was short or tall, fat or thin, handsome or homely—but it's unlikely that work-hardened fishermen and Zealot freedom fighters would have followed a gigolo rabbi or a first-century Rasputin.

I suspect that women liked Jesus primarily for one reason: he paid attention to them. He struck up conversations with them, listened to their problems, even paid them the supreme compliment of believing they were teachable—an assumption rare in those days, even among the most liberal Pharisees. In fact, though Jews had an obligation to teach Torah to their male children, their daughters routinely went uneducated.

In the town of Bethany, just a bit farther up the road from the olive orchard where Jesus would later be arrested, lived two sisters, Mary and Martha. Though over the centuries tradition has cast Mary in the role of mystical contemplative, she was also the intellectual one and a pupil of the rabbi's. When Jesus visited the sisters' home, where he appeared to be a frequent guest, she sat among the men listening to the Galilean rabbi's teaching. But while Mary is studious and reflective, her sister Martha does the talking—and rules the roost.

I know this woman. I work at a college run by nuns. I worship at churches managed by women. Martha is the church organist who never misses a service for thirty years. She's the head of the Outreach Committee, the president of the Hospital Auxiliary, the one who organizes potlucks and makes sure there're poinsettias at Christmas and lilies at Easter. While she's the power behind the pulpit, she does not aspire to ordination. Nevertheless, she is fully aware that without her behind-the-scenes support the whole spiritual enterprise would come crashing down around everyone's ears. We rarely worry about such bustling, practical people losing heart. We assume their very competence is itself a fortress against feelings of helplessness.

This indelible impression of Martha comes from Luke, who tells a story of an earlier visit Jesus made to her home in Bethany. The rambling rabbi used the village as a staging ground for his forays into Jerusalem, probably because he felt safer in that suburban setting among friends than in the city, surrounded by his powerful enemies. We never learn just how the rabbi came to be friends with Martha and her two siblings, Mary and Lazarus. We do know, however, that Martha owns the house in which they live. From that fact we deduce that she was the oldest child and either a widow or a spinster. I opt for the second choice, since women whose husbands had died were most often designated by the title "widow of," while this woman is always plain "Martha."

A spinster she may be, but in her house she calls the shots. She doesn't hesitate to complain to Jesus when her younger sister leaves all the dinner preparations to her. Though she is a homeowner, she obviously does not have a staff of servants to handle these chores. The rabbi defends the slacker, Mary, however.

"Martha, Martha," he says, shaking his head. "You worry too much. Didn't I tell you not to go to any trouble?"

Martha's face, already red from slaving over a hot stove, flushes even darker. Her lips tighten to a thin line.

"Look," he adds, "you can join us if you like. We can eat leftovers. Mary chose something else besides cooking—and I can't take that away from her."

"Sure," Martha probably mutters as she bustles back into the kitchen. And left me with all the dirty work. Leftovers, indeed. As if she *had* enough leftovers to feed all that rowdy gang of the rabbi's. That's the trouble with men—they think food just magically appears out of thin air, that the tooth fairy washes the dishes. It never occurs to them that *someone* actually has to spend time cooking the food. Or shopping for it. Or cleaning up afterward.

But the Marthas of the world, for all their peevishness, never give up. That's why they're still at the organ thirty years later, having seen any number of pastors come and go. That's why people turn to them in times of crisis—when the toilet overflows or the altar guild can't find the Pentecost paraments. They're the ones who know where everything is and the way it's always been done. They're aware that people snicker at them behind their backs, but that does not deter them. They know nothing would get done without them, that even their detractors depend on them. So they gather up the reins a bit more firmly and keep on heading for the moral high ground.

Which is why, when she later finds herself in the midst of a crisis she can't fix, Martha is dazed and dumbfounded. Her own

competence has betrayed her into believing all ills are curable, all
woes temporary.

When, as John records this story, her brother Lazarus falls ill,
Martha takes immediate steps. She puts him to bed, doses him
with her stock of herbal remedies, and forces fluids down his
fevered throat. But he only grows worse. Before long, Martha
sees that the disease has progressed past her ability to treat. She
still has confidence, however, that her friend the rabbi can take
care of the situation. After all, he's healed many a case worse than
this.

The rabbi, however, is at least a day's journey from Bethany at
this point. After an incident in Jerusalem that almost ended in his
stoning, he has retreated to the province of Peraea on the east side
of the Jordan. Rumor has it that the Temple officials plan to elim-
inate this troublemaker who consistently challenges their authority. Since she knows that the rabbi's return might well put his own
life in danger, Martha sends a messenger to Jesus in Peraea. She
does not beg him to come to Bethany, however. Oh, no. Not only
would she not jeopardize his safety, she knows he needn't be physically present to heal her brother. The message she sends, then, is
simply this: "Sir, I think you should know that your friend Lazarus
is quite ill." That should do it.

But it doesn't.

When the messenger returns, Martha is waiting for him anx-
iously. Lazarus as yet shows no sign of improving. She questions
the messenger: "What did Jesus say? What did he do? Did he give
any instructions?"

"Don't worry," he assures her. "The rabbi says it's not fatal. He
says it's all going to work out—and your brother's illness will in
the end bring glory to God."

Martha sighs in relief. Fine then. Everything's going to be fine.
She doesn't always understand the rabbi—not like Mary—but she
does believe in him. She knows he can do this. She stays by her
brother's bed, bathing his burning face to bring down the fever.
She never doubts the rabbi for a moment. If Jesus has promised recovery, then he'll make sure it happens.

But Lazarus continues to grows worse. And during the night he dies.

After that last breath has rattled in his throat, Martha sits there, holding the limp hand, feeling it grow cold as the fever drains away. She stares at her brother's body. This can't be happening. The rabbi promised. She *believed*. Her eyes are wide open and dry as dust. Betrayed by a promise, bereft of her brother. Like a sleep-walker, she gets up and leaves the room to start hunting for the nec-essary supplies—linen cloth, spices, a board on which to straighten the body. The law, she knows, requires that Lazarus be buried be-fore nightfall.

Martha moves like an automaton through that day and the next and the next. She lowers all the beds to the floor—the traditional sign of mourning—and accepts the food her neighbors bring in. A good thing too, because the house soon fills with mourners, and for once she doesn't feel like cooking. She doesn't feel like doing any-thing, in fact. It takes all her self-control to face the long week of official mourning and the curiosity seekers it brings from Jeru-salem. She's thankful that custom requires her to sit on the floor, her head covered with a shawl; that way she can avoid answering their questions. Nevertheless, she can't escape hearing them whis-per among themselves.

"Didn't they send for that wonder-worker they're so crazy about?"

"Isn't he supposed to be a big friend of theirs? Doesn't he stay here every time he's in town?"

"I wonder why he didn't come?"

"Where is he, anyway?"

Their questions are like hot knives through her heart because they are her questions too, the very protests she silently puts to the absent rabbi again and again in her head. But nowhere, not in her heart nor in her head nor in the deafening silence, can she hear an answer. I trusted him and he failed me, she keeps thinking. That's what I get for depending on someone else. I should have taken care of it my-self—found a doctor, maybe in Jerusalem. But no. I believed the message he sent. And now there's no undoing what's happened.

For she doesn't see this as simply the rabbi's failure. As the oldest, she's feels accountable for this loss. She trusted someone else to deal with a situation that it was her business to handle. Her friend has let her down, yes. And that disappointment in itself is bitter. But even worse is her own failure: her belief that she could simply give over her burden to him. Now she's going to have to live the rest of her life with the knowledge that she failed.

Finally, four days after the funeral, someone slips into the roomful of mourners and whispers in Martha's ear the message she has been dreading to hear: "The rabbi is coming. He wants to see you. Will you meet him at the tomb?"

Martha manages to slip out of the house unnoticed, grateful for once that the guests are paying more attention to Mary than to her own silent grief. Making her way over the rocky path to the cave-pocked cliffs that serve as the Bethany cemetery, she thinks how ironic that the rabbi should show up today. For at this point, death is the only thing she's certain of. She's already made the obligatory third-day visit to the tomb, when the body must be officially certified as dead.

The rabbi is standing at the mouth of the tomb, his ragtag ruffians hanging back among the rocks, obviously too ashamed to look her in the eye. Martha, always plainspoken, has, without even realizing it, been waiting for this moment. Her grief finally finds an outlet in anger.

"So," she says, looking the rabbi up and down with a freezing stare, "I see you finally made it." Her breath explodes in what passes for a bitter laugh. "It's a little late now, don't you think?" But even as she accuses the rabbi, her voice cracks. "If only you'd been here, this wouldn't have happened. Why did you let him die? Why? God always gives you everything you want. My brother—your friend—would have been spared if only you'd asked. Don't you care? Didn't you love him?"

The rabbi's face is like a mirror of her own grief. She sees reflected there not the defensive wariness she might have expected, not even shame or guilt. Only undisguised, naked grief. So that suddenly, as if the pressure of her unshed tears has finally broken through the wall of rancor she's raised around her heart, Martha at last begins to weep.

Jesus puts out a hand and grips her shoulder as she sobs. "Your brother is going to rise again," he says at last, giving her shoulder a little shake of affirmation.

But Martha has heard this kind of feeble comfort for days from her Pharisee friends. She pulls back from his grasp, not wanting this pie-in-the-sky consolation. "I know, I know. Just as they teach you in catechism class: 'The dead will rise again on the last day.'"

"No, Martha, that's not what I mean," the rabbi insists. "Look at me. *I'm* the resurrection. Life itself comes from *me*. As long as you believe in me, you don't have to worry about dying. In fact, you can't die. Not really. Don't you believe this?"

Martha frowns. She doesn't understand what he's talking about. How can you believe what you don't understand? What does that mean, *he's* the resurrection? The resurrection will only happen at the end of time. Or when the Messiah comes. Is that what he's getting at? Is the end actually as near as some of his followers claim?

"Well," she says cautiously, "I can believe that you're the Messiah. The one God has sent to rescue us."

He looks as if he might say something more, but before he speaks Martha turns away. "I'm going to get Mary," she calls back over her shoulder. Mary—the clever one, the sensitive one. Maybe she'll understand what he's talking about. For the first time in her life, Martha feels dependent on this younger sister. Maybe her impractical, flighty little sister can help her grasp what's going on here.

Though dazed by her meeting with the rabbi, when Martha gets back to the house she gathers her wits enough to slip quietly into the room where Mary sits on the floor surrounded by mourners. Bending down, Martha whispers, "Don't let on, but the rabbi has returned at last. He's out at the graveyard and he wants to see you."

Martha has intended for her sister to copy her own caution, but as usual Mary's emotions take over. She jumps up from the floor, whirls around with her hands pressed to her face in surprise and confusion, then rushes from the house.

The mourners look at one another and frown. "You think she's gone to the cemetery again?" they ask.

"I suppose we'd better go too," one of them offers. And before Martha can think of a way to head them off, they're pouring out the door and heading up the path to the cliffs.

Martha feels her heart sink even lower. She should have handled this better, found some excuse to take Mary outside to tell her about the rabbi's return. Now she's done it. All his enemies in Jerusalem will find out he's back. Everything is out of control at once, and it all seems to be Martha's fault. Martha, who's always prided herself on holding things together. She clutches her shawl under her chin and follows the pack of mourners back toward the graveyard. What else can she do?

When she gets to the cemetery, she finds everything in confusion. Mary is crying and clutching at the rabbi's knees. The mourners, as if put to shame by her sister's histrionics, are raising their own royal ruckus, howling and wailing in waves of ululating ritual grief. Even the rabbi is in tears. It's enough to wake the dead.

As she approaches, Martha sees someone gesturing toward the cave that holds Lazarus's body and Jesus pushing through the crowd of mourners toward it. "He's really broken up about this, isn't he?" she hears one man say. "I hear they were really close."

But his neighbor replies sardonically, "Yeah, well, if they were such good friends, why didn't he do something for him? After all, he gave that blind man in Jerusalem his sight—the one who'd been born blind. You'd think if he could do that, he could have healed Lazarus before it came to this."

Hearing her own sentiments mirrored so exactly by Jesus' critics has a strange effect on Martha. Less than an hour ago she was furious with the rabbi herself, blaming him in exactly those words. But now she feels like defending him from these outsiders. After all, Jesus did love her brother. He is weeping openly at the tomb. Martha has discovered what it feels like to fail. These people have no right to judge him.

She begins to have misgivings, in fact, about what the rabbi's grief may lead him to attempt. Sure enough, just as she struggles through the crowd to the mouth of her brother's tomb, she hears the rabbi say the words she dreads.

"All right," he gestures to some of the men standing by, "let's get this stone out of here. Roll it over to the side." His voice, no longer weak with tears, has taken on an angry edge.

The crowd is murmuring around her. "What's he going to do? What's he up to now? Hey, this could be good. I'm glad we stuck around."

No, Martha thinks, aiming her mental protest at the rabbi. Don't do it. I know you're angry too. But it won't change anything. You're only going to embarrass yourself if you try this. And you'll give your Jerusalem enemies more ammunition. She pushes through the crowd and throws her arms wide as if to block the men from approaching the cave.

"Wait, Rabbi. Think. The body's been lying here four days already. The spirit has already departed. The body will be stinking. That's not how we want to remember him. It's no use. Don't even try this."

Jesus turns and scowls at her. Grief and anger cloud his face. "Didn't I tell you, Martha? Didn't I send you word that if you have faith you will see the glory of God blaze out here today?"

Martha looks at him and lets her arms drop, defeated once again. She, who only last week was so competent, so in charge, now is powerless. She drops down on a rocky ledge and holds her head in her hands. She should have been the one to die, she thinks. She feels like she *has* died, like life will never be the same again.

She hears the stone blocking the entrance to the cave grate as it pivots into its stone channel. She listens to the undercurrent of muttering among the growing crowd of people. She looks up, trying to find Mary so they can cling together at this horrible moment. But as she raises her head, she finds the rabbi staring at her, his eye like an awl, boring into her own. Their eyes lock for a moment, and then he raises both his eyes and his arms to heaven.

"Father," he says, "I'm grateful. I know that you hear me all the time, that our connection is never broken off. But not everyone realizes this. Some people here don't understand that you are the one that gives me my instructions. I'm saying this out loud now for their benefit. Just so they'll know where my power comes from."

Slowly he lowers his arms and scans the crowd, his gaze resting once more on Martha. She holds her breath, afraid to move, to exhale, as if the merest displacement of air at this moment could disturb the universe. *Don't do anything!* Something flashes the message in her brain. And for once in her life, she sits still, doesn't strain to make it work. Just waits. Breathless.

Then she hears the words she has been dreading shouted so loud they reverberate against the stony cliffs.

"Lazarus! Come out!"

And in the echo, she realizes she has longed for these words even more than she dreaded them.

Did Martha really expect to see the unsteady figure appear like a white shadow at the dark mouth of the cave? Did she foresee the mixture of fear and euphoria which would fall upon them all as her brother, trailing his linen wrappings like a disintegrating rag doll, shuffled into the light? Can sitting still, waiting, forcing oneself not to interfere, be called faith? Or hope?

The rabbi, the cloud gone from his face now, turns to the astounded mourners edging closer and says, "What are you waiting for? Give this man a hand. You can't expect him to walk wrapped up like that."

Martha watches the others fumble with the linen bindings her own hands wrapped around her brother's corpse. Let someone else undo them now. For once, she will be still, let the others do the work, and, like Mary, savor this moment.

Chapter 28

Faced with Nothing:

Mary of Magdala

*O*nce again we are at the mouth of a tomb. Not many days have passed since the rabbi from Galilee called his friend Lazarus out of the cave in Bethany's limestone outcrop. This time the cemetery is just outside Jerusalem and the woman standing at the cave's entrance is Mary of Magdala. According to the three synoptic gospels, she arrived with two other women, though establishing who precisely these others were is tricky. Several women had watched the crucifixion and the removal of the rabbi's body from the Roman cross. Now they have returned early the morning after the Sabbath to attend to the body properly. These women are identified in different ways by the gospel writers. They are called "the mother of" or "the wife of" or once simply "the other Mary." After carefully sorting and matching these designations, I think the other two women must have been the rabbi's mother and Salome, identified by Matthew as the mother of James and John, Zebedee's sons.

But John begins his account with Mary of Magdala who was nobody's mother and nobody's wife. In fact, her identification by her hometown indicates that she was no longer even considered anyone's daughter. Both Mark and Luke say that Jesus had cast seven devils out of her. If the behavior of the Gerasene demoniac—also identified only by his town's name—is any indication of Mary's previous violent state, we can see why her family might no longer claim her. After Jesus had released the Gerasene from the demons' power, he refused the man's request to come with him and sent him back to his own people. Mary, on the other hand, he had allowed to join his entourage. Why?

We should not ignore the fact that the relationship between a female student and a male mentor can have erotic overtones. I would have died at the stake for my eighth-grade English teacher, Mr. Gunther, not because of his erudition (though that was certainly part of his attraction) but because he was tall, wore tweed jackets, and had black wavy hair and topaz eyes. We may assume that Jesus' hair was also black and his eyes brown, but we know nothing else about his physical appearance, other than his approximate age of thirty. Not only was he erudite, but he was willing to teach women, possibly the most countercultural aspect of his earthly career. He was also the man to whom Mary of Magdala owed her life and sanity. So she may well have felt a quite understandably passionate attachment to this teacher.

While we cannot deny that possibility—nor indeed should we find such feelings shameful—no scriptural basis exists for Mary's traditional depiction as a reformed prostitute. Nor for Nikos Kazantzakis's portrayal of her as Jesus' seductress. She was, in fact, only one among the group of "certain women, which had been healed of evil spirits and infirmities" who Luke tells us accompanied the rabbi. At least two of these women—Susanna and Joanna, the wife of Herod Antipas's steward—had private means from which they supplied funds for this peripatetic adventure. But Mary of Magdala had nothing. Except, perhaps, her experience of mental suffering.

Unlike the public deliverance of the crazed Gerasene, the details of neither Mary's nor any of these other women's liberation from inner demons is recorded in the gospels. But we do know that, once free, Mary put that past behind her and signed on with the rabbi's band. We also assume that Mary held a significant position on his staff, since she is, with only one exception, named first in every list of women around Jesus. She may not have had funds to contribute, but her experience with the shadowy realm of psychic oppression would make her a valuable assistant at exorcisms.

Nevertheless, it was a rare rabbi who allowed women to travel with him, and this peculiarity provoked charges of loose morals against him. His detractors sometimes hinted that these women were no more than camp followers, groupies for the guru. And for women, such as Zebedee's wife, with previously respectable reputations, joining the rabbi's entourage meant abandoning their secure social positions. But Mary of Magdala had no family to fret over her. In fact, the rabbi and his company offered her the only family she was ever likely to have.

Thus, when Jesus is finally arrested and tried in Jerusalem during Passover, Mary determines that she will not desert this man who has not abandoned her. During the radical rabbi's trial and crucifixion, the male disciples, with the exception of John, hide or watch from a distance, but the women, with Mary of Magdala at their center, stick it out there on the garbage dump where the cross is set up. Though powerless to save their leader, they will not leave him to suffer alone.

Even after his humiliating death, they stay, watching as more powerful people—Nicodemus, the Pharisee and member of the Sanhedrin, and Joseph of Arimathea—remove the body and have it carried to a new tomb in the nearby hillside. Then, over the Sabbath, they do what women always do at such times—they plan what they will do to start the clock again, what motions will make life seem normal or at least possible once more. They ponder what act will be fitting, what can fit this tragedy into life, how it can be got through, got over.

Today women bake casseroles and make Jell-O salads when someone dies. They write thank-you notes for the funeral wreaths. Send sympathy cards. And busy, important people often see these acts as inconsequential and even slightly ridiculous. No doubt some of the disciples, hiding in the upper room, felt the same way about the women's taking spices to the tomb. Emily Dickinson described "the bustle in the house" that necessarily occurs "the morning after death." The poet knew the bustle was neither small nor ridiculous, but "the solemnest of industries enacted upon earth." In performing these homely chores, we are actually "putting love away."

Which is exactly what Mary of Magdala and the other women are doing early that morning as they hurry to the tomb at sunrise. The loss of their leader has shattered their lives as surely as those

of the rabbi's men. But while the men are still immobilized by the
terrible turn of events, the women, familiar with frailty and defeat,
find picking up the pieces a natural response to ruin. They have
been left high and dry in an unfamiliar and hostile city, their future
even more tenuous than the men's. Peter and the sons of Zebedee
can go back to their boats and fishnets. But who will take back a
wife or mother who's run off with a rabbi? For Mary of Magdala
there is no place left to go.

John focuses his camera narrowly on this solitary woman
alone at the cave's gaping mouth. The circular stone, which she
watched being rolled into its groove by Joseph's men, now lies
off to one side. Grave robbers, she thinks when she sees it.
Tombs were frequently rifled for valuable objects that might
have been interred with the corpse. Well, she tells herself,
precious little they found in the grave of a man who owned nothing. But when she bends down to peer into the cave's gloom,
she's in for another shock. The body itself is missing. Vandals?
But what Jew would defile himself by dragging a dead body from
its grave? The Romans? Aren't they satisfied with having
tortured and killed the rabbi?

Whoever has done this and for whatever reason, Mary knows
she is no match for either grave robbers or Romans. She can't handle the situation without the men. Peter and John—they were the
rabbi's closest friends. Surely she can get them to help her find the
body. Mary hurries back into the city, knowing they're hiding upstairs in the same room where they'd shared their last meal with
the rabbi. She arrives breathless.

"They've taken the Rabbi out of the tomb," Mary gasps, "and
we don't know where they've put him."

Peter and John look at each other, then jump up and make for
the stairs. Mary follows. They don't wait for her, though, and she,
having made that trip twice already that morning, can't keep up
with them. She arrives just in time to find Peter emerging from the
dark cave.

The disciple looks stunned. John follows him out, blinking at
the morning light. "How is it possible?" he asks Peter. "The bind-

ings are still here. How could he just vanish out of them like that? And did you see the cloth his head was wrapped in? The folds aren't even disturbed." The two men stare at one another, then stagger off down the path again toward Jerusalem. They have completely forgotten Mary of Magdala.

She stands there, abandoned once again. Forsaken. She remembers what Jesus had cried out from the cross: *Why have you forsaken me?* The words might as well be hers. She hurls the same question at the gaping hole in the hillside. She is death-deserted by her beloved teacher, her champion and protector. Disregarded as well by the men he was training to take his place. There is no one now to acknowledge Mary of Magdala, no place on the face of the earth where she belongs. Weeping, she bends down to creep back into the tomb, thinking perhaps, if despair allows thought, to curl up on the same limestone shelf where his body had been stretched. She has followed him everywhere else. Why not follow him this last step into darkness, the only step left to her?

But as Mary hunches down to enter the cave, she sees a figure— no, two—inside, lounging on either end of the limestone shelf. She freezes. Are these the grave robbers? Why didn't Peter and John see them?

"Why are you crying?" one of the men asks her.

Mary answers cautiously, taking care not to accuse the men directly. "Someone has carried my master off, and I don't know where they have put the body." Then, before they can answer, she ducks quickly out of the cave again, sensing someone behind her. She whirls about, fearful, her hand to her throat. But, thank heaven, it's no outlaw—just a workman in the cemetery.

"Why are you crying?" the man asks. "Who are you looking for?"

He must think I've come to mourn a friend or relative, Mary thinks. He's offering to help me locate the grave. He doesn't realize I haven't a friend or relation left in the world. But maybe he saw whoever has stolen the body.

Mary wipes her eyes on her shawl. "Please, sir," she says, "if you've taken the body from this tomb, or if you know who did, just tell me where it's been put. I'll see to it properly then."

The workman straightens now, as if waiting for her to compose herself. Waits so long that she finally glances up. Just then he says her name. "Mary!"

The chalky hillside, the pale green tamarisk branches overhead, wisps of high cloud begin to spin, slowly at first, then to whirl about her in a sudden welter of color and light, as if the world itself were being remade out of chaos. She feels as if the top of her head is coming off. "Wha—" she stammers, blood suffusing her face, then, "Who?" And finally, "My master!" as she sinks to the ground, throwing her arms around his knees. She looks up at him, wondering how she could ever have doubted him, how her despair can be so completely swallowed by joy.

"No, Mary," he says, disentangling her arms. "You mustn't cling to me like this. I can't stay here." He pulls her to her feet. "I'm going to have to leave you again and return to the Father."

"No," she moans in protest.

"Now don't be upset. My Father is also your Father. My God is your God. I won't be deserting you."

Her God. Her Father.

"I have something I want you to do," he continues. "A commission."

Commission.

"I want you to go back to my brothers in Jerusalem and tell them the same thing. Let them know what's become of me."

But they were right here, she starts to say, Peter and John, the ones closest to you. Why didn't you tell them this yourself? Why me? But, looking at him one last time, she doesn't ask. She knows.

Yet not until she is hurrying back along the path into the city does it strike her—she is the only one in the world who knows. The first. John and Peter hadn't seen him. Why didn't he show himself to them, call their names instead of hers? She stops for a moment. Will they believe her now? Will the men question her message, think she's gone to raving again?

She closes her eyes, calling up the image of the man she hadn't at first recognized herself, the figure she'd taken for an ordinary workman, who had set the world spinning in a vortex of light. She hugs her secret knowledge to her. *My Father. . . your Father . . . . I won't be deserting you.* Not abandoned. Never abandoned. It doesn't matter what they think.

And with that assurance burning in her, she bursts into the upstairs hiding place, the first witness to the resurrection: "I have seen the Lord!"

Chapter 29

Too Good to Be True:

Doubting Thomas

*T*homas wasn't surprised at how the whole mad escapade had turned out. As soon as the rabbi started talking about suffering and dying, Tom had figured they would all come to a bad end. He had a built-in sensor for disaster. The others had ignored the doom and gloom in the rabbi's words, but Tom — the one they always scoffed at for being a worrywart, a wet blanket — had believed him. Just as he had believed his stories about the kingdom.

Tom had certainly never been known as a dreamer, but the rabbi's descriptions of a heavenly kingdom had lured him away from home and down the road to this foolhardy adventure. Tom had first heard the rabbi debating with scholars at the local synagogue. He had been instantly struck with the man's quick wit, his way of turning a question inside out so that his interrogators became the ones on trial. But mostly it was those little stories about the heavenly kingdom that kept Tom coming back. They weren't the usual fairy tales about golden palaces and heavenly choirs, but stories about everyday life, farmers planting seeds or lost sheep or hired workers — all with a curious twist to them. When the rabbi had moved on to the next town, he invited Tom to come along and hear more.

As long as the rabbi and his growing band of followers stayed in the countryside, everything had gone well. But then the teacher had made his first big mistake. He had gone to the capital during Passover and ended up causing a riot in the Temple. Not until they were safely back in Galilee out of harm's way did Tom breathe easy again. In the fall, the rabbi had insisted on returning to Jerusalem a second time, for the Feast of Tabernacles. The rabbi's brothers had egged him on, of course, telling him his miracle show needed a bigger audience, that his talents were wasted there in the sticks.

And Jesus went—not just for the fall feast but well into the winter. Given that long in the city, naturally he got in trouble with the establishment again, this time for healing people. On the Sabbath, of course. Tom had seen catastrophe coming. It's hard to miss when an angry crowd starts stoning you. Only by some miracle had they made it out of town alive.

For a few fleeting days after they escaped the mob in Jerusalem, Tom believed the rabbi had finally come to his senses. Abandoning his usual plan of retreating to the suburb of Bethany, Jesus had marched them all the way into Peraea, east of the Jordan River. He must have figured they would be safer there among the pagans than going back to Galilee to haggle with the Pharisees.

Tom agreed with him there. It had been a big mistake, making enemies of the Pharisees—the only party able to stand up to the Jerusalem priests and get away with it. If Rabbi Jesus had only been satisfied with doing like the Essenes—teaching the Torah the way he saw it, but staying out of harm's way, up in the hills. Not invading the Sanhedrin's turf in Jerusalem. Keeping a low profile.

The Baptizer's fate should have shown the rabbi what he could expect if he kept baiting the big guys. The prophet had kept out of Jerusalem, all right, but he just couldn't keep his mouth shut about Herod's private life. His accusations were true enough. It was no secret that Herod had stolen his brother's wife. But why make a big deal about it—especially if it cost you your head? Did it make life any better? How did it change anything? Those were the practical questions Tom preferred to ask. And if the answer was a big fat zero, then he usually opted to cut his losses.

But then, just as they were getting settled in Peraea, word had come from back in Bethany that the rabbi's friend Lazarus had fallen ill. "I've got to wake Lazarus up," the rabbi announced. "We're going back."

At that, Thomas had felt the chill grip of certainty: the whole absurd experiment was about to come crashing to a halt.

Even the other men had raised their eyebrows. If they went back to Bethany, the Jerusalem establishment was sure to find out they were in the neighborhood. "But don't you remember? They just tried to kill us in Jerusalem!" they protested. "Besides, if Lazarus is sleeping, that's a good sign he's on the road to recovery."

The rabbi shook his head. "No, you don't understand. Let me spell it out for you. D-E-A-D. Lazarus is dead." After a pause, he added, "And it's probably a good thing. You're going to learn something important from this experience."

No, they won't, Thomas had silently objected. You've been trying to teach these guys for years now, and they still don't get it. And who knows? Maybe I don't either. Maybe I've just been fooling myself, hoping you can make a difference. He shook his head, feeling the old dark misgivings creeping up on him again.

Tom looked around at the other men. That last incident in Jerusalem had frightened them. They felt safe here in Peraea. He could see they were hesitating about this change in plans, uncertain whether they wanted to take the risk of returning. Cowards, he thought. Deserting the rabbi now, after all we've been through together.

Suddenly Tom found himself on his feet. "Okay then. If the rabbi's determined to go back and get himself killed, we may as well go and die with him."

At first the other men had simply stared at him, amazed to hear Thomas the pessimist, Thomas the skeptic, Thomas the naysayer, sound so bold and decisive. Then, fools that they were, they'd begun to cheer, as if his impulsive words were some kind of brave battle cry.

On the road back to Bethany, Thomas noticed the mood of the other men begin to shift. They were getting charged up, convinced that the rabbi was using Lazarus as an excuse to make his move on Jerusalem. This is it, they whispered among themselves. He's finally decided to show his hand. That he's not just some dime-a-dozen rabbi but the Messiah, the great Liberator.

Tom, though, had been reluctant to turn Rabbi Jesus into King Jesus, headed for Jerusalem like some reincarnated David. For one thing, that scenario didn't fit with the kingdom stories the rabbi told. Tom wasn't sure he could have said exactly why; he just knew that no one who called the poor and meek blessed was likely to lust after palaces and power himself.

When they arrived in Bethany, the rabbi turned out to be right again. They could hear the wailing of the mourners even before they reached the cemetery. Lazarus had died three days before, just as they had been packing up to leave Peraea. The rabbi, obviously overcome with grief, called for someone to roll the stone away from the mouth of the tomb. Then he shouted for his friend to come out. Thomas held his breath. Then a shroud-wrapped figure had slowly shuffled into the daylight.

At that moment, his heart in his throat, Thomas had felt that Jesus might actually pull it off, that dream kingdom he'd told them about. A man who can raise the dead can do anything, right? For once Tom felt drunk with unaccustomed joy, gripped by the ecstasy of a dream coming true. That intoxication carried him into Jerusalem, marching with the rest of the disciples as the masses shouted hosannas. And Tom had shouted just as loud as any other fool in the crowd.

But neither Tom's momentary burst of bravery back in Peraea nor his elation in Bethany lasted much beyond the Jerusalem gates. Tom could feel it begin to envelop him again, that cold cloud of doubt and fear he'd come to accept, through bitter experience, as the truth about the world. This wasn't going to work. The rabbi might have special powers, might even raise the dead. But he wasn't going to change anybody's mind about power. Altering human nature was even harder than transforming a dead body into a living one. The fat cats on the Sanhedrin were never going to roll over and play dead. They wouldn't go without a fight. And then there were the Romans. How could a handful of backwoods protesters take on the whole Empire?

But would anyone listen to him? Oh no. All the big shots in the organization—the insiders like Peter and John and his brother James—still thought the rabbi could pull it off. "Where's your confidence?" they kept asking him. "For once in your life, show a little optimism, Tom." He wondered just how perky the Big Three were feeling now.

"Don't worry," the others kept telling him. "When the time comes, the rabbi will just call down fire from heaven, like Elijah on Mount Carmel when he went up against the pagan priests. Or like David. You remember how the peasants rallied around David and made him king. It could happen again, Tom. There's historical precedent. You gotta believe."

Right.

By the time they assembled for what turned out to be their last meal together, Tom was having serious doubts about the future of the movement. They were still lounging around the table when the rabbi made the really depressing announcement that someone at the table would betray him to the authorities. Talk about a downer.

Later, the rabbi tried to cheer them up. "Don't be downhearted or afraid," he told them. "Trust me. Just as you trust God. I'm going to have to leave you in a little while—"

Great, Tom thought. I knew it.

"But there's plenty of room for you where I'm going. And I'll come back for you. We'll be reunited then. You know where I'm going"—he spread out his hands as if it should be perfectly obvious to everyone. "And you know how to get there."

"What?" The exclamation had jumped out of Tom's mouth before he could stop it. "What are you talking about? We haven't the foggiest notion where you're going. So how do you expect us to find the way?"

Startled by this outburst from his usually silent student, the rabbi stopped. Then he sat up, planting his feet on the floor and opening his arms even wider, as if offering himself as some kind of illustration of his murky point. "I'm the only road map you need. I contain all the directions, just as I contain truth and life itself. If you want to get to the place where my father lives, into his kingdom—in fact, if you want to know what he's like—then watch me act that out for you. Like father, like son. You'll see."

Tom sank back against the cushion. He didn't like the sound of that. It left him with a sense of vague foreboding while the others—who had, as usual, drunk too much—went off singing into the night.

And sure enough, after they'd made their way to a nearby olive orchard where they'd planned to spend the night in a cave, the rabbi's prediction came true once again. A little after midnight Tom had been waked by the sound of angry voices, curses, a cry of pain. He heard the rabbi's voice, lower but steady. Tom crept forward in the shadows, but he caught only one glimpse of the man he had followed so far before he disappeared into the night, surrounded by a contingent of Roman soldiers. Huddled inside the cave, shivering, Tom had watched as the flames from their torches wavered down the hillside.

That was the last Tom had seen of the teacher. It was, in fact, the last of everything. The end of the affair. John and Peter had managed to sneak through the city gates, but Tom had headed off in the opposite direction. No point in prolonging the agony. The rabbi had surrendered, plain and simple. If Jesus had given up, what was the point of his followers putting up a fight?

After that, there was only the ultimate fact to face. The rabbi was dead.

The other men had retreated to that secret upstairs room where they had eaten that last meal, too scared to make a break for it. Why didn't they just go on home? Admit it—the party was over. It had been fun while it lasted—marching up and down the countryside with thousands cheering at their heels. But it had all been a dream, and it was time to wake up now. Get on with their lives—or what was left of them.

Still, Tom was finding it hard to sleep now. Every time he closed his eyes, he kept seeing that torchlight parade down the hillside. And hearing his own words come back to mock him: *Let us go with him and die*. He'd been a fool for following the one dream he'd ever allowed himself. He could admit that now. But what really hurt was finding out he was just as big a coward as the others when the crunch came. He'd never even lifted a hand.

Several more days went by before word from Jerusalem reached him through the Galilee grapevine: *We have seen the rabbi*. For a moment his heart had started to race. Then he clamped down on it, trying to stop the hope before it got out of hand again.

But hope continued to haunt him, and finally he decided he would go back and try to find his old companions. Otherwise, I'll never sleep again, he thought. Not that I actually believe those boneheads, but maybe I can talk some sense into them, convince them to go home, get on with their lives.

When Tom arrives in Jerusalem, he remembers perfectly the way to the house they used that last night. Philip opens the door, pulls him inside, and throws his arms around him. "Hey, buddy. Glad to see you're back. We knew you'd come when you heard the news."

"About the rabbi?"

"Yes. We've seen him, Tom. Right here in this very room. It was awesome!" The whole bunch breaks into a cacophony of confirmation.

"It was wonderful, just wonderful. He stood right there where you're standing now."

Tom stares at the floor. "How'd you know it was him, not just your imagination?"

"You're not going to believe it, but he even showed us the wounds, the nail holes in his hands and where they stuck him in the side with a spear."

This kind of enthusiasm always makes Tom nervous. People can convince themselves of anything when they're this worked up. "You're right," he says, shaking his head, "I'm not going to believe it. Not unless I see it for myself. No. More than see. Anybody can see a ghost. I have to *feel* it—actually touch the wounds."

A storm of protest breaks out at this, but Peter holds up his hands for quiet. "Hey, guys. Don't forget. We didn't believe it either when the women first came back and told us." They subside into murmurs of reluctant assent.

At first nothing happens. A week goes by. Tom is surprised to find himself still there, hanging out with the rabbi's old gang. Why don't I go back home? he asks himself. But his friends keep urging him to stay. "Remember," they tell him, "how he said he'd come back? Don't leave now. Don't give up."

"Frankly, I think you've all gone batty, cooped up like this," he tells them. "You've worked yourselves into a state. You're just seeing things. But I'll give it one more day. If this ghost of yours doesn't show up by then, I'm outta here."

And wouldn't you know it? That very evening, just as they're all sitting down to supper, the door locked for the night, Tom suddenly feels the stale air of the overcrowded room grow slightly cooler, as if a breeze has just swept through and freshened the atmosphere. Everyone glances at his neighbor, and their eyes begin to shine. Then Tom senses, in a shadowy corner of the room, someone standing and waiting. He puts down the bread he has just broken and sits up very carefully. The figure steps closer to the center of the room.

"Be at peace," the figure says to them all. Then to Thomas, "I told you that you knew the way."

Thomas swallows. He can't, literally, believe his eyes. Looks, after all, are deceptive.

"Here," the figure says, holding out one hand, palm up. The ragged puncture wound is rusty with dried blood. "Stick your finger in that hole." With the other hand, he points to a slit in his side. "And there. Put your hand right here."

Tom sees that the wound has long ago stopped bleeding, though it has not healed.

"Give up this everlasting mistrust, Thomas. It's cutting you off from life. You needed proof. I'm giving it to you."

Slowly Thomas extends his hand toward the ragged edges of those injuries, wondering if he's about to touch a ghost or God.

Chapter 30

Hope:

Seeing, Not Seeing, and Believing

Lasciate ogni speranza, voi ch'entarte. Abandon all hope, ye who enter here. This is the last and most remembered line inscribed above the gate to Dante's Inferno, but several other lines precede it:

> I AM THE WAY INTO THE CITY OF WOE.
> I AM THE WAY TO A FORSAKEN PEOPLE.
> I AM THE WAY INTO ETERNAL SORROW
>
> . . .
>
> ONLY THOSE ELEMENTS TIME CANNOT WEAR
> WERE MADE BEFORE ME, AND BEFORE TIME I STAND.

According to Dante, Hell is balanced on a razor's edge between time and eternity. If we want to step beyond time and reach eternity, the razor must cut us loose from everything we love in this life. If we cling to those things, they drag us down into the City of Woe where we will forever wander among the forsaken, those who cannot turn loose of old loves, old sins, old griefs. Nothing in eternity is old; there all things are forever new. But to get there, you have to leave everything else behind. Lose everything or lose your soul. That seems to be the final, paradoxical choice we're offered.

Martha, for instance, had to lose her brother, had to watch Lazarus burn with fever, decline, and die. Hoping to save him, she sent for Jesus. But instead of the relief he seemed to grant with such ease to utter strangers, Martha got only the numb misery of bereavement, made worse by knowing her friend had ignored her plea for help. Note that Martha was not lacking in faith. But instead of that faith being rewarded, her very trust in Jesus' healing powers set her up for disappointment. His failure to respond to that faith doubled her anguish.

By the time Jesus finally arrived in Bethany, Martha had indeed abandoned all hope. She wasn't even looking for Jesus anymore. What good was his coming after the final fact of death? When she finds the rabbi at her brother's tomb, her bitterness turns to accusation. When he tries to restore her hope by promising to revive Lazarus, Martha can only respond indifferently: "Yes, I know. . . ."

Martha's reaction—first anger, then apathy—indeed the entire scene, shows the psychological realism of John's gospel. Anger frequently follows disillusionment. She blames the friend who's failed her, then brushes aside his promise of resurrection for Lazarus as no more than the standard funeral condolence. People who have *lost* hope are rarely capable of looking for it—or recognizing it, even when it's poked under their noses.

Does Jesus react defensively to Martha's accusation? No. He calls her attention to how he plans to resurrect her brother. When she still doesn't get the message, he doesn't take back his promise. Do her accusations hurt, though? Quite possibly. Twice during the ensuing action, Jesus "groans inwardly," first in response to her sister Mary's tearful indictment and then to the accusations of the Jerusalem mourners. When his friends verbally lash out against him, he absorbs the blow, just as he will later offer no resistance to the physical blows of his enemies. But this forbearance doesn't mean their words don't sting. Though some scholars claim that John's gospel shows us Jesus as a spiritual superman, omniscient and impervious to pain, here we see him made miserable by his friends' reproach.

For Mary of Magdala, the tomb where she went to find Jesus might as well have been the gateway to Hell, inscribed with Dante's words: *Abandon all hope*. The cave's dark mouth had swallowed her world. Mary and Martha, grieving for their brother, still have each other, have their position, their home in Bethany. But this woman, adrift in the world without her protector, has no one and no place to go. She has watched the temporal remains of her spiritual master disappear into the limestone tomb. The man who had mastered her seven devils has left her now with only this gaping wound in the earth down which all her hope has vanished.

If she could bring back the one who freed her from its spell, she would be willing to descend, like Eurydice, into the underworld. She knows those regions of darkness only too well. Instead, Mary has to be satisfied with scenting the putrid air of the sarcophagus with spices. Like a parent who preserves a dead child's room untouched, she clings to the physical shreds of her old life with the rabbi. But when she finds his body is missing, it seems even that small solace has been taken from her. Her only thought is to find the body; she doesn't recognize as angels the two men inside the cave. In fact, so intent is she on looking for a dead Jesus, that she mistakes the living one for a workman in the cemetery garden.

Again, I'm impressed with the gospel's psychological realism. The movement from despair to hope never appears to happen automatically or instantaneously. Emotional time progresses at a slower pace than our synapses carry simple visual stimuli. Just as it takes a while to absorb the fact of loss, hope takes time to digest. Skeptics are right in observing that we see what we want to see. But the psychological phenomenon works the other way too; sometimes, especially after we've abandoned all hope, we're blind to what we previously longed for.

Jesus appears to understand this. He doesn't shout, "Hey, it's me! Look, I'm back!" Instead, he asks Mary why she is crying, focusing on her current emotional state. Then he moves her attention to something outside herself: "Who are you looking for?"

When Mary still fails to recognize him and mistakes him for the gardener, how does Jesus react to her blindness? With the world's most convincing word—her name. That is her doorway out of Hell, just as Lazarus's name had summoned him from his tomb. Our own name is the one word we all long to hear echoing down whatever wormhole connects time to eternity. It rolls our most abiding desire into a single irresistible sound, reassures us more than a week's worth of reasoned argument.

But along with that reassurance came Jesus' injunction not to touch him, or more accurately, not to cling to him. A strange request, perhaps, followed by his equally puzzling explanation that he has not yet ascended to his Father. Could this warning have something to do with the mysterious mechanics of the spiritual realm? Possibly. But since *cling* implies a certain desperation, his words could also be an admonition to Mary that she must no longer rely on physical signs of his presence. He is, as he cautioned his followers before the crucifixion, going to leave them. But not alone. Mary must learn to discern his presence—and not lose hope—even when she can't see him.

And what of Thomas, who prided himself on his pragmatism, who built a barricade of rational defenses against the inevitable disappointments of this life, who was not afraid to demand evidence? He was, after all, the only one among Jesus' followers who took the rabbi at his word and expected the debacle in Jerusalem. Not swept away by the emotional tidal wave of triumphalism that engulfed the other disciples, Thomas went to Jerusalem fully expecting to die along with Jesus. And after the scene played itself out exactly as predicted, he was more determined than ever not to let hope beguile him again. We might even say that Thomas never lost hope because he never had any to begin with.

Except how would we then explain his leaving home to follow the radical rabbi? Why try to get Jesus to give clearer directions to the place he was going unless Thomas hoped to go there too? Thomas, as much as Martha or Mary of Magdala, wanted something from Jesus. We have a fairly clear picture of what the women wanted. But what exactly did Thomas want? Why did he finally rejoin the rabbi's other followers in that upper room? Why was he still hanging around a week later?

Though he might never have admitted it, Thomas was waiting for the other half of the rabbi's prediction to come true. The pupil had already observed the first part, his teacher's death. Now he lingered to see the unthinkable antithesis—his return. Martha made it clear that Jesus had thwarted her hopes. Mary of Magdala felt hers had died with her master. But Thomas could not admit he still hoped that Jesus had told them the truth: that he would return. If that last hope were shattered, what would be left? So Thomas doggedly doubts the eyewitness reports supplied by the other disciples. It has to be his own eyes that see, his own hand that touches.

Again, Jesus does not condemn Thomas's refusal to hope. He gives the skeptic exactly what he demands. Despite the fact that he earlier told Mary not to cling to him, he now invites Thomas to probe his wounds. But he has an admonition for this disciple, so determined to doubt. He supplies what is needed—physical evidence—to restore his hope. But he also points out the greater gift of those who trust without proof.

I have always found that admonition strangely comforting: "Blessed are those who have not seen . . . " For us, even seeing isn't always enough; we have learned the limits of evidence. Though we might ask for a shroud sample, a blood test, not even carbon-dating or DNA testing would supply enough evidence of the resurrection. Behind every test lies yet another series of questions, like receding reflections in an infinity of mirrors. However much the evidence, in the end you either believe or you abandon all hope.

Still, all these responses to loss remain familiar after twenty centuries. Anger, apathy, defensiveness, denial, despair. A peculiar blindness descends on those who lose hope. They can no longer recognize what is right under their noses: Martha brushes aside Jesus' promise to raise Lazarus; Mary can't recognize the very man she's looking for; Thomas willfully rejects out of hand the witness of his friends—testimony a reasonable person would at least consider. Nevertheless, Jesus responds without anger or condemnation to the blindness of despair. He restores her brother to Martha, opens Mary's eyes, provides the evidence Thomas demands. All three got what they desperately needed from him— even when they couldn't ask for it.

The same pattern unfolds during an encounter on the first Easter afternoon, when two of Jesus' former followers are hurrying along the road from Jerusalem to the village of Emmaus. A shadowy figure joins them and asks what they're discussing so intently.

The pair stare at the stranger. "Are you the only person in the whole city who hasn't heard?" they ask incredulously. Then they relate the events of the past few sad days, describing Jesus, not as the Messiah, but as a prophet. "We had hoped that he was the one who would redeem Israel," they finish.

They *had* hoped. But no longer. It takes several more hours and a meal at an inn before their eyes are opened to their companion's identity.

Such is the nature of despair. In its grip, the hopeless cannot help themselves. They can see no way out of their prisons, can lift up their eyes no more than their hearts. It takes something, someone, outside themselves to restore both hope and sight.

Conclusion: Finding Jesus
What a Mystery Looks Like

As soon as I could understand language, Jesus was handed to me on a silver platter, like a fish already gutted, cooked, and garnished. People who loved me worked hard to prepare that dish, and it nourished me and made me strong. What it couldn't give me was what those same people called a "personal relationship with Jesus." For that, I needed a live fish. So I had to reverse the process that had first brought him to me—throwing out the parsley, retrieving the entrails, stitching up the slits—trying to get back to the original, elusive fish slipping through deep water.

Such a task would be impossible except for these stories where he has left his traces. Despite two millennia and countless interpreters, they stand up remarkably well. Though I will never hear these passages in the fresh and stunning way their original audiences did, though they will always come to me through a dozen different filters of familiarity, nevertheless they make up a fine-webbed matrix in which to net the fish. Every generation, rightly skeptical of the Jesus it inherits from a previous age, returns to these stories to see if they can seine the protagonist for themselves.

For me, the process involved making myself familiar with biblical scholarship, an undertaking not without its own hazards. I found that some biblical scholars mix a generous amount of devotional writing in with their research. Their sentences often end with exclamation points, a rhetorical device that leaves me uneasy and unconvinced. Other academics seem determined to prove that the expedition is doomed from the outset. They begin with the assumption that their efforts are futile, that this Galilean rabbi is a fossilized fish so deeply embedded in literary limestone that no

amount of chiseling can ever release him. One must negotiate
these scholarly waters with care, dodging between the overeager
enthusiasts and the overanxious skeptics.

Strangely enough, it has always been people with the most religious education, whether the scribes of two millennia ago or biblical scholars today, who have the hardest time with Jesus. More
committed to refining their methodology than finding the quarry,
their analysis often ends up being an autopsy. Disgruntled blue-
collar workers, dispossessed women, and desperate parents of sick
children, on the other hand, have less trouble finding Jesus. And
indeed, his own words encourage us to look for him among the
hungry, homeless, sick, and suffering.

Still, I readily acknowledge that cultural components color
these stories. Jesus was a man, a provincial Jew, a speaker of Aramaic. There's no getting around those limitations. Theology and
philosophy can afford to do away with the embarrassing clutter of
culture and deal with the smoother surface of abstractions. But in
the process they also have to sacrifice character, setting, action, dialogue—all those narrative elements that give us a sense of lived
experience.

To those of us who find time and space our natural, if inconve-
nient, element, stories remain as essential as they are exasperating.
Narrative is our primary mode of making sense of our own lives,
of all that has happened to us and the ways we have been shaped
by those events. If I'm looking for Jesus, rather than an idea, I still
think these stories are the best waters to fish.

A brief description of Jesus that takes those cultural components into account might sound something like this: Like the many
other Jewish holy men who inhabited Palestine during the Roman
occupation, Jesus drew people to him for a variety of reasons—curiosity, physical need, longing for vindication, spiritual itchiness.
He launched his teaching and healing vocation not in a void, but
from his religious tradition, using the texts he inherited with authority and without apology. (Modern sensibilities might even say
with arrogance.) Having no official credentials to certify his position, he nevertheless attracted large crowds as a roving rabbi. In

his native region of Galilee, the local religious leaders took him seriously enough to engage him in public debate, the traditional forum for first-century Judaism. While he proved to be a skilled and forceful opponent, over time these debates escalated into nasty confrontations, especially as he extended his reach to Judea, the seat of Jewish power in the provinces.

Given this description of Jesus' public face, it is easy to see why he, like so many other dissenters of his day, ended up a victim of imperial security measures. What it doesn't explain is why the size of his following continued to expand after his execution. This anomaly sets him apart from the other insurrectionists and holy men of his time. Examining cultural information alone won't tell us the answer. For that, we need to know something of Jesus as a person. That's why these stories of individual encounter are important.

So what has this search for Jesus yielded? Has tracking him through these stories given me a clearer picture of this person from whom we measure time itself? In recounting these encounters, I have imagined how he might have looked to people in ancient Palestine. How does he look to me now?

Perhaps it will be easier to begin with what I didn't find.

First of all, I uncovered nothing to reinforce Mrs. Batcher's version of the socially acceptable Jesus, a genial Mister Rogers who swapped his cardigan for a bathrobe and sandals. True, Jesus not only liked, but valued children—another characteristic making him unusual among first-century holy men. Also, he was amazingly accessible to people in distress and found it impossible to turn them away. At the same time, he could be painfully blunt. Anyone who came to him with a hidden agenda could expect to feel his razor-edged tongue. He broke many of his own culture's taboos and offended the social conventions of our day as well—calling people names, breaking up families, even assaulting businessmen. If what you want is a figure to model social skills and decorum for your children, don't look for him in these stories.

What about the rebel Jesus of my youth then, the Che Guevara look-alike? At twenty, I had cast Jesus as a student activist challenging defense contractors on campus. I had used the scene where he sacks the Temple as evidence that he was ready to storm the establishment's barricades. Looking at these stories three decades later, did I find a champion who could fix the world's evil systems, an apocalyptic hero to rectify the injustices of society?

Not really. As I examined these scenes again, I could find none where Jesus directly challenged the forces occupying his native Palestine. On the contrary, when civil or military representatives of Rome came looking for him in the provinces, he treated them rather well. His anger in the Jerusalem Temple appears to have been directed not against the occupying Romans, but the indigenous religious leadership.

Recently, some scholars have attributed this tolerant treatment of Romans not to Jesus, but to the gospels' editors. They argue that those in the nascent Christian movement did not want to portray their founder as an enemy of the Empire, lest it imperil their precarious standing with Rome. Yet these stories show that Jesus was clearly aware of the politicized climate in which he operated. He makes many more references to Roman soldiers and puppet kings than the other roving rabbis of his day. He openly debates such obviously political issues as paying taxes and other conflicts between religious practice and state decrees.

Jesus seems not so much ignorant of as indifferent to politics, even though many of his followers evidently believed he would take up arms against Rome at some point. His inner circle professed their willingness to die for his cause and haggled over their roles in his new government. But Jesus stubbornly resisted their pressure and tried—unsuccessfully, as it turns out—to redirect their focus. He agitates people, uses political metaphors for spiritual matters, foments radical change, but not for political ends. Thus my Jesus-of-the-barricades deflates considerably when thrown against the solid backboard of these gospel accounts.

What, then, of Jesus the stabilizer? As I had watched political upheavals around the globe bring more suffering but little relief to oppressed people, social equilibrium came to look more appealing. Divorce, abortion, child abuse, drug testing, armed intervention, genocidal slaughter, environmental disasters—in the face of such chaos, what could forestall complete social disintegration? How could we discern the boundaries between what was tolerable and intolerable? Where were the guidelines that would restore at least a modicum of decency and order to civilization? Could Jesus provide a shelter from the storm threatening to undo us all? Earlier, I'd wanted a Jesus who would evict the mighty from their thrones; now I wanted him to hand over a blueprint for a better society. Did I find such a design in these stories?

First of all, remember that we are talking about a man who neither married nor had children. (I still find this the most frustrating aspect of Jesus.) Add to that the fact that he deserted his widowed mother, leaving her to the care of his younger siblings. In addition, he enticed a number of men—and women—away from their families and homes. What kind of model for family values is that? Kant's moral imperative—that one must only act in ways that one would apply to the rest of humanity—is not the code by which Jesus operated. If everyone went on the road like Jesus, society would quickly disintegrate. If we are looking for a paradigm of responsible citizenship, we better look elsewhere.

Jesus will frustrate anyone trying to make society function smoothly. On the one hand, he comes out strong against divorce; on the other, he rescues the adulterous woman from the punishment prescribed by Torah. He is likewise lenient with the oft-married woman at the Sychar well. Though he repeatedly affirms the Ten Commandments, he brushes aside their infractions with irritating ease. Rather than firming up the rules that maintain social order, he flexes them. He dissolves social boundaries, accumulates followers from unsavory backgrounds. Instead of crusading for moral or social reform, as a number of other rabbis did, he reprimands respectable community leaders and makes friends with the Mafia of his day. Thus, Jesus the social strategist, dear to liberals and conservatives alike, is not to be found in these stories.

So what about the Jesus who could at least assure me personal peace? If life, as it appears to be, is inevitably a voyage on a sea of troubles, maybe he could teach me to sail them serenely. After all, Jesus' own words assure us of eternal rest, light burdens, seeking and finding, receiving what we ask for. Perhaps those who focus on the personal, even private nature of the spiritual life were right.

But what happens when Jesus' promises of rest and peace are balanced against his own actions in these stories? Was he imperturbable in the midst of disorderly crowds? Did he keep his guru's gaze serenely fixed on the invisible sphere of the spirit? Was the Jesus in the Gospels as coolly composed as the actor portraying him in the perpetual Easter rerun, Zefferelli's *Jesus of Nazareth*?

Not in these stories. Though he appears to have been a patient teacher and a quick and clever debater, he also got tired, grew intermittently irritable or even angry, was on different occasions ironic, inquisitive, moved to tears, disappointed, brusque, apprehensive, and sorrowful. I am hard-pressed to remember a scene, except when he goes to sleep in the middle of a storm on the Sea of Galilee, where Jesus appears perfectly serene and dispassionate.

Also, his words of comfort and reassurance must be weighed alongside his other, seemingly contradictory statements. Peace, yes. But not as the world gives it. Instead of domestic tranquillity, he said to expect families torn apart by divided loyalties. And always, of course, the cross that he himself faced, not with calm equanimity, but sweating blood.

Thus, discovering a foolproof formula for serenity in these stories remains tricky. The Jesus I find here cares about the troubles of this world. Most of his encounters with people occurred as a result of their immediate physical distress—hunger, illness, bereavement. They came to Jesus wanting him to fix their lives in *this* world, and he did not belittle that desire. He himself may have gone without food for forty days in the wilderness, but he refused to let the crowds who followed him there go unfed for even one day.

So much for the Jesus I didn't find. What about the one I found? How did he look?

My own earthly troubles are pretty much the same as those people brought to him two thousand years ago. Ill health, psychic turmoil, death—my own or my family's and friends'. So I was comforted to find a Jesus who never told people their suffering was an illusion, that pain didn't matter in the ultimate scheme of things, or that they should simply rise above the situation by concentrating on the spiritual realm. I like that.

But ironically, I also discovered that spending too much time with Jesus can be dangerous. Those people with whom this Galilean rabbi had only a fleeting encounter often got more than they bargained for—and with very little commitment on their part. Bring him your body and he fixed it. Bring him your empty stomach and he filled it. But bring him your spiritual conundrums, your philosophical riddles, and you often went away smarting. He demanded a lot from those with leisure and resources to contemplate the spiritual realm—the religious scholars, the well-to-do intellectual, the powerful Nicodemus. The more interest you showed in his invisible kingdom, the more Jesus expected of you. That scares me.

By setting out on a search for Jesus, equipped with a religious education and a spiritual itinerary, I have put myself in jeopardy. Jesus appears to have infinite patience with beginners, those he calls "the little ones." They get basic words of encouragement from him. But his advanced class, the disciples, often get a dressing down for their spiritual sluggishness. Judging from the way Jesus keeps raising the stakes, one might conclude that it's better to stick with the slow learners. This worries me.

For how am I to undo my past, unravel my conditioning, forget what I have already learned? How do I wipe the slate clean and start over? I hear Nicodemus's old ironic question echoing in my own. *Shall a man enter again a second time into his mother's womb?* Finding Jesus may well depend on diminishing, sloughing off, stripping down. Some days I think only the desperate and reckless find Jesus, those who have had everything taken away. Is the end of my rope the only place I'm sure of finding Jesus?

Other days, however, I take heart from the fact that Jesus' closest companions, the ones who spent the most time with him and who followed him many a dusty mile, also had trouble adjusting their preconceptions to the living reality before them. They were just as baffled by their leader as the religious scholars or the rich young ruler.

In fact, the only thing that set the disciples apart from those more speculative seekers was their sheer doggedness. They may not have understood Jesus very well, but they stuck with him—at least until his arrest. And despite all their deficient comprehension, even their flagrant opportunism, Jesus never broke off his friendship with them. He sometimes railed at their slow understanding, but he never sent them away. Even after they had abandoned him in Gethsemane, Jesus returned to them, gathered them together, and, in spite of their former failure, entrusted them with his own mission. Though the struggle to understand continued, none of their failures were final. Who could have expected that Peter, after cravenly denying his visible friend, would later die for the invisible one?

Strangely, this realization cheers me. Should I find myself at the end of my rope, at least I can count on Jesus not letting go the other end. He hangs on, doesn't turn loose. Spiritual stupidity or moral dereliction—no failure is final with him.

I confess, however, some lines are not yet drawn in my composite sketch of Jesus and not all questions are resolved. What *don't* these stories tell me—or at least what have they not yet revealed? Even after considering all the ancient evidence I can scrape together, what gaps remain to be filled?

Questions about definition, for one thing. These are more easily asked than answered. The stories may reveal how Jesus acted, what sort of person he was, but do they draw a clear and defining line around his figure? Unfortunately, the gospels do not spell out just how Jesus perceived his own destiny. For a long time after he began using his healing power, he tried to keep it secret. He was very cagey with his circle of insiders as well. Was there some strategic reason for this secrecy, or was he himself only gradually discovering the path that lay before him?

The scenes I've investigated here show us a person with access to power beyond our understanding, someone who purports to communicate familiarly, even familialy, with the creator of the universe. They reveal something about the nature of the power he wields, the kingdom from which it emanates, and the paradoxical ways that realm penetrates our own temporal experience. But is

Jesus that kingdom's envoy? Its messenger? Its heir apparent? God in disguise? The many different titles by which he calls himself make this a difficult question to answer.

And what was his earthly function? Was he an umbilical cord linking matter to spirit? An exemplar, the perfect pattern we should struggle to copy? The ground wire for God's wrath? An extensionless point, passing through which, in some metaphysical acrobatics we have dubbed redemption, all wrongs turn inside out? Is he, as Paul later calls him, the pioneer of our faith—the first one to get it right? The scriptures are full of names for this Palestinian rabbi, many of them as disturbing as they are illuminating, none of them containing all the possible definitions.

And is this even a soluble problem? After all, there is more to any person than can be reduced to a formula. The pleasure I take in my friends and family does not depend on my ability to define them. I suspect the same is true of Jesus, about whom, John's gospel claims, the earth itself could not contain all the stories. Maybe this is why, even though the Jesus I find may be limited by what I'm looking for, and despite my misgivings about ever capturing him completely, I am not disappointed in my search.

True, every time I think I have him pinned down, he slips through my fingers once more, just as he slipped away from those disciples who stopped to eat with a mysterious stranger at the Emmaus inn. They only realized who he was after he had disappeared. But it was the resurrected Jesus, the one who walks through walls, who came looking for his erstwhile followers, not the other way around.

This, I suspect, is the Jesus I'm really after. The one who is looking for me. The one I sense at times—often when I'm desperate, but sometimes not—the way a chloroplast, equipped with consciousness, might sense the sun. The Jesus not limited by the constraints of time and space.

Yet however much I want to transport myself to his celestial habitat, I do not believe I can, at will, reach through time to lay hold of that ethereal figure. He lives now on the far side of these earthbound stories and comes and goes as he will. He can walk through walls, but I can't. He may no longer be limited by time and space, but I am. And who knows when he'll next penetrate the membrane between heaven and earth? Some people make Jesus seem as easily accessible as ordering a Happy Meal. But at times I find my attempts to contact him to be, as Gerard Manley Hopkins put it, "like dead letters sent/To dearest him that lives alas! away."

Even then, though, I still have the stories, locked, like myself, in time and space. This is the place where I can indeed count on finding Jesus. So I continue to search for him there, watching him change as the decades pass, though his transformations are actually a result of my own metamorphoses. It's against these stories that I continue to measure the truth of my own experience. Looking for Jesus, I have found, is also a way of looking for myself. Or rather, like Peter, I am looking for those words which contain life itself. These stories are not simply historical documents, pins to hold down a dead specimen for my examination. They are living breath, expanding, their perspective shifting as I move through them and through time. And such an enterprise, I find, is proving to take, even as it gives, my whole life.

One final note of caution. Looking for Jesus is an undertaking fraught with danger. As I intimated earlier, the closer you get to finding him, the higher the stakes become. He is no mere passive object to be circled and appraised like a piece of sculpture. You look at him and he looks back. You may begin the search for Jesus with your own agenda, but be warned: he has one too. As the disciples discovered, you pay a price for finding Jesus.

He may, in fact, one day turn to you, as he did to those feckless first-century followers, and ask, "But you—who do you say that I am?" Then you will either have to abandon his company altogether or spend the rest of your life trying to answer that question.

A Bibliographical Farewell

*E*very year books about Jesus continue to pour from the presses. When I checked the Amazon website this morning, it listed over a thousand books in this category currently in print. I have included only a few titles here, both to indicate the sources from which I took much of my information and to suggest other reading that might illuminate this figure for you.

The best place to read about Jesus, of course, is the four gospels. But which gospel? And which translation? The answer to the first question has been argued for centuries. Most scholars believe that Mark was composed earliest, perhaps using the memories of the disciple Peter. Matthew and Luke were written later, both incorporating material that does not appear either in Mark or John from a source scholars have named Q. Many of Jesus' parables come from this source; thus, though written later, both Matthew and Luke are important to understanding Jesus. Most scholars also agree that Matthew's gospel shows signs of being written for Jewish Christians, since it takes pains to connect Hebrew scriptures and practices to Jesus. Luke, on the other hand, is written to a much more cosmopolitan audience and emphasizes Jesus' broad sympathies for the diverse peoples living in Palestine. While most scholars date John as the latest of the gospels, I, along with A. N. Wilson and the late J. A. T. Robinson, find exceptional traces of an eyewitness account embedded in this work. Yet, each of the four gospels has something unique to contribute to a detailed picture of Jesus.

The question of which translation or version to use is harder to answer. In many ways the Authorized Version (best known as the King James Version) is the closest word-for-word translation available in English. However, in the nearly four hundred years that separate us from its composition, the English language has

changed so much that readers today sometimes have difficulty understanding it. Also, over the centuries scholars have learned a bit
more about the ancient texts, which, at least in a few instances,
makes later translations more accurate. If you have a hard time
reading Shakespeare, then the Revised Standard Version or the
New International Version can help you.

When using some of the latest translations or versions, such as
The Living Bible or Today's English Version (developed in 1976
for nonnative speakers of English), remember that each was composed with a specific audience in mind. This inevitably affects the
final product. Realize too, however, that in this these translators or
revisionists are doing the same thing that the original four evangelists did—making these stories about Jesus accessible to people
in a language they can hear and respond to. Some, such as Eugene
Peterson's *The Message* (1993) and Reynolds Price's *Three
Gospels* (1996) may seem highly individualistic (Price's third
"gospel" is, in fact, his own "apocryphal gospel"), but these are
generally written with passion and may make the words come
alive for you in a new way.

To provide a context for these stories of Jesus' encounters with
citizens of ancient Palestine, I wanted more understanding of first-
century Jewish life and the cultural matrix within which it func-
tioned. Since the ancient historian Josephus was a contemporary of
Jesus, I went first to sections of his *Antiquities, The Wars of the
Jews,* and his treatise *Against Apion.* These are all usually collected
in the various translations of *The Works of Josephus.* My edition,
translated by William Whiston, contains a helpful index as well.

Hyam Maccoby's *Early Rabbinic Writings* (vol. 3 of the Cam-
bridge Commentaries on Writings of the Jewish and Christian
World 200 B.C. to A.D. 200) includes selected passages from the
Mishnah, various midrashim, Targums, and other liturgical and
mystical literature either written or widely read during this period.
The editor supplies an informative introduction to these selections,
as well as thoughtful commentaries on them.

Secondary material—books *about* the gospels or first-century
Palestine—should be selected with several considerations in mind.

The prose of some academic tomes is so impenetrable as to drive away the uninitiated reader. Don't despair if you can't plow through these. Other quite reputable scholars have probably made the same interesting and important information available to the general reader. In addition, be aware that all writers have a particular theological approach to this subject. Some are simply more obvious than others. On the other hand, don't dismiss an important source of information just because you don't agree with its underlying assumptions. Merely take those into consideration when weighing its conclusions. Try to diversify your reading, including books from various sorts of publishing houses—secular, academic, and religious.

Fortunately, I had a library of biblical reference books left over from seminary to rely on as I wrote this book—several dictionaries of the Bible, a Bible atlas, a Greek New Testament, four concordances, and more commentaries than I knew what to do with. Readers with more than a cursory interest in the gospels will eventually add similar works to their libraries.

For books that not only supply information but interpret the data about this crucial period, as well as explain how Jesus fit into that milieu, I consulted several sources. For a broad overview of Palestine in the first century I read *Customs and Controversies: Intertestamental Jewish Backgrounds of the New Testament,* by J. Julius Scott Jr. I found its summaries of the geography, history, culture, and religious crises of Jews in first-century Palestine both objective and readable. Irving M. Zeitlin's *Jesus and the Judaism of His Time* emphasizes the many varieties of religious experience in first-century Judaism, as well as considering several hypotheses about Jesus' true agenda. A helpful bibliography is supplied also.

John Wijngaards' *Handbook to the Gospels: A Guide to the Gospel Writings and to the Life and Times of Jesus* is a simple little paperback I found at the library, yet it served as a practical, easy reference from a Catholic perspective. It also provided useful background about settings in which Jesus operated and included useful pictures, maps, and diagrams.

A work that both provides information and interprets that data,

Jesus' Jewishness: Exploring the Place of Jesus in Early Judaism, collects essays by contemporary Protestant, Catholic, and Jewish scholars, all representing widely divergent viewpoints about Jesus' relation to his culture. Besides giving the reader much to ponder, it concludes with a helpful annotated bibliography of major works about Jesus—again from multiple perspectives.

For a contemporary slant on Jesus by Jewish scholars I read individual authors who develop their arguments at greater length and depth. Geza Vermes's landmark work, *Jesus the Jew: A Historian's Reading of the Gospels,* links Jesus to his time, culture, and the religious institutions that inevitably shaped his ministry. Considerably more polemical, but imaginative and fun to read, is Jacob Neusner's *A Rabbi Talks with Jesus: An Intermillennial, Interfaith Exchange.* Though the author is, besides a rabbi, the Distinguished Research Professor of Religious Studies at the University of South Florida, this book is not a dry academic product, but an impassioned rabbinical debate of the very sort Jesus might have engaged in following his Sermon on the Mount. Neusner respects and appreciates Jesus, but gives a sturdy defense for not following him.

For someone interested in how stories work—biblical ones in particular—Robert Alter's *The Art of Biblical Narrative* will prove instructive. Perhaps more esoteric but nevertheless intriguing is Northrup Frye's *The Great Code.* By using the indexes, particularly the one for biblical passages, you can maneuver to relevant portions.

Finally, for two very dissimilar contemporary assessments of Jesus that draw on historical data for their conclusions, read both A. N. Wilson's *Jesus: A Life* and Philip Yancey's *The Jesus I Never Knew.* The first is an attempt by a British novelist to reconstruct a biography of Jesus. It may be compared with his earlier work, *Jesus: The Evidence,* written before his recent rejection of his Christian beliefs. Yancey's book starts by stripping away accreted assumptions that have accumulated around the figure of Jesus over two millenia, then starts afresh, trying to reconstruct Jesus' identity. It provides interesting links to literature and our own popular culture.

This is admittedly a very elementary and limited road map. Like medieval cartography which left some patches blank and others marked only with the warning "Dragons are here," it leaves a good bit up to you and whatever spirit you choose to guide you. That only seems proper, however. Looking for Jesus is, after all, a voyage of discovery, full of uncertainty and a sense of danger, yet one driven by hope.